GUIDE
TO THE
LEED® AP

Operations and Maintenance (O+M) Exam

Michelle Cottrell, LEED AP O+M

WILEY

John Wiley & Sons, Inc.

For general information on our other products and services, or technical support, please contact our Customer Care Department within the United States at 800-762-2974, outside the United States at 317-572-3993 or fax 317-572-4002.

Wiley also publishes its books in a variety of electronic formats. Some content that appears in print may not be available in electronic books.

For more information about Wiley products, visit our Web site at http://www.wiley.com.

Library of Congress Cataloging-in-Publication Data:

Cottrell, Michelle

  Guide to the LEED AP Operations and Maintenance (O+M) Exam / Michelle Cottrell.

     p. cm.

  Includes bibliographical references and index.

  ISBN 978-0-470-60830-2 (pbk.); ISBN 978-1-118-09802-8 (ebk); ISBN 978-1-118-09803-5 (ebk); ISBN 978-1-118-09937-7 (ebk); ISBN 978-1-118-09969-8 (ebk); ISBN 978-1-118-09970-4 (ebk)

  1. Leadership in Energy and Environmental Design Green Building Rating System–Examinations–Study guides. 2. Buildings–Maintenance–Examinations–Study guides. I. Title.

  TH880.C679 2011

  658.2–dc22

                                        2011009741

Printed in the United States of America

10 9 8 7 6 5 4 3 2 1

Guide to the
LEED® AP Operations and Maintenance (O+M) Exam

Contents

Acknowledgments

STEFANO, ALTHOUGH YOU WERE TRAVELING and accomplishing your own endeavors, you were always there to support and encourage me each day as I wrote. You will never know how much I appreciate you and your understanding and patience (especially when we were traveling across Europe)!

Next, I would like to thank each and every one of the image contributors, as the exam prep series would not be the same without your added visual integrity. Each of you helped to maintain my excitement about the book with your great images and photos.

To all my students, thank you so much for all the insight for the content for this study guide. Your questions and eagerness to learn inspired me throughout the process.

Zach Rose, Assoc. AIA, LEED AP, LEED Green Associate, thank you for your encouragement and support for not only this book and the others, but for your continued motivation. Thank you to the rest of my team at Green Education Services for your excitement and interest in the exam prep series!

John Czarnecki, Assoc. AIA, thank you for another opportunity and your support along the way. Thank you to my team at Wiley for always keeping me on schedule and the great editing. Thank you, Lisa Ryan at Stellar Searches for helping me with another thorough index!

Many thanks to my family and friends for granting me the time and space again to write yet another book! You all have been so understanding and patient with my frequent disappearances. I cannot ever tell you how much it meant to be "guilt free" while writing! Your continued accolades with every status update was so appreciated!

And finally to my mom! You never cease to amaze me with your creative ways to encourage, motivate, and help me achieve my goals! I will never be able to thank you enough for all you do for me each and every day!

Introduction

GUIDE TO THE LEED®*AP OPERATIONS AND MAINTENANCE (O+M) EXAM* is the resource to prepare for the Leadership in Energy and Environmental Design (LEED®) Accredited Professional (AP) Operations + Maintenance (O+M) exam. This exam prep guide provides a road map to studying for the LEED AP O+M exam as administered by Green Building Certification Institute (GBCI). The *Guide to the LEED AP Operations and Maintenance (O+M) Exam* is aimed at those professionals seeking more information about the basic knowledge and understanding that is required in order to pass the exam and earn the LEED AP O+M accreditation.

As a means to introduce myself, I am a LEED consultant and an education provider, focused on sustainable design and building operation concepts. I have traveled the country helping hundreds of students to prepare for the LEED Green Associate and LEED AP exams. The LEED AP O+M classes typically are two-day seminars that review all of the information as presented in this book. During these classes, I share my LEED project experiences and study tips in order to help make sense of this challenging information and present it in a logical format to help streamline the studying efforts for my students. This book breaks down the difficult information to be retained into a coherent and straightforward approach, as compared to simply repeating what would be found in the study reference material outlined by GBCI.

 TIP Keep an eye out for these **STUDY TIPS!** as they will point out the intricacies and nuances to remember.

EXAM PREP GUIDE STRUCTURE

Guide to the LEED AP Operations and Maintenance (O+M) Exam is organized into three parts as a method to break down the information one can expect to see on the exam. First, an introduction is needed to review the concepts and process covered in the LEED Green Associate exam in order to then understand the next part, which covers the technologies and strategies to implement as detailed in each prerequisite and credit. Finally, the appendices include charts and diagrams summarizing the critical information, as well as other resources to narrow down the amount of information to be studied as preparation to sit for and pass the LEED AP O+M exam. The composition of the book is as follows:

Part I: Ramping Up is composed of the following information:

Chapter 1: Understanding the Credentialing Process

Chapter 2: Sustainability and LEED Basics Review

Chapter 3: The LEED EBOM Rating System

 TIP Be sure to review the eligibility requirements described in Chapter 1 to apply for the LEED AP O+M exam.

Part II: Diving In: The Strategies and Technologies of LEED details the overlying concepts of the primary categories and the strategies to achieve each basic concept within. Part II is focused on organizing the information to remember and also to provide the concepts behind each prerequisite and credit. It is intended to work in tandem with the coordinating study worksheets included at the end of each chapter to help you remember the details, such as the intents, requirements, documentation requirements, and required calculations of each prerequisite and credit. In Part II, the following LEED categories are reviewed:

Chapter 4: Sustainable Sites

Chapter 5: Water Efficiency

Chapter 6: Energy and Atmosphere

Chapter 7: Materials and Resources

Chapter 8: Indoor Environmental Quality

Chapter 9: Innovation in Operations and Regional Priority

Part III: Study Tips and Appendices is dedicated to summarizing the critical information, details, and concepts to retain, as well as providing an overview of the testing center environment. The appendices include additional resources to help summarize the information presented in Parts I and II, such as scorecards and summary charts.

STUDY TIPS! are located throughout the book as tools to help stay focused on the pertinent information. They will include things to remember and point out side note types of information. While reading through this book, be sure to also keep an eye out for **FLASHCARD TIPS!**, as they will help to distinguish the important aspects for the exam and act as an indicator to create critical flashcards. All of the FLASHCARD TIPS! referenced throughout the book are collected at the end, following the index, although it is suggested to create your own to enhance your studying. It is recommended to purchase plain white note cards, as well as the color-coded note cards (i.e., pink, yellow, blue, green, and purple). Use the white ones for the information to be covered in Part I and the color-coded cards for Part II of this exam prep book. The FLASHCARD TIPS! suggest a starting point for flashcard creation, but feel free to make more as needed. If you decide to make your own with the help of the FLASHCARD TIPS!, be sure to refer to flashcards at the end for some additional flashcard suggestions. If you decide to use the flashcards from the book and not make your own, you can always use markers or highlighters to color-code them for streamlined studying.

One of the main concepts of sustainable design is the integrative fashion in which green buildings are designed and constructed. It is critical to understand how strategies and technologies have synergies and trade-offs. For example, green roofs can have an impact on a construction budget but can help save on operational energy costs, which may present a breakeven or surplus. Green roofs, as seen in Figure I.1, also have synergistic qualities because they can not only help reduce the heat burden on a building, but also help to manage stormwater. These types of concepts will be discussed in greater detail in Part II of this exam prep guide, but for now be sure to look for these **BAIT TIPS!** throughout Part II to help bring the concepts together.

Be sure to spot these **FLASHCARD TIPS!** to create flashcards along the way. Use the white cards for Part I and the color-coded ones for Part II.

Be sure to look out for these **BAIT TIPS!** as well. These tips will reinforce the important concepts and **B**ring **A**ll of **I**t **T**ogether as synergies and trade-offs are pointed out for green building strategies and technologies.

Figure I.1 Holy Wisdom Monastery project in Madison, Wisconsin, by Hoffman, LLC, reduces the amount of stormwater runoff from the site, increases the amount of open space, promotes biodiversity, reduces cooling loads, and reduces the impacts of the urban heat-island effect by implementing a vegetated roof. *Photo courtesy of Hoffman, LLC*

STUDY SCHEDULE

Week	Chapters	Pages
1	Part I: Ramping Up (Chapters 1–3)	1–30
2	Part II: Sustainable Sites (Chapter 4)	31–78
3	Part II: Water Efficiency (Chapter 5)	79–108
4	Part II: Energy and Atmosphere (Chapter 6)	109–152
5	Part II: Materials and Resources (Chapter 7)	153–196
6–7	Part II: Indoor Environmental Quality (Chapter 8)	197–254
8	Part II: Innovation in Operations and Regional Priority (Chapter 9) and Part III: Study Tips	255–276
9	Study flashcards, rewrite your cheat sheet a few times, and take online practice exams	
10	Register and take the LEED AP O+M Exam!	

As the preceding table shows, it is recommended to read through Parts I and II of this exam prep book within eight weeks. Introductory terminology from Part I should be absorbed to get on the right path to understand the more critical exam-oriented information presented in Part II. The goal is to create a complete set of flashcards during the first eight weeks while reading through the material, thus allowing the following week (ninth week of studying) to focus on memorizing and studying the flashcards, followed by taking a few online practice exams, which are available at www.GreenEDU.com.

TIP After taking some practice exams, you may want to add to your cheat sheet and/or your flashcards.

Although the exam format and structure will be reviewed in Part III of this book, there is one component that should be revealed up front. When at the testing center and about to take the exam, you will be prompted to take a tutorial on the computer. You will be allotted 10 minutes for the tutorial but will probably need only 4 to 5 minutes. It is highly advised to take advantage of those extra 5 to 6 minutes and jot down some thoughts and make a "cheat sheet" of sorts prior to starting the exam. Although you will not be allowed to bring any paper, books, or pencils into the exam area, you will be supplied with blank paper and a pencil (or a dry-erase board and a marker). So now that you know this opportunity is there, let's take advantage of it! Therefore, as a concept, strategy, referenced standard, or requirement is presented in this exam prep guide, make note of it on one single sheet of paper. At the end of Part II, this "cheat sheet" should be reviewed and then rewritten with the critical information you determine that you might forget during the exam. You are the only one who knows your weaknesses in terms of the information you need to learn—I can only make recommendations and suggestions. During Week Nine, you should rewrite your cheat sheet two to three more times. The more you write and rewrite your cheat sheet, the better chance you will have for actually retaining the information. It is also advised to monitor the time it takes to generate your cheat sheet, as time will be limited on exam day.

If you maintain the recommended study schedule, eight weeks from now a set of flashcards will be created and your cheat sheet started. Then you will have one week of consistent studying time to focus on the material in your flashcards. After studying your flashcards, it is recommended to take a few online practice exams to test your knowledge. The approach to these sample exams is described in Part III, Chapter 10, of this book, including the next steps for the cheat sheet. After a few practice exams, an assessment of your preparation should be completed to determine if you are ready for the exam. Your exam date should be scheduled at that time, as appointment times are readily available.

Before focusing on the exam material, be sure to read through Chapter 1 to understand the application requirements of the LEED AP O+M exam to ensure your eligibility and to understand the exam application process.

Guide to the
LEED® AP Operations and Maintenance (O+M) Exam

PART I

RAMPING UP

CHAPTER 1

UNDERSTANDING THE CREDENTIALING PROCESS

BEFORE DIVING INTO THE EFFORT OF STUDYING and preparing for the Leadership in Energy and Environmental Design (LEED®) Accredited Professional (AP) Operations + Maintenance (O+M) exam, there are quite a few things to review to ensure your eligibility. Whenever I teach an exam prep course, this topic is not typically addressed until the end of the class, as it is easier to digest at that point; but it is important to present this information here in the first chapter, to make sure the test is applicable and appropriate for you. This chapter will provide the important concepts of the tiered credentialing system to ensure that the components, the exam application process, and the requirements for eligibility are understood.

This initial information begins with the credentialing system for LEED accreditation, as it involves three tiers:

1. LEED Green Associate
2. LEED Accredited Professional (AP) with Specialty
3. LEED Fellow

THE TIERS OF THE CREDENTIALING PROCESS

The first step of comprehending the credentialing process begins with a brief understanding of the basics of LEED. LEED is the acronym for Leadership in Energy and Environmental Design, signifying a green building rating system designed to evaluate projects and award them certification based on their performance. U.S. Green Building Council's (USGBC®) created the LEED Green Building Rating System back in the 1990s as a tool for the public and private commercial real estate markets to help evaluate the performance of the built environment.

 TIP Notice the LEED acronym does **not** contain an "S" at the end. Therefore, please note this first lesson: when referring to LEED, please do not say "LEEDS," as it is quite important to refer to the acronym correctly.

The First Tier of the Credentialing System: LEED Green Associate

The **LEED Green Associate** tier is applicable for professionals with a basic understanding of green building systems and technologies. Green Associate professionals have been tested on the key components of the LEED rating systems and the certification process. This level of credentialing is the first step to becoming a LEED Accredited Professional (AP).

The Second Tier of the Credentialing System: LEED Accredited Professional with Specialty

The next tier, **LEED AP with Specialty**, is divided into five types (of specialties):

1. *LEED AP Building Design + Construction* (BD+C). This exam includes concepts related to new construction and major renovations, core and shell projects, and schools. This specialty will also cover retail and health care applications in the future.
2. *LEED AP Interior Design + Construction* (ID+C). This exam contains questions related to tenant improvement and fit-out project knowledge for commercial interior and retail professionals.
3. *LEED AP Operations + Maintenance* (O+M). This exam covers existing building project knowledge specific to operations and maintenance issues.
4. *LEED AP Homes.* This exam applies to professionals practicing in the residential market.
5. *LEED AP Neighborhood Development* (ND). This exam tests whole or partial neighborhood development project knowledge.

LEED project experience is required in order to be able to sit for any of the LEED AP specialty exams. These exams cover more in-depth knowledge of each of the prerequisites and credits; the requirements to comply, including documentation and calculations; and the technologies involved with the corresponding rating system. These exams are, therefore, applicable for those professionals working on LEED registered projects or those who have worked on a project within the last three years that has earned certification.

The Third Tier of the Credentialing System: LEED Fellow

Finally, the third tier of the credentialing system, **LEED Fellow**, is the highest level of credentialing. It is meant to signify a demonstration of accomplishments, experience, and proficiency within the sustainable design and construction community. These individuals will have contributed to the continued development of the green building industry.

THE APPLICATION PROCESS

TIP GBCI updates the candidate handbooks for each of the exam types at the beginning of each month, so make sure to have the most current version.

Now that there is an understanding about the three tiers of the credentialing system, whom each tier is geared for, and the eligibility requirements of each exam type, it is time to review the process for applying for the exam. The first step involves visiting the Green Building Certification Institute (GBCI®) website at www.gbci.org and downloading the *LEED AP O+M Candidate Handbook* found in the Professional Credentials section of the website.

Although the intention of this exam prep book is to consolidate all of the information needed to prepare for the LEED AP O+M exam, some of the references are updated from time to time. Therefore, this book contains similar information to that found in the handbooks for added efficiency, but you are best advised to refer to the latest version of the handbook appropriate to the LEED AP O+M credential for the most up-to-date exam information, especially as related to the exam application process.

APPLY...

REGISTER...

SCHEDULE!

Figure 1.1 The steps to register for the LEED AP O+M exam.

APPLY!

Assuming that an account is already established with GBCI, the next step is to apply for eligibility. On the GBCI website, visit the "My Credentials" section to begin the process after logging in. Make sure the profile is correct, and select the intended credentialing path. It is assumed that you have already passed the LEED Green Associate exam, and therefore you will only need to have worked on a LEED project within the past three years to be eligible to sit for the LEED AP O+M exam. Be sure to refer to the candidate handbook for more information about the requirements for project participation. Next, enter in the project information, such as name, location, and rating system in which it was registered or certified under and upload the documentation proving eligibility as described in the *LEED AP O+M Candidate Handbook.* You will then need to pay the non-refundable $100 application fee. Within seven days, you should receive an email indicating approval or denial, in order to move to the next step of the exam registration process. "Five to seven percent of all applications will be audited; you will be notified immediately if you are chosen for an audit and will be notified of your eligibility within seven days."[1] Should indication of ineligibility be received, you will be required to wait 90 days to apply again.

REGISTER!

Your application is valid for up to one year, once approval notification is received. At this point, the next step of registering for the exam should be seen as an option within the "My Credentials" section of the website. Here, verification is required for the test to be registered for and confirmation of membership status. Remember, USGBC national company members can take advantage of reduced exam fees. This means the company in which you work for must be a national member of USGBC. To receive the discount, you will need to ensure your USGBC/GBCI account profile contains the corporate ID associated with the company in which you for.

SCHEDULE!

The next step is scheduling an appointment to take the exam at a Prometric testing center. As stated previously, it is advisable to refrain from selecting an exam date until further along in the preparation for the exam. In the introduc-

TIP To reschedule or cancel an exam date, please consult the *LEED AP O+M Candidate Handbook* for explicit instructions. They are quite meticulous about the procedure, so it is advisable to be aware of the details to avoid risking a loss in fees paid.

tion of this exam prep book, a study and reading schedule is suggested. It is highly recommended that you start studying and determine the level of knowledge of the test content before scheduling an exam date.

When you are ready to schedule an exam date, visit www.prometric.com/gbci, or if you are at the GBCI website, follow the links to the Prometric website to schedule a day to take the exam, from the "My Credentials" section. Remember, the eligibility code from GBCI is required to schedule an exam date. After an exam date is scheduled, a confirmation code is displayed on the screen. Keep this code! It will be needed should you need to cancel, confirm, or reschedule the selected exam date with Prometric. A confirmation email containing your confirmation code will be sent from Prometric shortly after scheduling.

CHAPTER **2**

SUSTAINABILITY AND LEED BASICS REVIEW

AS MENTIONED EARLIER, it is critical to be on the right path by remembering the basic concepts tested on the Leadership in Energy and Environmental Design (LEED®) Green Associate exam before jumping into the details of the LEED categories as seen on the LEED Accredited Professional (AP) Operations + Maintenance (O+M) exam. For example, what is sustainability? When referring to green buildings, it is understood that the buildings are sensitive to the environment, but one might wonder, how exactly? Green buildings are more efficient and use resources wisely, as they take energy, water, and materials into account (Figure 2.1). But one might ask, "How do they use resources more efficiently?"

Figure 2.1 Reasor's Supermarket in Owassa, Oklahoma, incorporates daylighting strategies and polished concrete floors, together helping the project to earn multiple LEED credits within different categories, including Materials and Resources, Energy and Atmosphere, and Indoor Environmental Quality. *Photo courtesy of L&M Construction Chemicals, Inc.*

7

To answer this question, it is important to think of the different aspects of a building, for instance:

- *Site selection.* Is the project a redevelopment in an urban area, or does it support urban sprawl? How close is the project to public transportation to reduce the number of cars coming and going? How is the building situated in order to take advantage of the natural breezes for ventilation and daylight to reduce the need for artificial lighting within the building? Does it contribute to the heat island effect? How is stormwater managed?

- *Design of the building systems, such as mechanical equipment, building envelope, and lighting systems.* How do the systems work together? Were they designed independently of each other? Is the heat emitted from the lighting fixtures accounted for? Are there gaps in the envelope that allow conditioned air to escape?

- *Construction processes.* For a new construction project or an existing facility undergoing an alteration or addition, think about the people on site during construction—are they being exposed to harmful fumes and gases? Are precautions being taken to reduce the chances for mold growth or other contaminants?

- *Operations of the building.* What kinds of items are purchased to support business? What about cleaning procedures for the exterior and indoor environments?

- *Maintenance.* When was the last time equipment was tested to ensure that it is performing appropriately? Are there procedures in place to monitor for leaks?

- *Waste management.* How is construction waste addressed? What about the garbage generated during operations? Is it going to the landfill? Who knows where those containers are going?!

> **TIP** When thinking of green buildings, it is important to think of not only how the building is designed to function and how it is constructed, but also the environmental impacts from operations and maintenance.

THE TRIPLE BOTTOM LINE

The USGBC website summarizes the benefits of green buildings in three components: environmental, economic, and health and community benefits, as shown in Table 2.1. In the green building industry, these three concepts are defined as

Table 2.1 The Benefits of Green Buildings[1]

Environmental Benefits	Enhance and protect ecosystems and biodiversity
	Improve air and water quality
	Reduce solid waste
	Conserve natural resources
Economic Benefits	Reduce operating costs
	Enhance asset value and profits
	Improve employee productivity and satisfaction
	Optimize life-cycle economic performance
Health and Community Benefits	Improve air, thermal, and acoustic environments
	Enhance occupant comfort and health
	Minimize strain on local infrastructure
	Contribute to overall quality of life

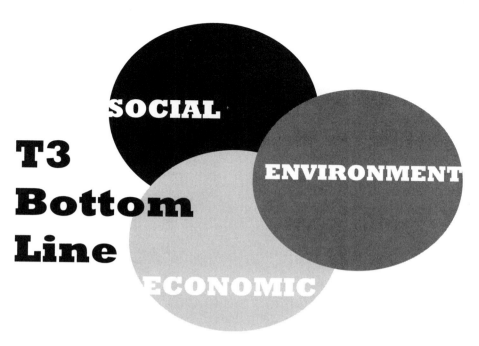

Figure 2.2 The triple bottom line.

the *triple bottom line* (see Figure 2.2). A conventional project usually assesses only the singular component of the economic prosperity for the project. However, when determining the goals for a project seeking LEED certification, the process typically begins with assessing the goals in comparison to the *triple* bottom line values. For example, should a client wish to install a green roof on their building, the team would assess the financial implications as compared to the environmental impacts versus the community benefits. These types of details will be discussed later, but understanding the three types of benefits is important at this time.

DO GREEN BUILDINGS COST MORE?

USGBC has promoted many studies, including one from Davis Langdon (as found in the references listed in the LEED AP O+M candidate handbook), indicating that green building does not have to cost more. This is especially true if the project starts the process early in the planning phases. It is also important to bridge the gap between capital and operating budgets to understand the value of green building technologies and strategies. For example, the first or up-front cost of installing photovoltaic panels, high-efficiency mechanical systems, or an indoor water wall to improve indoor air quality may not fit in a typical budget, but if the utility cost savings were considered and evaluated, either one might make more sense. Another case in point, first costs may also be higher in a traditionally planned project because of the lack of integration. Remember, the economic bottom line is important, but a green building project team also evaluates the environmental and social impacts and benefits (see Figure 2.2).

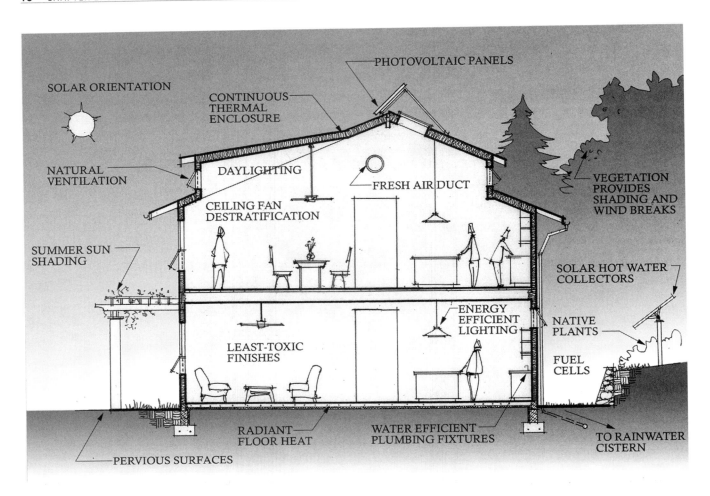

Figure 2.3 The EcoDorm at Warren Wilson College in Swannanoa, North Carolina, earned Platinum certification under the LEED for Existing Buildings™ rating system after a thorough investigation of credit synergies of the sustainable concepts implemented, such as shading and the photovoltaic system installed to save on energy costs. *Photo courtesy of Samsel Architects*

USGBC AND GBCI

Although Chapter 1 briefly introduced USGBC, it is important to remember the organization as "a 501(c)(3) nonprofit composed of leaders from every sector of the building industry working to promote buildings and communities that are environmentally responsible, profitable and healthy places to live and work," as posted on the USGBC website.[2] Remember also, USGBC created GBCI in January 2008 to "administer project certifications and professional credentials and certificates within the framework of the U.S. Green Building Council's Leadership in Energy and Environmental Design (LEED®) Green Building Rating Systems™," as indicated on the GBCI website.[3]

 Make a flashcard to remember what a TAG is.

As indicated in Figure 2.4, USGBC is focused on developing the LEED Green Building Rating Systems, as well as providing education and research programs. In order to develop the rating systems, USGBC created a LEED Steering Committee composed of five **technical advisory groups** (TAGs) to help the main

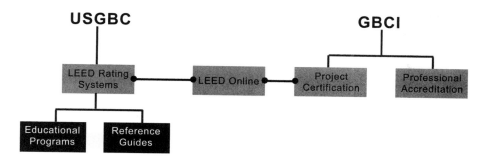

Figure 2.4 The Roles of USGBC and GBCI.

categories evolve. Eight regional councils are also a part of USGBC to help with the regional components of the rating systems.

GBCI was created in order to separate the rating system development from the certification and credentialing process. Therefore, GBCI is responsible for administering the process for projects seeking LEED certification and for professionals seeking accreditation credentials.

Now that you have an understanding of the roles of the two organizations, the next chapter will lay out the details of the certification process as related to the LEED for Existing Buildings: Operations & Maintenance (EBOM) rating system.

CHAPTER 3

THE LEED FOR EXISTING BUILDINGS: OPERATIONS & MAINTENANCE RATING SYSTEM

THE LEADERSHIP IN ENERGY AND ENVIRONMENTAL DESIGN (LEED®) Accredited Professional (AP) Operations + Maintenance (O+M) exam tests participants' knowledge of the LEED for Existing Buildings: Operations & Maintenance™ (EBOM) rating system contained within the *LEED Reference Guide for Green Buildings Operations and Maintenance*. Not only is it important to know which reference guide contains which rating system, but it is also important to know when to use each of the LEED rating systems for the purposes of the exam.

LEED FOR EXISTING BUILDINGS: OPERATIONS & MAINTENANCE (LEED EBOM)

The LEED EBOM rating system was developed for all commercial and institutional buildings and residential buildings of four or more habitable stories. This includes offices, retail, and services establishments, libraries, schools, museums, religious facilities, and hotels. In addition to the components of the other rating systems, LEED EBOM also encourages those responsible for buildings to evaluate their exterior site maintenance programs, purchasing policies for environmentally preferred services and products, cleaning programs and policies, waste stream, and ongoing indoor environmental quality.

The rating system is aimed at single, whole buildings, whether multi-tenanted or single owner–occupied. Although the owner is encouraged to seek participation from all the tenants, those responsible for a multi-tenanted building can exempt up to 10 percent of the total gross floor space and still pursue certification.

LEED EBOM is the only certification that can expire and is therefore the only rating system that can be recertified. The program is applicable to projects seeking certification for the first time or to projects that were previously certified under another rating system (See Figure 3.1), such as LEED for New Construction and Major Renovations™ (LEED NC), LEED for Schools™, or LEED Core and

Figure 3.1 Bill Stoller, the owner of Stoller Vineyards in Dayton, Ohio, holds the first LEED Gold plaque awarded to a winemaking facility. *Photo courtesy of Mike Haverkate, Stoller Vineyards*

 Create a flashcard to remember the details of initial certification versus recertification.

Shell™ (LEED CS). The LEED EBOM certification is valid for five years, although recertification can be applied for every year. Should a project not be recertified within five years and the certification expire, the next application for certification is considered to be initial.

Alterations and Additions

Project teams may find themselves questioning when is it appropriate to seek certification under the EBOM rating system as opposed to the LEED for New Construction and Major Renovations. For the purposes of LEED, there is a definitive difference between a *major renovation* and a *building alteration and addition*. Knowing the differences will help a project team determine the appropriate rating system. The *O&M Reference Guide* allows maximum and minimum determination for alterations and additions to establish the boundaries for when to use the EBOM rating system:

- "Maximum. **Alterations** that affect no more than 50 percent of the total building floor area or cause relocation of no more than 50 percent of regular building occupants are eligible. **Additions** that increase the total building floor area by no more than 50 percent are eligible."[1]

- Minimum. **Alterations** are required to involve more than one construction trade, impact at least 1 entire room, and impact the building occupants requiring isolation of work for the duration of construction. Building **additions,** on the other hand, must increase the total building floor area by at least 5 percent.[2]

Therefore, if any alterations or addition to projects exceed the maximum scope as defined, those responsible for the project should pursue certification under the LEED NC rating system. Should an alteration or addition project not meet the minimum requirements, one can still pursue EBOM certification for the existing building. In this case, the only hindrance would pertain to the pursuit

 Create a flashcard to remember the maximum and minimum scope of work requirements in order to pursue EBOM certification.

of certain credits. Specifically, the scope of work would not be eligible for points under MR Credit 3: Sustainable Purchasing – Facility Alterations and Additions, MR Credit 9: Solid Waste Management – Facility Alterations and Additions, and EQ Credit 1.5: IAQ Best Management Practices – IAQ Management for Facility Additions and Alterations.

CATEGORIES OF LEED

Just as with most of the other rating systems, the LEED EBOM rating system, included in the O+M Reference Guide, has five main categories:

- Sustainable Sites (SS)
- Water Efficiency (WE)
- Energy & Atmosphere (EA)
- Materials & Resources (MR)
- Indoor Environmental Quality (EQ)

The rating system also includes two other categories, which provide bonus points: Innovation in Operations (IO) and Regional Priority (RP).

PREREQUISITES AND CREDITS

As shown in Figure 3.2, within each category of each of the rating systems, there are prerequisites and credits. For certification, it is critical to remember that prerequisites are absolutely required, while credits are optional. Not all categories

 Make a flashcard to remember the differences between credits and prerequisites. Be sure to include the following: credits are optional components that earn points, while prerequisites are mandatory, are not worth any points, and address minimum performance features.

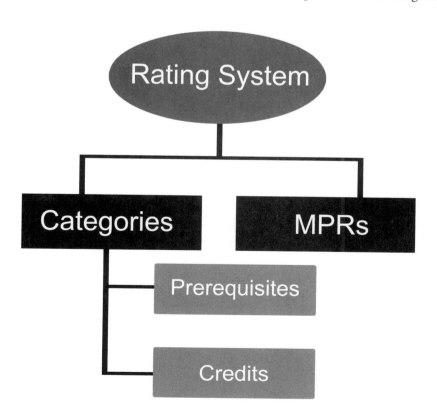

Figure 3.2 The components of a rating system.

contain prerequisites, but all of the categories have credits. All of the prerequisites of each primary category, required by the majority of the rating systems, are noted in the following list. These minimum performance features will be discussed in Part II, within each chapter, broken out by category. It does not matter if a project intends to pursue credits in every category—*all* prerequisites are required and are mandatory within the rating system the project is working within.

The prerequisites covered in the EBOM rating system are sorted by category:

Water Efficiency
> Minimum Indoor Plumbing Fixture and Fitting Efficiency

Energy & Atmosphere
> Energy Efficiency Best Management Practices
> Minimum Energy Efficiency Performance
> Fundamental Refrigerant Management

Materials & Resources
> Sustainable Purchasing Policy
> Solid Waste Management Policy

Indoor Environmental Quality
> Minimum Indoor Air Quality (IAQ) Performance
> Environmental Tobacco Smoke (ETS) Control
> Green Cleaning Policy

Each prerequisite and credit is structured the same way, and they include the same components.

The components of prerequisites and credits:

Credit name and point value

Intent: Describes the main goal or benefit for each credit or prerequisite.

Requirements: Details the elements to fulfill the prerequisite or credit. Some credits have a selection of options to choose from to earn point(s).

Benefits and issues to consider: Discusses the triple bottom line values to the credit or prerequisite.

Related credits: Indicates the trade-offs and synergies of credits and prerequisites.

Referenced standards: Lists the standard referenced for establishing the requirements of the credit or prerequisite.

Implementation: Suggests strategies and technologies to comply with the requirements of the credit or prerequisite.

Timeline and team: Outlines which team member is typically responsible for the credit and when the effort should be addressed.

Calculations: Although most calculations are completed online, this section describes the formulas to be used that are specific to the credit or prerequisite.

Documentation guidelines: Describes the necessary documentation requirements to be submitted electronically for certification review.

Examples: Demonstrates examples to satisfy requirements.

Exemplary performance: Think of these as bonus points for achieving the next incremental level of performance,

Regional variations: Speaks to issues as related to project's geographic location.

Resources: Provides other tools or suggestions for more information on the topic.

Definitions: Provides clarification for general and unique terms presented.

Credit Weightings

Since prerequisites are required, they are not worth any points. All credits, however, are worth a minimum of one point. Credits are always positive whole numbers, never fractions or negative values. All prerequisites and credits are tallied on scorecards (also referred to as checklists) specific to each rating system.

Any project seeking certification must earn a minimum of 40 points, but this does not mean 40 credits must be earned as well; because different credits are weighted differently, they have varying point potentials. To determine each credit's weight, USGBC referred to the U.S. Environmental Protection Agency's (EPA's) 13 Tools for the Reduction and Assessment of Chemical and Other Environmental Impacts (TRACI) categories for environmental and health concerns including: climate change, resource depletion, human health criteria, and water intake. Once the categories of impact were determined and prioritized, USGBC referred to the National Institute of Standards and Technology (NIST) for their research to determine a value for each of the credits by comparing each of the strategies to mitigate each of the impacts.

As a result of the credit weighting and carbon overlay exercise, LEED values those strategies that reduce the impacts on climate change and those with the greatest benefit for indoor environmental quality, focusing on energy efficiency and carbon dioxide (CO_2) reduction strategies. For example, transportation is a very important element within LEED, and therefore any credits associated with getting to and from the project site are weighted more than others. Note Credit 4 in the Sustainable Sites category is worth up to 15 points, more than half of all the point opportunities within the category! Water is an invaluable natural resource, and therefore water efficiency and consumption reduction is weighted appropriately to encourage project teams to design accordingly to use less. Providing renewable energy on a project's site will lessen the burden on fossil fuels, and therefore it is also suitably weighted.

In summary, USGBC created a simplified, 100-base-point scale for the four different certification levels.

- *Certified:* 40–49 points
- *Silver:* 50–59 points
- *Gold:* 60–79 points
- *Platinum:* 80 and higher

The 100 base points are totaled from the five main categories: SS, WE, EA, MR, and EQ. The last two categories make up 10 bonus points for a total of 110 available points. See Table 3.1 for a breakdown of credits and point opportunities per category for the EBOM rating system. The Credit column provides the number of credits consistent with the scorecard while the number in parentheses provides the actual number of credits available. For example, SS Credit 7: Heat Island Reduction is one credit but has two different opportunities to earn points: one

TIP Remember, prerequisites are not worth any points but are mandatory regardless of the strategy pursued within each category, in order for a project to receive certification.

TIP Refer to the LEED EBOM scorecard in Appendix A for a visual representation of how each category is composed of credits and prerequisites and the allocation of points.

Remember, credit weightings are based on environmental impacts and human benefits, such as energy efficiency and CO_2 reduction for cleaner air.

Make a flashcard so that you can quiz yourself of the certification levels and corresponding point range.

Table 3.1 Point Distributions for the EBOM Rating System

Credits	Category	Possible Points
8 (9)	Sustainable Sites	26
5	Water Efficiency	14
6 (9)	Energy and Atmosphere	35
9 (10)	Materials and Resources	10
3 (15)	Indoor Environmental Quality	15
	Subtotal	100
Innovation and/or Exemplary		6
Regional Priority		4
Total		110

for non-roof strategies (SSc7.1) and another for roof strategies (SSc7.2). Notice prerequisites are not addressed in the chart, as they are not worth any points.

QUIZ TIME!

 TIP Don't worry if some of the questions presented are unfamiliar territory. The questions in this book are meant to present you with new information to learn from and to prepare you for the real exam, as there is bound to be information presented for which you will need to use the process of elimination to determine the best answers.

 TIP Refer to Appendix G to review the answers to these quiz questions.

Q3.1. How long is the LEED EBOM certification valid for? (Choose one)

A. 2 years

B. 3 years

C. 4 years

D. 5 years

E. Forever, it never expires.

Q3.2. Which of the following statements are true in regard to credit weightings? (Choose two)

A. USGBC consulted with NIST and the U.S. EPA's TRACI tool to determine the credit weightings.

B. The LEED rating systems were reorganized, and new credits were introduced to recognize what matters most, such as transportation.

C. The LEED EBOM rating system is based on a 100-point scale.

D. All credits are worth two points within LEED NC, but only one point within LEED CS.

Q3.3. If an existing facility wishes to undergo a renovation, they could look to LEED for New Construction or LEED for Existing Buildings: Operations & Maintenance rating systems and determine which one is more applicable. (Choose two)

A. If the alteration impacts more than 50 percent of the total building floor area, the project must use LEED NC.

B. If the alteration impacts more than 50 percent of the total building floor area, the project must use LEED EBOM.

C. If the alteration affects less than 50 percent of the building occupants, the project must use LEED NC.

D. If the alteration impacts less than 50 percent of the building occupants, the project must use LEED EBOM.

Q3.4. Which of the following is true about credit weightings and the carbon overlay? (Choose one)

A. Considers the impact of direct energy use

B. Considers the impact of transportation

C. Considers the impact of embodied emissions of water, solid waste, and materials

D. All of the above

Q3.5. Incorporating green building strategies, such as high-efficiency mechanical systems, on-site photovoltaic systems, and an indoor water wall to help with the indoor air quality and air conditioning, plays a role in what type of cost implications? (Choose one)

A. Increased life-cycle costs

B. Increased first costs

C. Reduced construction costs

D. Increased soft costs

E. Reduced soft costs

Q3.6. If a project plans on earning silver certification under the LEED EBOM rating system, which point range would they aim for? (Choose one)

A. 50–59

B. 20–30

C. 40–49

D. 60–69

E. 30–39

THE LEED CERTIFICATION PROCESS

The typical project team members were previously outlined, but one member was not included: the LEED project administrator. The administrator is typically responsible for registering a project with Green Building Certification Institute (GBCI®) and for the coordination between all of the disciplines on the project team, by managing the documentation process until LEED certification is awarded. The LEED project administrator can be one of the team members previously mentioned in Chapter 2 and, therefore, would serve a dual-purpose role, or they can be an addition to the team. In either case, the administrator would grant access to each of the team members to LEED-Online, the online project management system.

LEED-Online

TIP To learn more about LEED-Online, be sure to check out the demo video at www.youtube.com/watch?v=fS3yzjZxcUA.

LEED-Online is a web-based tool used to manage a project seeking LEED certification. It is the starting point to register a project with GBCI and communicate with the certification bodies, and it is used to review the documentation submitted for both prerequisites and credits during design and construction. All projects seeking certification (except LEED for Homes™) are required to utilize LEED-Online to upload submittal templates and any required supporting documentation, such as drawings, contracts, and policies for review by the assigned certification body. Project teams receive reviewer feedback, can check the status of application reviews, and learn the certification level earned for their project through LEED-Online. Credit interpretation requests (CIRs) and appeals (both to be discussed later in the chapter) are also processed through LEED-Online.

When a team member is invited to a project on LEED-Online, he or she needs to log in to the LEED-Online website to gain access. Once signed in, the team member is greeted with the "My Projects" page, which shows a list of active projects that person is assigned to. Upon selecting one of the projects, the "Project Dashboard" page appears. This dashboard serves as a project's home page and provides access to:

TIP Remember, only invited team members can see a project's LEED-Online page, after a project is registered.

- The project's scorecard, which shows which credits the team is pursuing and their status.

- CIRs and rulings.

- LEED submittal templates—think of these as the "cover page" for each credit and prerequisite. There is a submittal template for every prerequisite and credit, which must be submitted through LEED-Online. If a calculation is needed to show compliance, the template contains a spreadsheet with built-in functionality that automatically completes the calculation after the required data is input according to the requirements described in the reference guides.

- A timeline, which shows when a project administrator would submit information for certification review

- Postcertification—to purchase plaques, certificates, and the like

Registration

TIP Remember, USGBC members pay a reduced fee for project registration and certification.

The LEED certification process for projects begins with project registration. To register a project, the team administrator would sign in to LEED-Online and click on the "Register New Project" tab and follow the instructions provided. The registration process begins with a review of eligibility criteria, including contact and USGBC membership verification. The next step involves selecting a rating system. LEED-Online provides assistance through a Rating System Selector to help the team to decipher which rating system is best suited to the specific project seeking certification. Before advancing to the Rating System Results step, the team administrator is prompted to confirm compliance with the seven minimum program requirements (MPRs) to be described in the next section. After MPR compliance is confirmed, the applicable LEED scorecard appears. The next step of registration is entering specific project information, including owner contact information, the project's address and square footage, and the anticipated construction start and end dates. All of the information is then presented on screen for review, the payment is processed, and the registration information is confirmed. The project administrator is then awarded access to the project's LEED-Online page through the My Projects tab and assigned a certification body for customer service.

Minimum Program Requirements

Just as there are prerequisites that must be achieved in each rating system, there are seven MPRs that must be met in order for a project to receive certification. MPRs pertain to all the rating systems except LEED for Homes and LEED for Neighborhood Development™ (LEED ND), but the following MPRs are specific to the EBOM rating system. MPRs are critical components that are not listed on a project scorecard, but instead are confirmed when the administrator registers a project on LEED-Online. Should noncompliance with any of the seven mandated MPRs be found at any time, a project could risk losing its certification, including any fees paid for registration and certification. The USGBC website details the following seven MPRs[3]:

MPR 1. Must comply with environmental laws
This MPR must be fulfilled from the beginning of the performance period through the date the LEED certification expires.

MPR 2. Must be a complete, permanent building or space
LEED projects must include at least one existing building, all-inclusive.

 MPR 2 prohibits mobile homes, trailers, and boats from pursuing LEED certification.

MPR 3. Must use a reasonable site boundary
The LEED project boundary must include and be consistent with all of the property as part of the scope of work of the new construction or major renovation, including any land that will be disturbed for the purpose of undertaking the LEED project during construction and operations.
The LEED project boundary may not include land that is owned by another party.
Campus projects seeking LEED certification must have project boundaries equal to 100 percent of the gross land area on the campus. If this causes a conflict with MPR 7, then MPR 7 takes precedence.

MPR 4. Must comply with minimum floor area requirements
A minimum of 1,000 square feet of gross floor area must be included in the scope of work.

MPR 5. Must comply with minimum occupancy rates
Full-Time Equivalent Occupancy. The LEED project must be occupied at least one full-time equivalent (FTE) occupant. If there is less than one annualized FTE, EQ credits will not be awarded, although compliance with EQ prerequisites is required.
Minimum Occupancy Rate. The LEED project must be occupied and operating during the performance period, and a minimum of one year before submitting the first certification review to GBCI.

MPR 6. Commitment to share whole-building energy and water usage data
Five years of actual whole-project utility data must be shared with U.S. Green Building Council (USGBC) and/or Green Building Certification Institute (GBCI) from the date certification was awarded to the EBOM project.

 Remember, all MPRs must be met in order to certify a project and to keep the certification once earned.

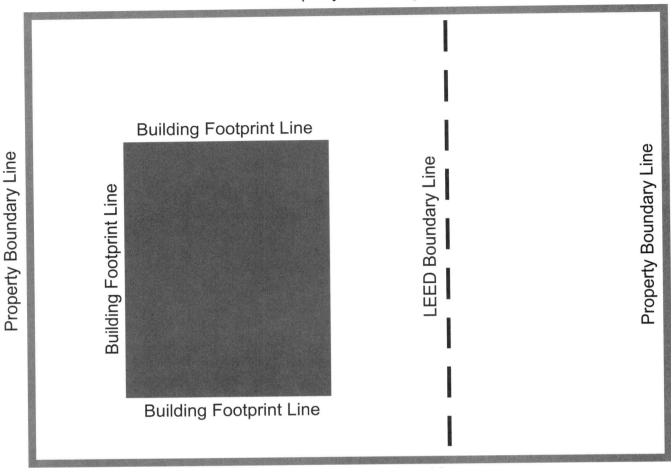

Property Boundary Line

Property Boundary Line

Property Boundary Line

Property Boundary Line

Building Footprint Line

Building Footprint Line

Building Footprint Line

LEED Boundary Line

Figure 3.3 The different types of boundaries for a LEED project.

Be sure to make flashcards to remember the seven MPRs.

Make a flashcard to remember the three types of boundaries associated with LEED projects.

MPR 7. Must comply with a minimum building area to site area ratio

The project's gross floor area must be no less than 2 percent of the gross land area within the LEED project boundary.

MPR 3 refers to the LEED project boundary. There are three types of boundaries to be aware of for the purposes of LEED: property boundary line, LEED project boundary line, and the building footprint (Figure 3.3). The property boundary line refers to the land owned according to a plot plan or legal property deed. The LEED project boundary line may or may not be the same as the property boundary. For example, a university may own acres of land but may wish to develop only a portion of it for one academic building. Therefore, the LEED project boundary line sets the limits for the scope of work to be included in the documents for certification. The building footprint is the amount of land on which the building resides.

Local municipalities are responsible for establishing sections of their towns for different uses and then characterizing these areas into different zones, such as commercial, residential, and industrial. These sections of land are regulated in reference to:

- Building type (commercial, residential, mixed-use, etc.)
- Building height
- Footprint, impervious versus pervious development
- Parking
- Setbacks
- Open space

Project teams should be mindful of local regulations for land and the allowable uses. For the purposes of the exam, it is important to remember, although many credits may reference zoning, LEED will never override local, state, or federal requirements.

 TIP Be sure to check out Appendix B for an MPR summary chart.

Credit Submittal Templates

After a project is registered, the project administrator invites the other team members to the project's LEED-Online site and assigns each member their coordinating prerequisites and credits they will be responsible for. This means each prerequisite and credit has one responsible party assigned to it, and that person will generate and upload the required documentation specific to each prerequisite and credit.

 TIP Remember, a submittal template acts as a cover page of sorts for each prerequisite and credit.

When a team member is assigned a credit or prerequisite, they become the **declarant** to sign the credit submittal template. Each of these templates summarizes how the project team has satisfied the requirements for the specific credit or prerequisite. There is a submittal template for every prerequisite and credit, which must be submitted through LEED-Online. If a calculation is needed to show compliance, the template contains a spreadsheet and automatically completes the calculation after the required data is input according to the requirements described in the reference guides. It is suggested to visit the USGBC website to download the sample submittal templates (the link is available through the candidate handbook from GBCI).

 TIP One team member can be assigned to more than one credit or prerequisite. Additional team members can be invited to LEED-Online and not be assigned any credit or prerequisite.

Remember, all prerequisites and credits require a submittal template, and some may require additional documentation. The additional documentation may be exempt if the design team opts to use the **licensed-professional exemption** (LPE) path. This optional path is determined on the submittal template.

 Make a flashcard to remember LPE!

Credit Interpretation Requests and Rulings

For those in the design and construction industry, it is helpful to think of **credit interpretation requests** (CIRs) like requests for information (RFIs). Just as a contractor may issue an RFI to a design team for clarification about a detail to be constructed, a project team can issue a CIR to their assigned certification body in an effort to obtain clarification or more information. CIRs can be submitted any time after a project is registered via LEED-Online. Because the certification bodies are an integral part of the certification process, they are responsible for answering and responding to CIRs.

 TIP When a CIR is responded to by a certification body, the reply is referred to as a **credit interpretation ruling.**

For a fee, team members of registered projects seeking LEED certification can submit CIRs for clarification about a credit or prerequisite within a LEED rating

 TIP Be sure to check out the CIR guidelines on the GBCI website at www.gbci.org/Libraries/Credential_Exam_References/Guidelines-for-CIR-Customers.sflb.ashx.

system. It is important to remember that CIRs are issued specific to *one* credit, prerequisite, or MPR. Note that CIR rulings are not considered final, nor are they definitive in determining if a particular strategy is satisfactory. Therefore, project teams are encouraged to upload their ruling with the coordinating credit, prerequisite, or MPR when submitting for a certification review through LEED-Online.

The USGBC website contains a database on previously issued CIRs for teams to query for more information before submitting a new one. Although these CIR postings serve as useful tools for a project team, they will no longer be used as supporting documentation for projects other than the one that submitted the CIR. For projects registered under the 2009, version 3 rating systems, CIRs are project specific and will not be posted to the database. With this change, teams are still encouraged to refer to the reference guides and the CIR database, as well as to contact their certification body before submitting a CIR, since there is a fee associated with issuing a new CIR. As of the print date for this Guide, USGBC has unofficially announced a change of the CIR process, but this update is not currently reflected in the exam.

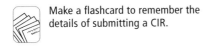 Make a flashcard to remember the details of submitting a CIR.

Certification Review

At the time of a review submission, the LEED project administrator will need to pay a fee for the certification review. This certification review fee is based on the rating system the project is seeking certification with, the project's square footage, and whether the project was registered under a corporate membership account

Figure 3.4 The certification review process.

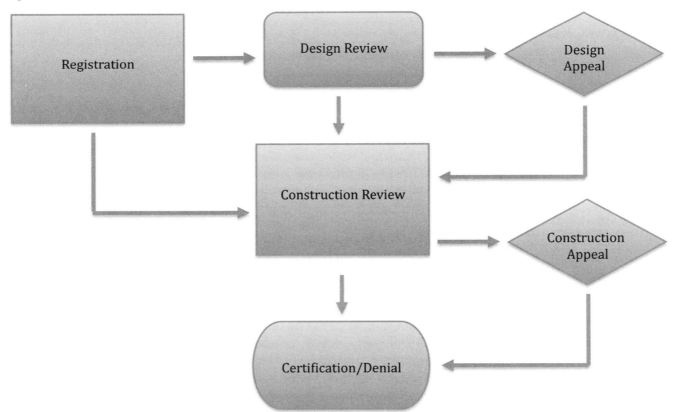

with USGBC. The project administrator will be required to submit a short project narrative to provide the certification body a background of the project, the intended use of the project, the location and surrounding areas, and any other details deemed appropriate for clarification purposes. Project photographs or renderings, elevations, floor plans, and any details should also be uploaded to LEED-Online.

 Make a flashcard to remember the three components on which a project's certification fees are based.

Performance Period

Although projects registered under the LEED EBOM rating system use LEED-Online just like most other LEED registered projects (except LEED for Homes), there are some key differences with the process for certification. When a project is registered under the NC, CI, CS, or LEED for Schools rating systems, the project is certified for the design and construction of a green building (See Figure 3.4). EBOM projects, however, are certified for a particular performance period (see Figure 3.5). A **performance period** is a continuous period of time in which a building or facility's performance is measured. A performance period is required to be at least 3 months long with a maximum length of 24 months for all prerequisites and credits. This minimum requirement confuses some, as EA Prerequisite 2 and Credit 1 require a facility's performance to be measured for at least 12 months. Therefore, the performance period is not necessarily consistent across all credits and prerequisites (although suggested), but the different periods associated with the prerequisites and credits must end within the same seven-day interval. They must be continuous without any gaps in data, although they can be paused for a maximum of one week.

Since design-side and construction-side prerequisites and credits do not exist within the EBOM rating system, as opposed to most of the other rating systems, there is not an opportunity for a split review (i.e., one at the end of the design phase and another one at the end of the construction phase) process with the GBCI certification body. EBOM projects must be submitted for certification review within 60 days after the performance periods are completed.

 Make a flashcard to remember the characteristics of a performance period.

The Time Frames of Certification Review

Table 3.2 outlines the schedule associated with the submission and review times during the LEED certification review process. Once a project team submits a request for review, they must then wait 25 business days to hear back from their assigned certification body. The certification body updates LEED-Online

TIP Remember, USGBC members pay a reduced rate for registration and certification.

Table 3.2 Certification Review Schedule

Process	Days
Certification review	25 business days
Team reply	25 business days
Final review	15 business days
Team reply	15 business days
Appeal (if necessary)	25 business days
Appeal review (if necessary)	25 business days
Certification awarded	

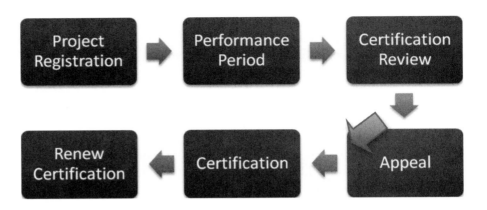

Figure 3.5 The LEED certification review process for an EBOM project.

to indicate whether a credit or prerequisite is "anticipated" or "denied," or it will issue clarification requests to the team specific to any credits or prerequisites in question. The team then has 25 business days to respond with more information to explain how they satisfy the requirements of the credit or prerequisite requiring clarification. At that time, the team must wait 15 business days to receive indication whether the credit or prerequisite clarified is either "anticipated" or "denied." Should the team receive a "denied" status, they can issue an appeal to GBCI for a fee within 25 business days. GBCI would then have 25 business days to review the appeal and issue a ruling to the project team. Although GBCI leaves CIRs to the certification bodies to respond to and manage, they remain directly responsible for administering the appeals process. Once the appeal process ends, certification is awarded.

THE EBOM PROCESS

Understanding the details of the certification process is the first step of learning more about how a project team works toward earning certification under the EBOM rating system. In the previous chapter, the process was described for a typical design and construction project, but an EBOM project approaches the process differently. For example, instead of kicking off a project with a programming exercise, an EBOM project would start with an audit. The **audit** phase includes a gap analysis, an initial cost-benefit analysis, and buy-in from the owner. This phase would establish the current performance of a facility and determine the opportunities for improvement. The next phase, **plan**, typically involves a charette, refinement of the cost-benefit analysis, developing a plan for improvements, and establishing roles and responsibilities. The third phase, **program development**, requires the critical plan elements to be verified while best practices of the plan are initiated, data is collected, and the set goals are completed. The next phase, **performance period/certification**, includes the completion of the actual performance periods, the process of submitting all of the documentation for certification review, and the awarding of certification. The last phase, **education/recertification**, might include sharing the successful certification with the building's occupants and the community and/or the process of recertifying the facility.

 Make a flashcard to remember the five phases of an EBOM project: audit, plan, program development, performance period/certification, and education/recertification.

Policies

The EBOM rating system includes the project team's submitting a number of policies to prove compliance with the prerequisites and credits. The O&M Reference Guide defines the following six components to be included in each of the policies as a minimum requirement:

1. *Scope.* How does the policy apply to the facility, operations, building components, systems, or materials?
2. *Performance metric.* How will the performance be measured?
3. *Goals.* What are the goals of the policy?
4. *Procedures and Strategies.* How will the goals be met?
5. *Responsible Party.* Define roles and responsibilities.
6. *Time Period.* What is the time period for the policy?

QUIZ TIME!

Q3.7.   Credit interpretation requests (CIRs) provide which of the following? (Choose two)

   A. Responses to written requests for interpretation of credit requirements

   B. Determination of whether a particular strategy can be used to satisfy two different credits at once

   C. Clarification of one existing LEED credit or prerequisite

   D. Definitive assurance that a particular method or strategy permitted on a previous project will be applicable to other projects in the future

Q3.8.   Which of the following meets the MPR regarding minimum gross floor area for LEED EBOM rating system? (Choose one)

   A. 250 square feet

   B. 500 square feet

   C. 1,000 square feet

   D. 2,500 square feet

Q3.9.   Which of the following statements are not true regarding MPRs? (Choose two)

   A. The LEED project boundary must include all contiguous land that is associated with normal building operations for the LEED project building, including all land that was or will be disturbed for the purpose of undertaking the LEED project.

   B. The owner must commit to sharing whole-building energy and water usage data for 10 years.

   C. LEED projects located on a campus must have project boundaries such that if all the buildings on campus become LEED certified, then 100 percent of the gross land area on the campus would be included within a LEED boundary.

D. Any given parcel of real property may only be attributed to a single LEED project building unreasonable shapes for the sole purpose of complying with prerequisites.

E. Gerrymandering of a LEED project boundary is allowed.

Q3.10. How many years must a project commit to sharing whole-building energy and water use? (Choose one)

A. 7 years

B. 10 years, unless the building changes ownership

C. 6 months

D. 1 year

E. 5 years

Q3.11. Which of the following statements are true? (Choose two)

A. Appeals are mailed to GBCI.

B. Appeals can be submitted within 25 business days after final certification review.

C. Appeals are free.

D. Appeals can pertain only to credits, not prerequisites or MPRs.

E. Appeals are submitted through LEED-Online.

Q3.12. Which of the following is new to all LEED rating systems under LEED 2009? (Choose one)

A. Minimum program requirements

B. Credit interpretation requests

C. The Regional Priority category

D. The Awareness and Education category

Q3.13. Design reviews can prove to be a beneficial option for a team to pursue since the project can be awarded points before construction begins. True or False?

A. True

B. False

Q3.14. LEED project registration provides which of the following? (Choose two)

A. Three credit interpretation requests (CIRs)

B. One preapplication USGBC review of project submittals and documentation

C. One point toward LEED certification for registration prior to the development of construction documents

D. Access to online LEED credit submittal templates for the project

E. Establishment of contact with GBCI and the assigned certification body

Q3.15. An application for LEED certification must contain which of the following? (Choose two)

A. Project summary information, including project contact, project type, project cost, project size, number of occupants, estimated date of occupancy, and the like.

B. A list of all members of the design and construction team, including contact information, documented green building industry experience, and indication of all LEED Accredited Professionals

C. Completed LEED credit submittal templates for all prerequisites and attempted credits, plus any documentation specifically required to support those templates

D. Detailed documentation for all credits pursued, including full-sized plans and drawings, photocopies of invoices for all purchased materials, records of tipping fees, all energy modeling inputs and assumptions, and evidence of all calculations performed in support of LEED credits

Q3.16. When should LEED credit submittal templates and documentation be submitted for certification review? (Choose one)

A. Beginning of a performance period

B. One year after the performance periods have been completed

C. 30 calendar days after the performance periods have been completed

D. 60 calendar days after the performance periods have been completed

E. 90 calendar days after the performance periods have been completed

Q3.17. Regarding the application process for LEED certification, which of the following is a correct statement? (Choose one)

A. LEED credit submittal templates and documentation may be submitted only after the performance periods are completed.

B. All LEED credit submittal templates and documentation must be submitted prior to the completion of the performance periods.

C. LEED credit submittal templates and documentation must be submitted to USGBC.

D. LEED credit submittal templates and documentation must be submitted via certified mail or an independent mail carrier service.

E. A team must submit any appeals after certification has been awarded.

Q3.18. How long does a project team have to submit an appeal after receiving certification review comments back from GBCI? (Choose one)

  A. 15 business days

  B. 25 business days

  C. 45 business days

  D. 1 week

  E. 1 month

Q3.19. Which of the following correctly characterizes credit interpretation requests (CIRs)? (Choose three)

  A. Can be viewed only by the primary contact for a registered project

  B. Can be submitted any time after a project is registered

  C. Must be requested through LEED-Online

  D. Can be requested only in a written request mailed to GBCI

  E. Can address more than one credit or prerequisite

  F. Are relevant to one specific project and will not be referenced in the CIR database

Q3.20. Who is responsible for the appeals process? (Choose one)

  A. GBCI

  B. USGBC

  C. Certification bodies

  D. None of the above

Q3.21. Regarding performance periods, which of the following is an incorrect statement? (Choose one)

  A. Performance periods must be at least 3 months long.

  B. Performance periods can start at different times, overlap, and not be stopped for more than one week.

  C. None of the prerequisites or credits requires a duration of less than 6 months.

  D. Performance periods must stop within the same seven-day interval.

  E. Performance periods are not to be longer than 24 months.

PART II

DIVING IN: THE STRATEGIES AND TECHNOLOGIES OF LEED EBOM

CHAPTER 4

SUSTAINABLE SITES

THIS CHAPTER BEGINS THE DETAILED STUDY OF THE INTENTIONS, requirements, and strategies described within the Sustainable Sites (SS) category's credits. The main topics include the factors applicable to site design and location, management and maintenance, transportation impacts, and stormwater management of a site. As with making any other decision while working on a green building project, all components within the SS category are weighed on the triple bottom line values of environmental, economic, and community effects.

Where a project is located and how it is maintained can have multiple impacts on the ecosystem and water resources required during the life of a building. The site's location can have an impact on a building's energy performance with respect to orientation, and stormwater runoff strategies could also be affected by the site's location. How much of the site is developed and how much was preserved or restored as open space? Does the site reduce the heat gain from the sun for the entire site, including rooftop areas? Are there strategies to reduce light pollution? Carbon emissions should be evaluated as well, as they increase because of the transportation required to get to and from the site. Is access by public transportation available? How much parking is available for cars? Does accessing the project site require the use of cars? If so, are there incentives for using carpools or vanpools?

These concepts and questions help to illuminate some of the important factors to consider when evaluating a site's true sustainable value. Sustainable

 Dedicate one color to all your flashcards within the SS category. That way anytime you see that color, you will associate that flashcard question with Sustainable Sites concepts and strategies.

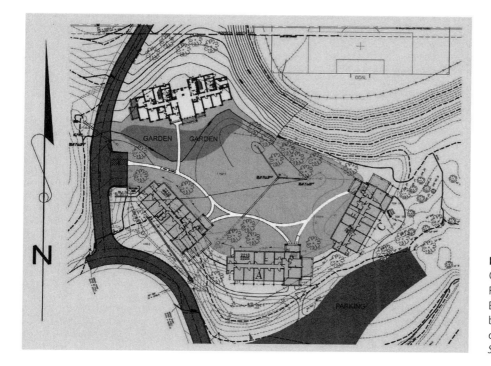

Figure 4.1 The EcoDorm at Warren Wilson College in Swannanoa, North Carolina, earned Platinum certification under the LEED® for Existing Buildings rating system as the fourth building of a master plan of dormitories adjacent to trails and ball fields. *Image courtesy of Samsel Architects*

strategies will aid the project in successfully earning Leadership in Energy and Environmental Design (LEED®) certification, as proven by the project team for the EcoDorm at Warren Wilson College (see Figure 4.1).

The SS category is composed of the credits shown in Table 4.1. Notice that there are no prerequisites, and the largest opportunity to earn points falls under Credit 4: Alternative Commuting Transportation. Use the table as a summary of the available credits, but for the purposes of the exam and to break down the information to remember, the category information is presented in this chapter according to general categories instead of on a credit-by-credit basis as shown in the reference guide. Therefore, when preparing for the LEED Accredited Professional (AP) Operations + Maintenance (O+M) exam, it is helpful to remember that the SS category is broken down into the following four areas and the associated credits:

1. Site design
2. Site management and maintenance
3. Transportation
4. Stormwater management

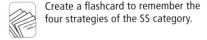 Create a flashcard to remember the four strategies of the SS category.

SITE DESIGN

A site's design lays the groundwork for sustainable management and maintenance strategies (see Figure 4.2). A site's sensitivity to vegetation, wildlife, water, and air quality provides the opportunity to implement sustainable strategies to maintain the grounds in an efficient manner. In addition, these strategies can mitigate the long-term detrimental effects a site can have on the environment.

From an environmental perspective, a sustainable site avoids the destruction of wildlife habitats to help lessen the threat to wildlife's ability to survive, as the goal is to preserve land and, thus, preserve plant and animal species. From an economic standpoint, a sustainably designed site is more efficient to maintain,

TIP Remember to use the study worksheets at the end of each chapter to recall the details of each credit, such as the intent, requirements, and documentation and calculation requirements.

Table 4.1 The Sustainable Sites Category

Timeframe	Credit	Title	Points
Audit	Credit 1	LEED Certified Design and Construction	4
Program Development	Credit 2	Building Exterior and Hardscape Management Plan	1
Program Development	Credit 3	Integrated Pest Management, Erosion Control, and Landscape Management Plan	1
Performance Period/Certification	Credit 4	Alternative Commuting Transportation	3-15
Audit	Credit 5	Site Development, Protect or Restore Open Habitat	1
Audit	Credit 6	Stormwater Quantity Control	1
Audit	Credit 7.1	Heat Island Effect, NonRoof	1
Audit	Credit 7.2	Heat Island Effect, Roof	1
Audit	Credit 8	Light Pollution Reduction	1

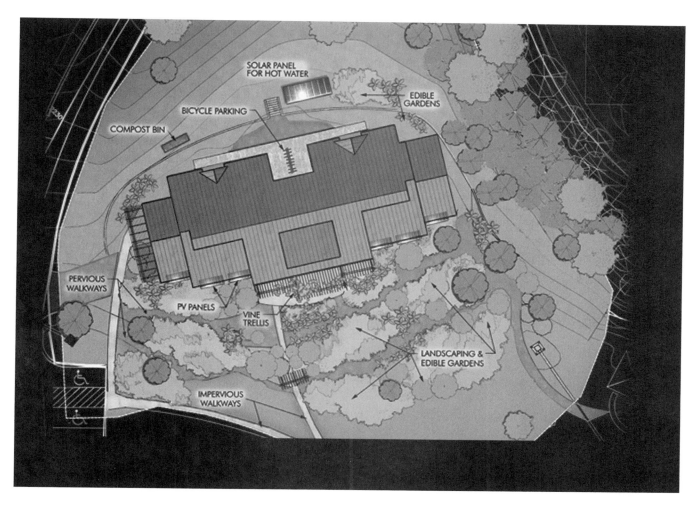

Figure 4.2 The EcoDorm project earned two points for the implementation of native and adaptive plantings under SS Credit 5 of the LEED for Existing Buildings version 2.0 rating system. *Image courtesy of Samsel Architects*

as less water and fertilizer are required. Reducing site's lighting or the duration of its use also can lower maintenance costs. The social equity of the proper site design could include the protection of the natural environment to be enjoyed and observed by future generations for ecological and recreational purposes.

Site Design in Relation to LEED Compliance

Project teams are encouraged to utilize the concepts of sustainable landscaping techniques, including using **native and/or adaptive plantings** with water-efficient irrigation systems, the preservation or restoration of open space, and the reduction of the heat island effect and light pollution. The following five credits address the sustainable strategies that project teams should be aware of when working on a project pursuing LEED for Existing Buildings: Operations & Maintenance™ (EBOM) certification.

SS Credit 1: LEED Certified Design and Construction. This credit is available for projects that were certified under the LEED for New Construction and Major Renovations™ (LEED NC), LEED for Schools™, or LEED for Core & Shell™ (LEED CS) rating systems. LEED CS projects are only eligible to pursue this

Create a flashcard to remember the definition of **building footprint:** the amount of land the building structure occupies, not including landscape and hardscape surfaces, such as parking lots, driveways, and walkways.

Monoculture plantings (e.g., turf grass) do not count, even if they are considered native or adaptive.

Preserving natural, ecologically appropriate features, such as exposed rock, water bodies, and unvegetated and bare ground, can also contribute to earning this credit and provide wildlife habitats for different animal and plant species.

Project teams should consult the regional listing of native and/or adaptive plantings in order to confirm compliance or to select plantings in order to comply with this credit.

Create flashcards to remember each of the definitions for **native and adaptive plantings** and **potable water.**

credit if at least 75 percent of the interior floor area was certified under the LEED for Commercial Interiors™ (LEED CI) rating system.

SS Credit 5: Site Development, Protect or Restore Open Habitat. During the performance period, the project team will need to ensure that a minimum of 25 percent of the site area (*not* including the **building footprint**) is covered with native or adaptive plantings. If a minimum of 5 percent of the total site area (*including* the building footprint) is covered with native or adaptive vegetation, the team can also pursue this credit as long as it is greater than the latter option. Projects that maintain off-site areas covered with native and/or adaptive plantings can include the off-site areas in the calculations, proving compliance with this credit. When completing the compliance calculation for this strategy, the team would use 1 square foot of on-site area for every 2 square feet of off-site area. Therefore, eligible off-site square footage contributes at half value. The off-site area does not need to be owned by the same owner of the project seeking certification, but a contract would be required to present a maintenance agreement. Therefore, project teams can seek out other undeveloped properties to maintain in order to increase the open space square footage to meet the minimum percentage threshold of this credit.

Exemplary Performance may be achieved for this credit if the team is able to double the percentage increment defined previously or if the project earned SS Credit 5.1: Site Development, Protect or Restore Habitat during the design and construction of the project while pursuing certification under a different rating system. Therefore, if a project with 50 percent of the site (excluding the building footprint) or 10 percent (including the building footprint) is covered with native and/or adaptive plantings, the project team can pursue an Exemplary Performance credit under the Innovation in Operations (IO) category.

Native plantings refer to local vegetation that occurs naturally, whereas **adaptive plantings,** once introduced, can adapt to their new surroundings. Both can survive with little to no human interaction or resources, such as irrigation or fertilizers. Project teams should select plants that will not only require less water and maintenance but also improve the nutrients in the soil and deter pests at the same time. Implementing these measures reduces the amount of chemicals introduced into the water infrastructure and, therefore, improves the quality of surface water and saves building owners from purchasing fertilizers and pesticides. **Xeriscaping** can also be used as a sustainable landscaping strategy, as it uses drought-adaptable and minimal-water plant types along with soil covers, such as composts and mulches, to reduce evaporation.

Eliminating or reducing **potable water** (drinking water supplied by municipalities or wells) used for irrigation decreases the overall quantity of water required for building sites and, therefore, reduces operation costs as well. Water-efficient irrigation and other water efficiency strategies will be discussed in the next chapter, but for now it is important to connect site design decisions, such as vegetation selection, with environmental and economic operating and maintenance impacts.

Other strategies to comply with this credit include the reduction of the threat that windows can potentially pose to birds. Project teams need to address both landscaping and façade treatment options to reduce collisions. For example, plants that attract birds should be placed less than 3 feet away from windows or far enough away to avoid glazing reflection. The building can also incorporate bird-safe treatments, including exterior shading devices, patterned glass,

Figure 4.3 This green roof at the Allegany County Human Resources Development Commission's community center in Cumberland, Maryland, minimizes impervious areas to reduce stormwater runoff. *Photo courtesy of Moshier Studio*

or implementing a sufficient number of visual markers. Visual markers can encompass varying "planes, materials, textures, colors, opacity, or other visually contrasting features that help fragment window reflections and reduce overall transparency and reflectivity."[1]

Green roofs (see Figure 4.3) have many synergies, including maximizing open space, creating a habitat for wildlife, and reducing stormwater runoff and the heat island effect, but they also help to insulate a building and, therefore, reduce energy use. For urban projects with little or a zero lot line, project teams are encouraged to incorporate a green roof to add biodiversity to the site. Green roofs can contribute to earning this credit for urban projects if the vegetation complies and the vegetated roof surface covers at least 5 percent of the total site area.

 The trade-offs with green roofs could include installation cost and maintenance.

 TIP Open space is considered pervious and vegetated land. Wetlands, natural ponds, and green roofs are included.

Heat Island Effect

Although energy use will be discussed in more detail in Chapter 6, materials used for site design and rooftops can have an effect on how efficient the use of energy is for two reasons. Think of summertime at the grocery store parking lot and how you can see heat emitted from the black asphalt surface. The sunlight is absorbed by darker surfaces, and heat is retained. Multiply this effect in a downtown, urban area to truly understand the impacts of the urban **heat island effect**. By specifying and using materials with a high **solar reflectance index (SRI)**, green building projects can reduce the heat island effect and the overall temperature of an area. A material's SRI value is based on the material's ability to reflect or reject solar heat gain measured on a scale from 0 (dark, most absorptive) to 100 (light, most reflective). Building materials are also evaluated according to their ability to reflect sunlight based on visible, infrared, and ultraviolet wavelengths on a scale from 0 to 1 (see Figure 4.4). This solar reflectance is referred to as **albedo**; therefore, the terms *SRI* and *albedo* should be thought of synonymously for the purposes of the O+M exam.

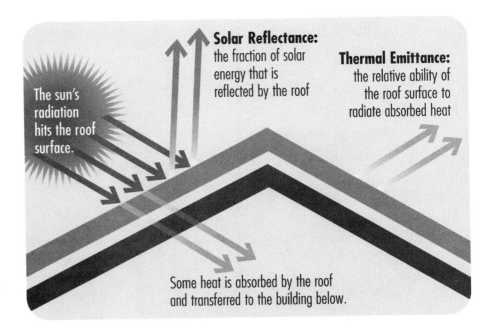

Figure 4.4 Diagram illustrating solar reflectance and thermal (or infrared) emittance. *Image courtesy of Cool Roof Rating Council*

 Besides low-albedo, nonreflective surface materials, car exhaust, air conditioners, and street equipment contribute to the heat island effect, while narrow streets and tall buildings make it worse.

 Create two more flashcards to remember the definitions of **solar reflectance index (SRI)** and **albedo**. Also, remember the different scales for each. Remember higher is better for both!

 Create a flashcard to remember the different compliant shading strategies: trees or shrubs (within five years), "trellises or other types of exterior structures that support vegetation,"[2] "architectural shading devices and structures,"[3] and photovoltaic systems.

 TIP It is important for teams to determine ways to limit the number of impervious surfaces on the site, not only to reduce the heat island effect but to reduce stormwater runoff as well. For the purposes of the exam, it is important to remember these types of synergies for strategies and credits.

SS Credit 7.1: Heat Island Effect, Nonroof. Project teams have two options from which to choose to comply with this credit and reduce the heat island effect for site areas. Option 1 addresses the **hardscape** (e.g., walkways, roadways, sidewalks, and courtyards), and option 2 relates to a parking provision strategy. Teams have the option to provide a combination of shading (within five years), high-SRI paving materials (minimum of 29), and/or **open-grid paving** (see Figure 4.5) for 50 percent of the hardscape areas in order to comply with option 1. If high-SRI materials are used for surface paving and walkways, light can be distributed more efficiently at night to reduce the number of light fixtures required, which saves money during construction and later during operations. A maintenance program also needs to be implemented to maintain the hardscape areas at least every two years to maintain its reflectance integrity.

Projects with existing asphalt parking areas are encouraged to increase the SRI value in order to comply with this credit. "Light-colored surface coatings, slurry seals, emulsion seal coats, or chip seals,"[4] as well as white-topping, a 4- to 8-inch-thick concrete layer, can be applied to reduce the heat island effect.

Option 2 requires 50 percent of the parking to be provided under cover. In keeping with the other strategies, the roof of the parking structure must be covered with vegetation and/or solar panels, and/or the roofing material must have an SRI of at least 29. Just as with the hardscape areas, a maintenance program needs to be implemented to maintain the parking roof areas at least every two years to maintain its SRI value. If the top level of a multi-level parking structure is not covered, it is exempt from compliance, as it is not considered a roof.

If the team were seeking an Exemplary Performance credit, they would need to exceed the 50 percent threshold defined previously and provide at least 95 percent compliant hardscape areas or ensure at least 95 percent of the parking was covered.

SS Credit 7.2: Heat Island Effect, Roof. Whereas SS Credit 7.1 has 2 options, project teams have three options from which to choose when pursuing this credit.

Figure 4.5 Turfstone™ Open-Grid Pavers allow stormwater to pass through and encourage vegetation growth in each open cell, in order to recharge groundwater and reduce runoff. *Photo courtesy of Ideal*

The first addresses the roofing material. If a lighter roofing material is used, the mechanical systems do not have to compensate for the heat gain to cool a building, consequently reducing the use of energy. From a larger perspective, think of the reductions in heat caused by the urban **heat island effect** if more projects implemented the same strategy. Therefore, if at least 75 percent of the roof surface (not including equipment, photovoltaic solar panels, and penetrations) is covered with a material with a high SRI value, then the project team could be awarded this credit and earn one point. If the roof is low-sloped, the minimum required SRI is 78, while a steep-sloped roof can comply with an SRI material with a value of at least 29. Option 2 requires at least 50 percent of the roof surface to be covered with vegetation (see Figure 4.6). Option 3 allows the team to provide a combination of options 1 and 2 (see Figure 4.7). If a project has 95 percent of its roof surface covered with vegetation, the team can pursue an Exemplary Performance credit.

Create another flashcard to remember the definition of **heat island effect:** heat absorption by low-SRI hardscape materials that contribute to an overall increase in temperature by radiating heat.

Create a flashcard to remember the definition of **emissivity** as described in the O+M reference guide: "the ratio of the radiation emitted by a surface to the radiation emitted by a black body at the same temperature."[5]

Figure 4.6 The green roof at the CCI Center in Pittsburgh earned its gold certification under the LEED for Existing Buildings rating system for the sustainable strategies implemented, such as the green roof. *Image courtesy of Conservation Consultants, Inc.*

 TIP Notice that a minimum value of SRI 29 is used for both SSc7.1 and SSc7.2!

SS Credit 8: Light Pollution Reduction. "Light pollution is waste light from building sites that produces glare, is directed upward to the sky, or is directed off the site."[6] In terms of site lighting, traditionally little attention has been paid to the quality of the night sky and the effects on wildlife, or to the wasteful energy use for exterior lighting. It is inefficient to illuminate areas not used at night, light areas beyond a property's boundary, or overcompensate light levels (**footcandle** levels). If vertical footcandle levels are minimized, light pollution is reduced, dark night skies are preserved, visibility at night is improved by the reduction of glare, and nocturnal animal habitats remain unaffected from sky glow. To pursue this credit, project teams will need to comply with the following interior lighting requirements and then select one of the three options with which to comply for exterior lighting (see Figure 4.8).

For the interior lighting compliance, the team must provide automatic controls for any nonemergency built-in fixture with a direct line of sight to any transparent envelope opening(s) in any wall or ceiling. Direct line of sight is based on where light leaves a fixture and not the location of the lamp. The controls are expected

Figure 4.7 The roof at the LEED certified Villa Montgomery Apartments in Redwood City, California, reduces the urban heat island effect with the installation of a combination of a high-SRI roof material with photovoltaic systems (generating a portion of the electricity needed for operations), along with a green roof, including a playground that offers residents the opportunity to enjoy the outdoor environment. *Photo courtesy of FFA*

to turn off the fixtures during all after-hours time during the performance period so that the total yearly duration is equal to or exceeds 2,190 hours (50 percent of annual nighttime hours). Control types include occupancy sensors, programmed master lighting control panels, and sweep timers. If controls are not incorporated, project teams must follow one of the three defined lighting design rules in the reference guide for built-in fixtures in order to comply with and earn the credit.

 TIP Facilities that operate for 24 hours are exempt from the interior lighting requirement for shut-off after hours.

 TIP **Light trespass** is unwanted light shining on another's property.

Figure 4.8 The LEED Platinum certified EcoDorm at Warern Wilson College in Swannanoa, North Carolina, earned SS Credit 8 by providing very minimal exterior lighting and shielding for fixtures that would pollute the night sky. *Photo courtesy of Samsel Architects, Photography by John Warner Photography*

Figure 4.9 Using full cut-off exterior light fixtures helps to avoid polluting the night sky. *Photo courtesy of Tyler Kisro of L.E.C. & Company*

 A **partially shielded** fixture has a shield that extends at least half the height of the fixture (or to the center of the fixture).

 It might be helpful to think of the credit number (SS Credit 8) when trying to remember the 8 minimum measurement locations for Option 3.

Create a flashcard to remember the definition of a **footcandle**: a measurement of light measured in lumens per square foot.

There are three options in which a project pursuing LEED EBOM certification can select from when addressing exterior lighting:

- Option 1 confers compliance if the project has already earned SS Credit 8 under a different rating system. Just as with SS Credit 1 described earlier, if the project received LEED CS certification, at least 75 percent of the total floor area must have earned LEED CI certification, and the Light Pollution Reduction credit must have been achieved in both rating systems in order to be eligible for this credit.

- Option 2 requires all exterior fixtures 50 watts and over to be **partially or fully shielded** to avoid emitting light to the night sky (see Figure 4.9).

- Option 3 requires the night illumination levels to be measured at least eight locations along the perimeter of the property, spaced no more than 100 feet apart. Illumination levels shall be measured with the exterior site lighting on and off with the interior lighting on during all measurements. In order to be in compliance, the light level at each measurement point when the lights are on cannot exceed 20 percent above the light level documented with the lights off. Should the light level exceed the 20 percent threshold, the team can compare the levels with the maximum defined footcandles of IESNA RP-33 and still comply with this credit. The reference standard defines four different lighting zones, ranging from dark ambient illumination levels for rural areas (LZ 1) to high ambient illumination levels for urban areas (LZ 4), with acceptable footcandles ranging from 0.01 to 0.60 at the perimeter of a property.

 Another trick to help memorize the different scales for the exam is to remember a lower SRI value indicates a darker material; just with a lower number lighting zone indicates a darker area.

 Create a flashcard to remember the range of the four lighting zones.

 Create a flashcard to remember the five credits that address site design.

QUIZ TIME!

Q4.1. What is the foundation for sustainable design for individual buildings? (Choose one)

  A. Carbon emissions

  B. Location

  C. Water use

  D. Orientation

  E. Energy use

Q4.2. If a previously certified LEED CS project is seeking EBOM certification and is pursuing SS Credit 1: LEED Certified Design and Construction, what is the minimum percentage of the total floor area that is required to have earned LEED CI certification? (Choose one)

  A. 10 percent

  B. 20 percent

  C. 50 percent

  D. 75 percent

Q4.3. Which of the following characteristics are required of a green roof in order to contribute toward earning SS Credit 5: Site Development – Protect or Restore Open Habitat? (Choose three)

  A. Supports biodiversity

  B. Covers 95 percent of the roof

  C. Has varying sizes of plantings

  D. Vegetation meets the definition of native or adaptive plantings for the region

  E. Covers 50 percent of the roof

Q4.4. What is the maximum timeframe to maintain hardscape areas in an effort to ensure optimizing the SRI value of the materials and to comply with the policy requirements of SS Credit 7.1: Heat Island Effect, Nonroof? (Choose one)

  A. 30 days after the performance period

  B. 1 year after certification

C. 2 years

D. 5 years

E. 7 years

Q4.5. If using an off-site area toward compliance for SS Credit 5: Site Development – Protect or Restore Open Habitat, which of the following is true? (Choose two)

A. The area must be owned by the same building owner seeking LEED EBOM certification.

B. The area is not required to be owned by the same building owner seeking LEED EBOM certification.

C. The compliant area is calculated at full value.

D. The compliant area is calculated at half value.

E. The compliant area can be included only if the area within the LEED project boundary is at least 50 percent compliant with the credit.

Q4.6. Which of the following is the best landscape design strategy to implement as a means to reduce the heat island effect? (Choose one)

A. Evapotranspiration

B. Xeriscaping

C. Increased albedo

D. Deciduous trees

E. Increased imperviousness

Q4.7. The owner of a two-story office building has suggested that he is interested in the installation of a vegetated roof system and would like the design team to evaluate it as an option to better insulate the building. Which set of team members best represents all of those that might offer meaningful input to this evaluation? (Choose one)

A. Architect, landscape architect, and civil engineer

B. Architect, contractor, and structural engineer

C. Landscape architect, contractor, civil engineer, and structural engineer

D. Architect, structural engineer, landscape architect, and civil engineer

E. Architect, structural engineer, landscape architect, civil engineer, and mechanical engineer

F. Architect, structural engineer, landscape architect, civil engineer, mechanical engineer, and contractor

Q4.8. Emissivity is an indication of which of the following material properties? (Choose one)

A. Ability to reflect light from light sources

B. Ability of a transparent or translucent material to admit solar gain

C. Ability of a material to absorb heat across the entire solar spectrum, including all nonvisible wavelengths

D. Ability of a material to give up heat in the form of long-wave radiation

Q4.9. A project team has attempted to address 50 percent of the hardscape surfaces on the project's site to meet the requirements to reduce the heat island effect for LEED compliance. Which of the following strategies should the LEED Accredited Professional discuss with the team? (Choose three)

A. Effective tree-shaded area of hardscape features

B. Solar reflectance index for all nonstandard paving materials proposed

C. Percentage of permeability for proposed open-grid paving materials

D. Emissivity of all low-albedo hardscape features in the design

E. Runoff coefficients for impervious paving materials selected

Q4.10. Which of the following statements is not true concerning infrared (or thermal) emittance? (Choose one)

A. Most building materials have an emittance of 0.9.

B. Emittance ranges from 0 to 1 (or 0 percent to 100 percent).

C. Glass is an exception to the rule and has an emittance of 0.1.

D. Untarnished galvanized steel has low emittance levels.

E. Aluminum roof coatings have intermediate emittance levels.

Q4.11. Which of the following is not an option from which project teams can select when pursuing SS Credit 8: Light Pollution Reduction? (Choose one)

A. Prove the project was awarded the credit under another rating system

B. Shield all nonemergency light fixtures at all envelope openings

C. Measure light levels at the perimeter of the property line to prove less than a 20 percent variance from an ON and OFF operation

D. Measure light levels at the perimeter of the property line to prove less than a 20 percent variance from one measurement point to another

E. Measure light levels at the perimeter of the property line to prove compliance with appropriate IESNA RP 33 defined lighting zone

F. Shield all exterior light fixtures 50 watts or more

Q4.12. Which of the following is not a type of an ecologically appropriate feature for site design to comply with SS Credit 5: Site Development – Protect or Restore Open Habitat? (Choose one)

A. Exposed rock

B. Abandoned maintenance shed now serving as an animal habitat

C. Water bodies

D. Bare ground that does not contain any vegetation

SITE MANAGEMENT AND MAINTENANCE

The creation of natural, sustainable exterior environments that can be sustainably maintained, add to the economic, environmental, and social equity of their green building projects and are, therefore, promoted within the LEED rating systems (see Figure 4.10). Site management and maintenance strategies are developed based on the design strategies implemented. For example, if vegetation requires irrigation

Figure 4.10 The high-efficiency Duke Law Star Commons project in Durham, North Carolina, by Shepley Bulfinch, obtained its LEED Certification by providing access to public transportation and reducing site disturbance and its contribution to the heat island effect. *Photo courtesy of Kat Nania, Shepley Bulfinch*

and supplemental fertilizers, a maintenance team will need to comply with providing potable water, and chemicals to the vegetated areas. Should a project's site be designed with native and/or adaptive plantings, these efforts can be reduced, as irrigation and fertilizers may not be necessary. Sustainable site design strategies can also help to prevent soil erosion and sedimentation avoiding the degradation of nutrients, soil compaction, and decreased biodiversity of soil organisms.

Think about the environmental advantages if a maintenance team were to expose a more sensitive approach to cleaning, erosion control, equipment, pest management, or even snow removal. All of these tasks can be approached in a low-impact manner for building exterior and hardscape areas. For example, **chemical runoff** could be reduced to avoid polluting nearby waterways, threatening navigation, and degrading recreational opportunities. Chemical runoff is considered to be antifreeze, gasoline, oil, and salts; products used for snow and ice removal; and other operations and maintenance activities.

Site Management and Maintenance in Relation to LEED Compliance

When developing strategies for site management and maintenance, project teams can refer to the following two Sustainable Site credits in the LEED EBOM rating system. The management plans for the two credits will need to address **best management practices** (BMPs) to reduce "harmful chemical use, energy waste, water waste, air pollution, solid waste, and/or chemical runoff."[7]

SS Credit 2: Building Exterior and Hardscape Management Plan. Project teams will need to develop an exterior and building hardscape management plan that is appropriate for the region in which the project is located. Each of the following operational tasks must be included in the plan:[8]

- *Maintenance equipment.* Think about the noise and emissions associated with this type of equipment. Larger equipment has the potential to increase soil compaction. Replace with electric powered or low-volume models.

- *Snow and ice removal.* Chemical runoff contribution that can degrade water quality and harm vegetation. Replace with environmentally sensitive products, such as magnesium chloride, potassium acetate, and potassium chloride.

- *Cleaning of building exterior.* Just as with the chemicals used to melt snow and ice, these chemicals can also pollute nearby waterways and harm vegetation. Use biodegradable products and refer to EQ Credit 3.3: Green Cleaning – Sustainable Cleaning Products and Materials (see Chapter 8).

- *Paints and sealants used on building exterior.* Think about the toxicity of these products and the exposure to the staff members that are required to apply them. Using low-emitting products compliant with MR Credit 3: Sustainable Purchasing – Facility Alterations and Additions, such as adhesives, sealants, and sealant primers, is less harmful on the maintenance staff and environment.

- *Cleaning of sidewalks, pavement, and other hardscape.* Another source of chemical runoff potential. Strategies should only be implemented to ensure safety and aesthetics.

 Create a flashcard of the five operational tasks that must be included in an exterior and building hardscape management plan.

Project teams will need to document when the plan was implemented and the coordinating performance period. In order to comply with the credit, the management plan will need to be implemented for at least 20 percent of the time over the duration of the performance period. The variance is provided with the understanding that some strategies are not practical at all times. For example, the environmentally sensitive deicing strategies and products mentioned in the reference guide may not work during severe weather conditions.

SS Credit 3: Integrated Pest Management Plan, Erosion Control, and Landscape Management Plan. Following suit with the previous credit, best management practices will need to be implemented to earn this credit as well. More specific to this credit, the following two operational components must be addressed in the management plan:[9]

- BMPs for outdoor integrated pest management (IPM) strategies for plants, fungi, insects, and/or animals should include the least toxic chemicals to control populations in targeted locations for targeted species and block the pests from entering the building. Project teams should refer to EQ Credit 3.6: Green Cleaning – Indoor Integrated Pest Management for specific tasks to address, such as notification. Areas to be monitored and maintained include: envelope, landscaping elements, and invasive vegetation.

- Erosion and sedimentation control strategies for regular operations and future construction activities, including site soil and potential construction materials, should address methods to control dust and other particulates and keep them from polluting the air, and methods to restore eroded areas. Teams can implement structural control measures, such as earth dikes, silt fencing, sediment basins, and sediment traps, and/or implement stabilization control measures, such as temporary or permanent seeding and mulching.

The management plan should also address strategies to divert landscape waste, such as mulching or composting. Incinerating landscape waste is not a compliant option unless it produces biofuel to be used for energy. The plan also depicts methods to minimize the use of chemical fertilizers and if it is used requires it to be kept at least 25 feet away from any water body. If synthetic fertilizers are used, a slow-release product should be required by the management plan. Just as with SS Credit 2, the plan is required to be in effect for at least 20 percent of the performance period duration.

 TIP Universal notification requires building occupants to be notified at least 72 hours prior to a pesticide application under normal conditions and at least 24 hours for emergency conditions. This does not apply to self-contained nonrodent bait or if a least-toxic pesticide is used.

 Create a flashcard to remember examples of *structural* control measures and make another one to remember *stabilization* control measures.

 TIP Did you notice that neither of these credits offers an opportunity to earn exemplary performance?

Create a flashcard to remember the two credits that address sustainable site management and maintenance strategies.

QUIZ TIME!

Q4.13. Why is it important to implement environmentally sensitive strategies for landscape waste and maintenance equipment? (Choose three)

   A. Avoid added volume to landfills

   B. Reduce contamination of groundwater

   C. Reduce emissions

   D. Reduce noise pollution

   E. Avoid harming vegetation

   F. Avoid polluting nearby waterways

Q4.14. How long must a project team ensure best management practices are employed in order to pursue SS Credit 2: Building Exterior and Hardscape Management Plan or SS

Credit 3: Integrated Pest Management Plan, Erosion Control, and Landscape Management Plan? (Choose one)

A. 100 percent of performance period

B. 1 year after certification

C. 50 percent of performance period

D. 5 years after certification

E. 20 percent of performance period

Q4.15. Which of the following credits might a project team refer to when developing the plan to address the building exterior and hardscape management for SS Credit 2? (Choose two)

A. EQ Credit 3.6: Green Cleaning – Indoor Integrated Pest Management

B. EQ Credit 3.3: Green Cleaning – Sustainable Cleaning Products and Materials

C. MR Credit 3: Sustainable Purchasing – Facility Alterations and Additions

D. SS Credit 3: Integrated Pest Management Plan, Erosion Control, and Landscape Management Plan

Q4.16. Which of the following strategies might a groundskeeper pursue in order to divert landscaping waste from landfills and incineration facilities? (Choose three)

A. Composting

B. Mulching

C. Burning the waste on site

D. Wood chippers

Q4.17. Which of the following is not required to be addressed in a building exterior and hardscape management plan to be in compliance with SS Credit 2: Building Exterior and Hardscape Management Plan if it is not applicable to the project type? (Choose one)

A. Snow and ice removal

B. Maintenance equipment

C. Paints and sealants

D. Building exterior cleaning

E. Cleaning hardscape areas

TRANSPORTATION

Transportation is one of the key components addressed within the LEED rating systems, as it accounts for 32 percent of the total U.S. greenhouse gas emissions in 2007, according to the U.S. Energy Information Administration.[10] As buildings traditionally have contributed to the need for transportation, green buildings have the opportunity to have an impact on these statistics by reducing the "length and frequency of vehicle trips and encourage shifts to more sustainable modes of transportation."[11] The environmental benefits of sustainable strategies for transportation include a reduction in pollution, including vehicle emissions, which have a dramatic impact on climate change, smog, and acid rain, among other air quality problems, according to Wikipedia.[12] The economic benefits include the reduction of the need to build and maintain roadways. The social component to reducing transportation impacts includes an improvement of human health by increasing the accessibility and, thus, encouraging people to walk or bike from place to place.

Transportation is most affected by four factors[13]*:*

- *Location:* Number and frequency of trips
- *Vehicle technology:* Quantity and types of energy and support systems needed to move people and goods to and from the site
- *Fuel:* Environmental impact of vehicle operation
- *Human behavior:* A daily transportation decision combining the listed impacts

Transportation in Relation to LEED Compliance

The EBOM rating system within the Operations + Maintenance (O&M) reference guide offers SS Credit 4: Alternative Commuting Transportation to help reduce the detrimental impacts from the use of cars. If more people carpooled, walked, or biked to work or school, there would be less pollution, as vehicles contribute to air pollution, **greenhouse gas** (GHG) emissions, and smog (see Figure 4.11). GHGs "absorb and emit radiation at specific wavelengths within the spectrum of thermal infrared radiation emitted by the Earth's surface, the atmosphere itself, and by clouds."[14] The alternative transportation strategies suggested within SS Credit 4 reduce the use of the automobile by single occupants and the use of conventionally powered and fueled vehicles and, thus, help to reduce the affiliated detrimental environmental impacts. Project teams are encouraged to address the infrastructure to support the strategies, such as bike racks (see Figure 4.12), preferred parking areas (see Figure 4.13), and incentive programs, such as bicycle reimbursements and discounted parking rates for carpools or fuel-efficient and/or **alternative fuel** vehicles. The reference guide mentions "telecommuting; compressed workweeks; mass transit; walking; bicycles or other human-powered conveyances; carpools; vanpools; and low-emitting, fuel-efficient or alternative-fuel vehicles" as acceptable alternative transportation strategies to comply with this credit.[15]

To document compliance, project teams have three options from which to select:[16]

Option 1. Participate in a local or regional commute reduction program that meets the South Coast Air Quality Management District (SCAQMD) data collection and analysis procedures.

Option 2. Participate in a local or regional commute reduction program and comprehensively document the program and data collection and analysis procedures.

Option 3. Occupant Commute Survey based on data collection procedures in **SCAQMD Rule 2202**. The survey must be conducted each day over five

TIP Land use is the ultimate contributor to the demands on transportation.

TIP Zero- or low-emission vehicles (ZEVs) are standardized by California Air Resources Board (CARB).

Create a flashcard to remember the definition of an alternative-fuel vehicle: a vehicle that operates without the use of petroleum fuels, including gas-electric, or hybrid, vehicles.

TIP Fuel-efficient vehicles (FEVs) are defined by the American Council for an Energy-Efficient Economy in *The ACEEE Green Book®: The Environmental Guide to Cars and Trucks.*

Make a flashcard to remember **"stratified random sampling** categorizes members of a population into discrete subgroups, based on characteristics that may affect their responses to a survey. For example, a survey of building occupants' commuting behavior might separate people by income level and commuting distance. To yield representative results, the survey should sample subgroups according to their proportions in the total population."[17]

Figure 4.11 Mass transit in New Jersey is designed to meet the commuting needs of large groups of people. *Photo courtesy of David Cardella*

consecutive days or at the end of the five consecutive workdays. The project team has the option to survey every regular building occupant (**stratified random sampling**) or to survey randomly selected regular building occupants that statistically represents the building population (**systematic sampling**). With either survey option, an 80 percent response rate is

 Make a flashcard to remember "**systematic sampling** surveys every *x*th person in a population, using a constant skip interval. It relies on random sampling order or an order with no direct relationship to the variable under analysis (e.g., alphabetical order when sampling for commuting behavior)."[18]

Figure 4.12 Bike racks at the Animal Care and Protective Services facility in Jacksonville, Florida, provide the staff and visitors the opportunity to commute to the facility without a car. *Photo courtesy of Auld & White Constructors, LLC*

Figure 4.13 Providing preferred parking for car/vanpool vehicles could contribute to a reduction in the number of single occupancy vehicle trips.

 TIP Note the 752 constant in the calculation, it is a value as all project types will use the same number to calculate the required random sample size to survey.

 Create a flashcard to remember the three reference standards for this credit.

required. If the team pursues this credit with the random selection approach for the survey, they are required to use the following formula:[19]

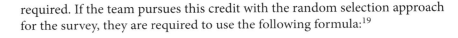

$$\text{Required Random Sample Size} = \frac{(\text{\# of Regular Occupants} \times 752)}{(\text{\# of Regular Occupants} + 752)}$$

The O&M reference guide includes information for project teams to convert the metric *average vehicle ridership* (AVR) into the metric *reduction in conventional commuting trips* (RCCT) in order to document compliance for this credit. This may or not be necessary, depending on the transportation program utilized. To determine AVR, the project team would divide the number of building occupants by the vehicles at the building based on a five-day time period. To determine RCCT, multiply the number of occupants by the expected commute trips each day (typically 2) for a total of five days.

Project teams will need to provide at least a 10 percent reduction in commuting round trips in order to earn this credit and be awarded three points. They have 10 opportunities to earn up to 15 points for a 75 percent reduction. They can earn another point for exemplary performance if they meet or exceed a 95 percent reduction in round trips.

QUIZ TIME!

Q4.18. How much of a percentage reduction in the number of commuting round trips could be expected from a four-day compressed workweek in which 80 percent of the 100 regular building occupants participate in? (Choose one)

A. 10 percent

B. 12 percent

C. 20 percent

D. 16 percent

Q4.19. Which of the following represent the major factors that affect transportation effects on the environment? (Choose three)

A. Vehicle technology

B. Fuel

C. Human behavior

D. Quality of roads

E. Suburban development

Q4.20. Which of the following are sustainable strategies that should be implemented on an auto-dependent green building? (Choose four)

A. Provide priority parking for carpools/vanpools.

B. Provide a mass transit discount program to employees.

C. Supply alternative-fuel vehicles and accessibility to recharging stations.

D. Offer discounted parking rates for multioccupant vehicles.

E. Incorporate basic services (such as a bank, gym, cleaners, or pharmacy) for occupant usage in the new building.

Q4.21. Which of the following are effective and sustainable strategies to address transportation for a LEED project? (Choose three)

A. Offer to reimburse occupants for bicycle purchases.

B. Install bike racks and showers.

C. Encourage carpooling.

D. Provide sport-utility vehicles (SUVs) for all employees.

E. Add a white-topping concrete coating to existing asphalt parking surfaces.

Q4.22. What is the minimum percentage response rate for a survey to comply with SS Credit 4: Alternative Commuting Transportation? (Choose one)

A. 25 percent

B. 50 percent

C. 75 percent

D. 80 percent

E. 90 percent

Q4.23. What is the time period used to determine AVR or RCCT? (Choose one)

A. 10 consecutive days

B. 5 consecutive days

C. 10 random days

D. 1 year

E. 5 random days

F. 1 week

STORMWATER MANAGEMENT

Create another flashcard to remember the definition of **stormwater runoff**: rainwater that leaves a project site, flowing along parking lots and roadways, traveling to sewer systems and water bodies.

In the previous section, strategies were presented to address LEED compliance while designing a sustainable site, including the reduction of impervious surfaces to lower heat island effects. Another benefit of minimizing impervious surfaces is the reduction of **stormwater runoff,** which causes degradation of the surface water quality and reduces groundwater recharge to the local **aquifer,** an underground source of water for groundwater, wells, and springs. The reduction in surface water quality is caused by both a decrease in filtration and the increase of hardscape areas containing contaminants. The increase of impervious surfaces and stormwater runoff has put water quality, aquatic life, and recreational areas at risk.

TIP Nonpoint source pollutants are one of the biggest risks to the quality of surface water and aquatic life.

Nonpoint source pollutants, such as oil leaked from cars or fertilizers from plantings, are one of the biggest risks to the quality of surface water and aquatic life. These pollutants typically contaminate rainwater flowing along impervious surfaces on the journey to sewer systems or water bodies, especially after a heavy rainfall. Once this polluted rainwater is in the sewer system, it then contaminates the rest of the water and takes a toll on the process to purify it or it contaminates the body of water into which it is discharged. These bodies of water also then suffer from soil erosion and sedimentation deteriorating aquatic life and recreational opportunities. Therefore, allowing rainwater to percolate through vegetation or **pervious** surfaces, such as pervious concrete or asphalt (see Figure 4.14), porous pavement, or open-grid pavers that allows at least 50 percent of water to seep through, reduces the pollution of surface water and is less of a burden on our ecosystem. For projects located in urban areas where space is limited, oil separators can be utilized to remove oil, sediment, and floatables. Within an oil separator, heavier solid materials settle to the bottom, while floatable oil and grease rise to the top.

Create a flashcard to remember the definitions of **impervious surfaces:** surfaces that do not allow 50 percent of water to pass through them, and **pervious surfaces:** surfaces that allow at least 50 percent of water to percolate or penetrate through them.

Stormwater Management in Relation to LEED Compliance

The triple bottom line benefits of managing stormwater include preserving the natural ecological systems that promote **biodiversity**, which in turn help manage stormwater, such as wetlands (see Figure 4.15). If the natural environment could manage stormwater, we could take advantage of the economic savings of creating manmade structures to do it for us, as well as the costs to maintain the structures. There is also social equity in managing runoff and maintaining clean surface water: the preservation of aquatic life and the ability to enjoy recreational activities. With

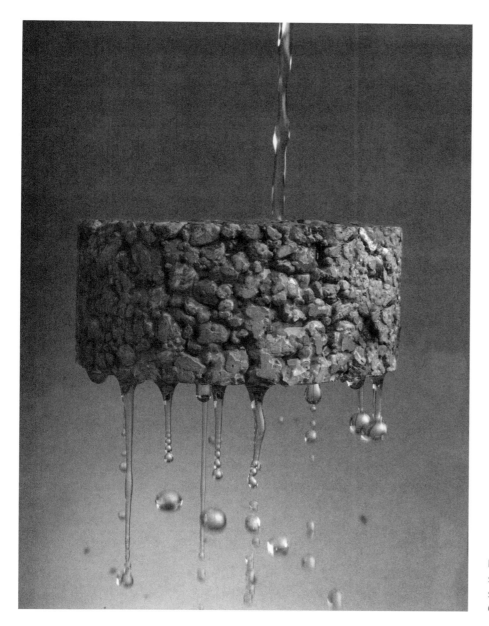

Figure 4.14 Installing pervious materials, such as pervious asphalt, helps to manage stormwater runoff. *Photo courtesy of BASF Construction Chemicals*

the importance of these triple bottom line benefits, LEED addresses stormwater management within the following credit:

SS Credit 6: Stormwater Quantity Control. Project teams will need to develop "a stormwater management plan to preserve or restore natural functions of the site and to manage stormwater based on the natural soil conditions, habitat, and rainfall."[20] Teams should ensure that the plan addresses the maintenance of features that mitigate stormwater problems and when to conduct inspections. The plan should indicate that all issues found as a result of an inspection must be addressed within 60 days of the inspection.

Project teams have a number of strategies from which they can choose to reduce the amount of stormwater that leaves a project site, such as **wet** or **dry retention ponds.** Both of these approaches use excavated areas to detain rainwater

Figure 4.15 The Utah Botanical Center's Wetland Discovery Point project, at Utah State University in Kaysville, earned LEED Platinum certification for its efforts to create biodiversity. *Photo courtesy of Gary Neuenswander, Utah Agricultural Experiment Station*

 TIP Be sure to review the six considerations of stormwater collection strategies in Chapter 5.

 Reducing the amount of impervious surfaces, and increasing pervious surfaces, helps to reduce stormwater runoff and, therefore, also helps to improve the quality of water.

and keep it from leaving the site, thus slowing runoff (see Figure 4.16). Some other options include on-site filtration methods. **Bioswales** (see Figure 4.17), or engineered basins with vegetation, can be utilized to increase groundwater recharge and reduce peak stormwater runoff. Vegetated filter strips and rain gardens are also an option, as they both function to collect and filter runoff while reducing peak discharge rates. Rooftops also contribute to the pollution of surface water, so implementing a green, or vegetated, roof would also reduce stormwater runoff and contaminating surface water. Another option is to collect the water from the roof and use it for irrigation purposes (see Figure 4.18) or toilet flushing.

The responsible party, or declarant, will need to perform a few calculations in order to document compliance with this credit. These calculations include the volume of captured runoff, the minimum **drawdown** rate, and determining rainwater runoff. The first calculation determines how much rainwater is being captured, the next one determines how much can be held, while the third calculation determines how much rainwater is leaving the site. In order to calculate how much water will leave the site, the declarant will need to determine the **2-year, 24-hour design storm** rainfall intensity (inches per hour).

To comply with the credit, the team will need to ensure that 15 percent of the precipitation falling on the whole project site both for an average weather year

Figure 4.16 The Armstrong World Industries Corporate Headquarters in Lancaster, Pennsylvania uses a catch basin to slow the rate at which stormwater is released into the adjoining wetlands, a strategy that helped the project earn Platinum certification under the LEED for Existing Buildings rating system. *Photo courtesy of Armstrong Ceiling and Wall Systems*

Figure 4.17 Bioswales, an on-site filtration strategy, can help to recharge the groundwater and reduce stormwater runoff. *Photo courtesy of Thomas M. Robinson, EDR*

and for the 2-year, 24-hour design storm was infiltrated, collected and reused, or evapotranspirated during the performance period. The declarant will need to define the different areas and surface types for the different conditions within the LEED project boundary.

Figure 4.18 Dick Sporting Goods corporate headquarters in Pittsburgh, Pennsylvania, designed by Strada Architecture, LLC, incorporates roof water capture to reduce the stormwater runoff and reduce the need for potable water for irrigation. *Image courtesy of Strada Architecture LLC*

Project teams that develop and implement a stormwater management plan during the performance period that permeates, captures, and reuses rainwater, or evapotranspirates runoff (at least 30 percent of the total rainfall within the LEED project boundary) will be eligible to pursue an Exemplary Performance point under the IO category.

QUIZ TIME!

Q4.24. Which of the following are strategies to reduce stormwater runoff? (Choose three)

A. Green roofs

B. Impervious asphalt

C. Pervious pavers

D. Bioswales

Q4.25. What roofing material would be best to comply with the EBOM rating system for heat island effect reductions? (Choose two)

A. Gray asphalt with an SRI of 22

B. Aluminum coating with an SRI of 50

C. Red clay tile with an SRI of 36

D. White EPDM with an SRI of 84

E. White cement tile with an SRI of 90

F. Light gravel on built-up roof with an SRI of 37

Q4.26. What is the minimum percentage of precipitation to be collected and reused (or evapotranspirates) in order to comply with SS Credit 6: Stormwater Quantity? (Choose one)

A. 5 percent

B. 10 percent

C. 15 percent

D. 20 percent

E. 25 percent

Q4.27. What is the maximum length of time in which issues found during inspections need to be addressed in order to be in compliance with SS Credit 6: Stormwater Quantity Control? (Choose one)

A. 24 hours

B. 2 years

C. 1 week

D. 30 days

E. 60 days

Q4.28. A project team is pursuing SS Credit 7.2: Heat Island Reduction, Roof. The total flat roof surface is 50,000 square feet, and they plan on installing 15,000 square feet of photovoltaic panels. The mechanical equipment occupies 5,000 square feet. How much of the roof surface has to be covered with a high-SRI material, and what is the minimum SRI of the material in order to comply with the credit? (Choose one)

A. 22,500 SF has to be covered with a roofing material with at least an SRI value of 78.

B. 15,000 SF has to be covered with a roofing material with at least an SRI value of 78.

C. 25,000 SF has to be covered with a roofing material with at least an SRI value of 78.

D. 25,000 SF has to be covered with a roofing material with at least an SRI value of 29.

E. 15,000 SF has to be covered with a roofing material with at least an SRI value of 29.

Q4.29. What strategy is defined in the reference guide that could earn a project a credit for Exemplary Performance for SS Credit 6: Stormwater Quantity Control if implemented? (Choose two)

A. Double the quantity reductions for runoff.

B. Improve the runoff quality by removing 90 percent of the total suspended solids.

C. Increase the number of best management practices from 5 to 10.

D. A strategy is not defined in the reference guide.

E. Decrease the runoff quantity by 30 percent by collecting and reusing the rainwater.

Q4.30. Which of the following is required in order to determine the rainwater runoff? (Choose one)

A. Two-year, 24-hour design storm

B. Minimum drawdown rate

C. Maximum drawdown rate

D. Volume of captured runoff

Q4.31. Which of the following is stormwater runoff based on? (Choose three)

A. Surface types

B. Areas

C. Collection system

D. Rainfall intensity

E. Conveyance system

Q4.32. Which of the following are stormwater management strategies based on? (Choose three)

A. Weather

B. Natural soil conditions

C. Rainfall

D. Seasons

E. Habitat

Q4.33. Which of the following are true regarding the lighting zones as defined by IESNA RP 33? (Choose two)

A. LZ1 is intended for rural areas.

B. LZ4 is intended for rural areas.

C. LZ6 is intended for rural areas.

D. LZ1 has an acceptable footcandle level of 0.01.

E. LZ4 has an acceptable footcandle level of 0.01.

F. LZ6 has an acceptable footcandle level of 0.01.

AUDIT	**SS Credit 1:** **LEED Certified Design and Construction**

PURPOSE

Reward _____ _____ projects for implementing sustainable strategies to help operating facilities to pursue high-performance goals.

REQUIREMENTS

Show proof of certification under the following rating systems:

- LEED for New _____
- LEED for _____
- LEED for _____ & _____ with _____% of leasable square footage certified under LEED for _____ _____

1 pt.

RESPONSIBLE PARTY:

OWNER

	SS Credit 1: **LEED Certified Design and** **Construction**

ANSWER KEY

PURPOSE

Reward **previously certified** projects for implementing sustainable strategies to help operating facilities to pursue high-performance goals.

REQUIREMENTS

Show proof of certification under the following rating systems:

- LEED for New **Construction**
- LEED for **Schools**
- LEED for **Core** & **Shell** with **75%** of leasable square footage certified under LEED for **Commercial Interiors**

| PROGRAM DEVELOPMENT | SS Credit 2:
Building Exterior & Hardscape Management Plan |

PURPOSE

To provide a clean, well-maintained and safe exterior by encouraging _____ -performance building _____ .

REQUIREMENTS

Implement an exterior and building _____ plan that includes best _____ practices to reduce:

harmful _____ use

energy and water use

air _____

solid waste

chemical _____

The plan must address the following to be implemented during at least _____% of the performance period:

_____ equipment

Snow and ice removal

Cleaning of building _____

Building exterior _____ and sealants

_____ of hardscape areas

1 pt.

RESPONSIBLE PARTY:

FACILITY/PROPERTY MANAGER

ANSWER KEY

PURPOSE

To provide a clean, well-maintained and safe exterior by encouraging **high**-performance building **operations**.

REQUIREMENTS

Implement an exterior and building **hardscape** plan that includes best **management** practices to reduce:

> harmful **chemical** use
>
> energy and water use
>
> air **pollution**
>
> solid waste
>
> chemical **runoff**

The plan must address the following to be implemented during at least **20%** of the performance period:

> **Maintenance** equipment
>
> Snow and ice removal
>
> Cleaning of building **exterior**
>
> Building exterior **paints** and sealants
>
> **Cleaning** of hardscape areas

PROGRAM DEVELOPMENT	SS Credit 3:
	Integrated Pest Management Plan, Erosion Control, and Landscape Management Plan

PURPOSE

To encourage high-performance facility operations and to support the integration into the adjacent _____ to protect the integrity of ecology, encourage natural _____, and safeguard wildlife.

REQUIREMENTS

Implement an exterior and building _____ plan that includes best management practices to reduce:

> harmful chemical use

> _____ and water use

> air pollution

> solid waste

> chemical _____

The plan must address the following _____ elements to be implemented during at least 20% of the _____ period:

> Outdoor integrated _____ management to control pest _____ and prevent pests from _____ building and requires the following:

>> _____ methods

>> Emergency conditions and _____ notification defined

>> Routine and inspection

>> Integrate with _____ Credit 3.6: _____ Cleaning, _____ Integrated pest management

> _____ and sedimentation control to include:

>> Ongoing landscape operations to _____ slopes and drainage infrastructure

>> Future construction activity for stabilization and structural controls, prevention of dust and particulate air pollution, and to _____ eroded areas

> Landscape waste _____ such as _____ or composting

> Minimize _____ fertilizer use

1 pt.	RESPONSIBLE PARTY:
	FACILITY/PROPERTY MANAGER

<table>
<tr><td colspan="1" align="right">**SS Credit 3:**

Integrated Pest Management Plan, Erosion Control, and
Landscape Management Plan</td></tr>
</table>

ANSWER KEY

PURPOSE

To encourage high-performance facility operations and to support the integration into the adjacent **landscape** to protect the integrity of ecology, encourage natural **diversity**, and safeguard wildlife.

REQUIREMENTS

Implement an exterior and building **hardscape** plan that includes best management practices to reduce:

harmful chemical use

energy and water use

air pollution

solid waste

chemical runoff

The plan must address the following **operational** elements to be implemented during at least 20% of the **performance** period:

Outdoor integrated pest management to control pest **population** and prevent pests from **entering** building and requires the following:

Nonchemical methods

Emergency conditions and **universal** notification defined

Routine and inspection

Integrate with **EQ** Credit 3.6: **Green** Cleaning, **Indoor** Integrated pest management

Erosion and sedimentation control to include:

Ongoing landscape operations to **maintain** slopes and drainage infrastructure

Future construction activity for stabilization and structural controls, prevention of dust and particulate air pollution, and to **restore** eroded areas

Landscape waste **diversion** such as **mulching** or composting

Minimize **chemical** fertilizer use

| PERF PERIOD/ CERTIFICATION | SS Credit 4: Alternative Commuting Transportation |

PURPOSE

Reduce the negative environmental impacts from _____ use, including _____ and _____ development by the use of _____, _____, and/or programs.

REQUIREMENTS

Reduce the number of _____ occupant commuting trips with _____-powered, conventionally _____ vehicles by participating in 1 of the 3 following options:

Options 1 and 2: Participate in a local or regional _____

Option 3: _____ occupants outside of local or regional program complying with the following rules:

Survey _____ regular occupant or by _____ selection of statistically representative sample

OR

Survey consecutively for _____ workdays (each day or at the end).

In either case, an _____% response rate is required,

POINT DISTRIBUTION

Percentage Reduction	Points
10.0%	3
13.75%	4
17.50%	5
21.25%	6
25.00%	7
31.25%	8
37.50%	9
43.75%	10
50.00%	11
56.25%	12
62.50%	13
68.75%	14
75.00%	15
95.00%	16

95.00% — 16 Exemplary Performance

EQUATION/DOCUMENTATION

To determine required minimum _____ size:

$$\text{Required Random Sample Size} = \frac{(\text{\# of } \underline{\hspace{2cm}} \text{ Occupants} * 752)}{(\text{\# of Regular Occupants} + 752)}$$

REFERENCED STANDARDS

_____ Air Resources Board, Definition of a _____-Emission Vehicle American Council for an Energy-Efficient Economy, The _____ Green Book®: The Environmental Guide to Cars and Trucks _____ Coast Air Quality Management District, Rule 2202

3-15 pts.

RESPONSIBLE PARTY:

FACILITY/PROPERTY MANAGER

ANSWER KEY

PURPOSE

Reduce the negative environmental impacts from **car** use, including **pollution** and **land** development by the use of **incentives**, **infrastructure**, and/or programs.

REQUIREMENTS

Reduce the number of **single** occupant commuting trips with **conventionally**-powered, conventionally **fueled** vehicles by participating in 1 of the 3 following options:

    Options 1 and 2: Participate in a local or regional **program**

    Option 3: **Survey** occupants outside of local or regional program complying with the following rules:

        Survey **every** regular occupant or by **random** selection of statistically representative sample

        OR

        Survey consecutively for **5** workdays (each day or at the end).

        In either case, an **80**% response rate is required,

POINT DISTRIBUTION

Percentage Reduction	Points
10.0%	3
13.75%	4
17.50%	5
21.25%	6
25.00%	7
31.25%	8
37.50%	9
43.75%	10
50.00%	11
56.25%	12
62.50%	13
68.75%	14
75.00%	15
95.00%	**16**

Exemplary Performance

EQUATION/DOCUMENTATION

To determine required minimum **sample** size:

$$\text{Required Random Sample Size} \quad = \quad \frac{(\text{\# of Regular Occupants} * 752)}{(\text{\# of Regular Occupants} + 752)}$$

REFERENCED STANDARDS

California Air Resources Board, Definition of a **Zero**-Emission Vehicle
American Council for an Energy-Efficient Economy, The **ACEEE** Green Book®: The Environmental Guide to Cars and Trucks **South** Coast Air Quality Management District, Rule 2202

AUDIT

PURPOSE

Promote _____ and provide _____ by conserving natural areas and restoring damaged areas.

REQUIREMENTS

During the performance period, ensure at least _____% of the site area (not including building _____ or _____% of the site area (including the building footprint)—whichever is greater—is covered with native or _____ landscaping.

_____-site areas can count but are treated with _____ value. Contract required for documentation.

_____ roofs can count for urban projects with little or no setback and plantings are native or adaptive. Roof surfaces must cover _____% of total site area to comply.

EXEMPLARY PERFORMANCE

_____ the percentage threshold: Cover at least _____% of the site area (not including building footprint) or _____% of the site area (including the building footprint)—whichever is greater—with _____ or adapted landscaping.

OR

If the project was certified under LEED NC and earned SS Credit 5.1: Site Development, _____ or _____ Habitat

1 pt.

RESPONSIBLE PARTY:

OWNER/FACILITY/PROPERTY MANAGER

SS Credit 5:

Site Development, Protect or Restore Open Habitat

ANSWER KEY

PURPOSE

Promote **biodiversity** and provide **habitat** by conserving natural areas and restoring damaged areas.

REQUIREMENTS

During the performance period, ensure at least **25%** of the site area (not including building **footprint**) or **5%** of the site area (including the building footprint)—whichever is greater—is covered with native or adapted landscaping.

Off-site areas can count but are treated with **half** value. Contract required for documentation.

Vegetated roofs can count for urban projects with little or no setback and plantings are native or adaptive. Roof surfaces must cover **5%** of total site area to comply.

EXEMPLARY PERFORMANCE

Double the percentage threshold: Cover at least **50%** of the site area (not including building footprint) or **10%** of the site area (including the building footprint)—whichever is greater—with **native** or adapted landscaping.

OR

If the project was certified under LEED NC and earned SS Credit 5.1: Site Development, **Protect** or **Restore** Habitat

AUDIT	**SS Credit 6:**
	Stormwater Quantity Control

PURPOSE

Increase _____ cover and on-site _____ to reduce _____ of runoff and the disruption of _____ hydrology.

REQUIREMENTS

Implement a _____ management plan during the performance period to infiltrate, _____, and reuse stormwater runoff or evapotranspirates runoff from at least _____% of precipitation falling on the total site area.

An annual stormwater management _____ program must be implemented.

EQUATIONS

Use the following 3 equations to determine of much water is being captured, how much can be held, and much is leaving the site:

Volume of _____ Runoff (Vr)

$$\text{Vr (cubic feet)} = \frac{(P)(Rv)(A)}{12''}$$

P = average rainfall event (inches); Rv = 0.05 + (0.009)(I), where I = % of impervious surface; A = area of collection surface (sq ft)

Minimum _____ Rate (Qr)

$$\text{QR (cubic feet per second)} = \frac{\text{Tank Capacity (cubic feet)}}{\text{Rainfall Event Interval (seconds)}}$$

Rainfall Runoff/Peak _____ Rate (Q)

Q = CiA

C = runoff coefficient; i = rainfall intensity (inches per hour); A = drainage area (acres)

EXEMPLARY PERFORMANCE

_____ the percentage threshold: Implement a stormwater management plan during the performance period to infiltrate, collect, and reuse stormwater runoff or evapotranspirate runoff from at least _____% of precipitation falling on the total. site area.

1 pt.

RESPONSIBLE PARTY:

OWNER/FACILITY/PROPERTY MANAGER

	SS Credit 6:
	Stormwater Quantity Control

ANSWER KEY

PURPOSE

Increase **pervious** cover and on-site **infiltration** to reduce **contamination** of runoff and the disruption of **natural** hydrology.

REQUIREMENTS

Implement a **stormwater** management plan during the performance period to infiltrate, **collect**, and reuse stormwater runoff or evapotranspirates runoff from at least **15%** of precipitation falling on the total site area.

An annual stormwater management **inspection** program must be implemented.

EQUATIONS

Use the following three equations to determine of much water is being captured, how much can be held, and much is leaving the site:

Volume of Captured Runoff (Vr)

$$\text{Vr (cubic feet)} = \frac{(P)(Rv)(A)}{12''}$$

P = average rainfall event (inches); Rv = 0.05 + (0.009)(I), where I = % of impervious surface; A = area of collection surface (sq ft)

Minimum Drawdown Rate (Qr)

$$\text{QR (cubic feet per second)} = \frac{\text{Tank Capacity (cubic feet)}}{\text{Rainfall Event Interval (seconds)}}$$

Rainfall Runoff/Peak Runoff Rate (Q)

Q = CiA

C = runoff coefficient; i = rainfall intensity (inches per hour); A = drainage area (acres)

EXEMPLARY PERFORMANCE

Double the percentage threshold: Implement a stormwater management plan during the performance period to infiltrate, collect, and reuse stormwater runoff or evapotranspirate runoff from at least **30%** of precipitation falling on the total site area.

AUDIT	SS Credit 7.1:
	Heat Island Effect, Non-Roof

PURPOSE

Minimize impacts on _____ and habitats by reducing _____ islands.

REQUIREMENTS

Option 1: Combine any of the following strategies for _____ percent of the _____ areas on site:
  Shade from _____

  Shade from solar panel covered structures or architectural structures with an _____ of at least _____

  _____-grid pavement system hardscape surfaces with an SRI of at least _____
Option 2:

  Place at least 50 percent of parking _____ or under cover by the means of either a green roof, roof surface with an
  _____ of at least _____, or solar panels.
Either option must include a _____ program to maintain SRI integrity.

DOCUMENTATION

Provide a _____ or _____ plan (depending on the compliance option pursued) depicting nonroof hardscape area square footage and SRI values and/or pervious capabilities for compliant areas.

EXEMPLARY PERFORMANCE

  Double the strategy for either compliance path option so that either _____ percent of the hardscape areas or
  _____ percent of all parking areas are addressed.

1 pt.	**RESPONSIBLE PARTY:**
	OWNER/PROPERTY MANAGER

	SS Credit 7.1:
	Heat Island Effect, Non-Roof

ANSWER KEY

PURPOSE

Minimize impacts on **microclimates** and habitats by reducing **heat** islands.

REQUIREMENTS

Option 1: Combine any of the following strategies for **50** percent of the **hardscape** areas on site:

Shade from **trees**

Shade from solar panel covered structures or architectural structures with an **SRI** of at least **29**

Open-grid pavement system hardscape surfaces with an SRI of at least **29**

Option 2:

Place at least 50 percent of parking **underground** or under cover by the means of either a green roof, roof surface with an **SRI** of at least **29**, or solar panels.

Either option must include a **maintenance** program to maintain SRI integrity.

DOCUMENTATION

Provide a **site or parking** plan (depending on the compliance option pursued) depicting nonroof hardscape area square footage and SRI values and/or pervious capabilities for compliant areas.

EXEMPLARY PERFORMANCE

Double the strategy for either compliance path option so that either **95** percent of the hardscape areas or **95** percent of all parking areas are addressed.

AUDIT	**SS Credit 7.2:**
	Heat Island Effect, Roof

PURPOSE

Minimize impacts on microclimates and _____ by reducing _____ islands.

REQUIREMENTS

Option 1: Cover _____ percent of the roof with roofing materials must have a minimum _____ value of:

_____ for low-sloped roofs

_____ for steep-sloped roofs

Option 2: Implement and _____ a _____ roof for at least _____ percent of the roof surface

Option 3: Combination of Option 1 and Option 2

DOCUMENTATION

Calculate total roof area _____ any equipment and penetrations, such as skylights.

Provide roof plan with slopes and roofing materials with SRI values and/or vegetated roof areas.

EXEMPLARY PERFORMANCE

Cover _____ percent of the roof with a green roof.

1 pt.	**RESPONSIBLE PARTY:**
	OWNER/PROPERTY MANAGER

ANSWER KEY

PURPOSE

Minimize impacts on microclimates and **habitats** by reducing **heat** islands.

REQUIREMENTS

Option 1: Cover 75 percent of the roof with roofing materials must have a minimum SRI value of:

78 for low-sloped roofs

29 for steep-sloped roofs

Option 2: Implement and **maintain** a **vegetated** roof for at least **50** percent of the roof surface

Option 3: Combination of Option 1 and Option 2

DOCUMENTATION

Calculate total roof area **minus** any equipment and penetrations, such as skylights. Provide roof plan with slopes and roofing materials with SRI values and/or vegetated roof areas.

EXEMPLARY PERFORMANCE

Cover **95** percent of the roof with a green roof.

AUDIT	SS Credit 8:
	Light Pollution Reduction

PURPOSE

Reduce light _____, sky glow, and the impacts on the nocturnal environment from the building and site, while _____ night sky access and visibility through _____ reduction.

REQUIREMENTS

INTERIOR LIGHTING with direct line of sight to Envelope Openings:

Implement _____ controls to shut off fixtures after hours with _____ override

Compliance based on shut off during 50% of annual _____ hours

EXTERIOR LIGHTING:

Option 1: Earned _____ Credit _____ under a different rating system

Option 2: Fixtures of _____ watts or more must be partially or fully _____

Option 3: Night illumination levels must be measured in _____ different perimeter locations of 100 feet apart not to exceed maximum illumination levels for Outdoor Lighting Zones LZ1 (_____) to LZ4 (_____)

1 pt.

RESPONSIBLE PARTY:

BUILDING ENGINEER

	SS Credit 8:
	Light Pollution Reduction

ANSWER KEY

PURPOSE

Reduce light **trespass,** sky glow, and the impacts on the nocturnal environment from the building and site, while **increasing** night sky access and visibility through **glare** reduction.

REQUIREMENTS

INTERIOR LIGHTING with direct line of sight to Envelope Openings:

Implement **automatic** controls to shut off fixtures after hours with **manual** override

Compliance based on shut off during 50% of annual **nighttime** hours

EXTERIOR LIGHTING:

Option 1: Earned **SS** Credit **8** under a different rating system

Option 2: Fixtures of **50** watts or more must be partially or fully **shielded**

Option 3: Night illumination levels must be measured in **8** different perimeter locations of **100** feet apart not to exceed maximum illumination levels for Outdoor Lighting Zones LZ1 **(Rural)** to LZ4 **(Urban)**

CHAPTER **5**
WATER EFFICIENCY

THIS CHAPTER FOCUSES ON THE STRATEGIES and technologies described within the Water Efficiency (WE) category of the Leadership in Energy and Environmental Design (LEED®) for Existing Buildings: Operations & Maintenance™ (EBOM) rating system, including methods to reduce the consumption of water, our most precious resource that is often taken for granted. As the demand for water continues to increase and supplies are decreasing, it is challenging for municipalities to keep up. The U.S. Geological Survey estimates that buildings account for 12 percent of total water use in the United States. **Potable water** that is delivered to buildings and homes is first pulled from local bodies of water, treated, and then delivered. This water is typically used for toilets, urinals, sinks, showers, drinking, irrigation, and for equipment uses, such as mechanical systems, dishwashers, and washing machines. Once the wastewater leaves a building, it is treated and then delivered back to the body of water. When the influx exceeds the capacity of the wastewater treatment facilities, overflow will result. This overflow can pollute and contaminate nearby water bodies, the sources of potable water, resulting in the need to build treatment facilities. Therefore, it is critical to understand how to reduce the amount of water we consume, to reduce the burden on the entire cycle, especially as we are threatened with shortages in the near future.

Remember to pick a new color for flashcards created for the WE category topics.

Green building design teams have the opportunity to specify efficient fixtures, equipment, and appliances that require less water. They also have the ability to implement rainwater-harvesting technologies to capture nonpotable water to use for multiple applications indoors and out. In order to capture stormwater, runoff is collected from the roof or a permeable surface and stored in a cistern onsite (see Figure 5.1).

Not only is it important to reduce the amount of potable water that is required, but green buildings also have the opportunity to reduce the amount of wastewater that leaves a project site. Implementing biological wastewater treatment technologies can be cost prohibitive, so teams are encouraged to assess the return on investment (ROI) through the means of triple bottom line evaluation.

Building and site designs can help to reduce the amount of water that is required for operations and the amount of wastewater that leaves a site. Within the LEED EBOM rating system, water efficiency for existing buildings is addressed in the following four components:

1. Indoor water use
2. Water consumption monitoring
3. Outdoor water use (for irrigation)
4. Process water for cooling towers

Each of these strategies is referred to in the prerequisite and/or credits of the category, as shown in Table 5.1. Notice Credits 2 and 3 are worth up to 5 points, while Credits 1 and 4 offer only 2 point opportunities each. Also notice that

Create a flashcard to remember the four strategies to address water usage and consumption as described in the WE category.

Figure 5.1 Capturing and storing rainwater to use for irrigation reduces the need for potable water. *Photo courtesy of Rainwater HOG, LLC*

Table 5.1 The Water Efficiency Category

Timeframe	Prereq./Credit	Title	Points
Audit	Prereq. 1	Minimum Indoor Plumbing Fixture and Fitting Efficiency	R
Performance Period/ Certification	Credit 1	Water Performance Measurement	1-2
Performance Period/ Certification	Credit 2	Additional Indoor Plumbing Fixture and Fitting Efficiency	1-5
Performance Period/ Certification	Credit 3	Water Efficient Landscaping	1-5
Program Development	Credit 4	Cooling Tower Water Management	1-2

Figure 5.2 The Utah Botanical Center's Wetland Discovery Point project is located within a natural habitat requiring the team to address environmental impacts, such as water quality. *Photo courtesy of Gary Neuenswander, Utah Agricultural Experiment Station*

Credits 1 through 3 are all addressed during the Performance Period and Certification phases. Do not worry about remembering the exact credit name and number, as the exam will list them together, but it is important to know which are credits versus prerequisites.

Similar to the strategies discussed within the Sustainable Sites category, there are triple bottom line values to water efficiency strategies. From an environmental standpoint, the more we build with impervious surfaces, the harder it is for the groundwater to recharge naturally. From an economic viewpoint, the more we contribute to sprawl, the more we increase the demand for more facilities and additional distribution systems to be built at a cost to the public. In addition, the energy required to heat water is in direct comparison to the amount of water used; use less hot water, use less energy, save money. Although the social equity of water is drastically understated, as its economic value does not reflect its importance, maintaining clean sources of water is imperative to future generations. The Utah Botanical Center's Wetland Discovery Point project earned Platinum level LEED certification for addressing each of the triple bottom line components for the project (see Figure 5.2).

 Water efficiency helps to reduce energy and, therefore, costs by reducing the amount of water that must be treated, heated, cooled, and distributed.

INDOOR WATER USE

Indoor water use typically includes the water used for water closets, urinals, lavatories, and showers. Break room or kitchen sinks are also included in the calculations for indoor water use. For the purposes of the exam, it is important to understand and remember the differences between a flush fixture and a flow fixture and how the consumption of the fixture is measured. Flush fixtures, such as toilets and urinals (see Figure 5.3), are measured in **gallons per flush** (gpf). Flow fixtures, such as sink faucets, showerheads, and aerators (see Figure 5.4), are measured in **gallons per minute** (gpm).

 Create flashcards to remember flow and flush fixture types and how they are measured.

Figure 5.3 Waterless urinals help to reduce the indoor water consumption. *Photo courtesy of SmithGroup, Inc.*

Indoor Water Use in Relation to LEED Compliance

When approaching the strategies to reduce water for a project seeking LEED certification, it is necessary for the project teams to calculate a **baseline** for water usage to compare to the amount the facility actually consumes. The WE prerequisite and Credit 2 utilize the Uniform Plumbing Code (UPC), 2006 or the International Plumbing Code (IPC), 2006 for flow and flush rates associated with conventional and efficient fixtures (see Table 5.2).

Figure 5.4 Aerators provide a low-cost solution to conserving potable water. *Photo courtesy of NEOPERL Inc.*

Table 5.2 Water Consumption Assumptions According to UPC and IPC for Baseline Calculations

Fixture Type	Standard Consumption Rate
Conventional water closet	1.6 gpf
Urinals	1.0 gpf
Showerheads	2.50 gpm
Public faucet	0.5 gpm
Private faucet	2.2 gpm
Kitchen and janitor sink faucets	2.20 gpm
Metered faucets	0.25 gallons per cycle

The team will need to determine when the original indoor plumbing system installation was completed in order to calculate the baseline consumption for the facility (see Table 5.3). If the fixtures' substantial completion date was prior to 1993, the baseline is calculated at 160 percent of the plumbing code. If substantial completion occurred during or after 1993, consumption is calculated

Create a flashcard to remember the UPC and IPC as the baseline standards for the WE prerequisite and indoor water use credits.

Table 5.3 Calculating Baseline Consumption for Water

Plumbing Fixture Install Year	Percentage of Plumbing Code
Before 1993	160%
During or after 1993	120%

TIP Notice that FTE is the acronym for **full-time equivalent** and not *full-time employee*. Make sure you account for part-time and transient occupants as well!

Create a flashcard to remember baseline versus design case: the amount of water a conventional project would use as compared to the design case. Remember, the baseline consumption is determined by the year in which the indoor plumbing system was substantially completed. Be sure to remember 1993 as the year with which to determine the calculation approach.

at 120 percent of the plumbing code. Teams are allowed to prorate consumption based on the substantial completion variation because of renovations and upgrades at different times to determine the baseline. For example, if 30 fixtures were installed prior to 1993 and 50 fixtures were replaced after 1993, the team would calculate $(30/80 \times 160) + (50/80 \times 120)$ to establish a 135 percent baseline level.

Once the fixture water consumption is determined for water closets, urinals, showerheads, and faucets, project teams need to account for the occupant usage to calculate how much water is required for the building. The full-time equivalent (FTE) occupancy is an estimation of actual building occupancy in terms of hours occupied per day and is used to determine the number of occupants for the building that will use the fixtures. Notice, FTE does not indicate full-time employee, but instead full-time equivalent. Therefore, to calculate an FTE, one would include regular building occupants (full-time and part-time) based on an occupancy period of 8 hours per day. For example, a full-time employee would have an FTE value of 1 because they spend 8 hours a day in the building and 8 divided by 8 is equal to 1. A part-time employee who works 4 hours per day would then have an FTE value of 0.5. Water consumption will also need to be calculated for transient occupants, such as visitors and guests.

Keeping within the lines of the basic concept to use less water, efficient indoor water strategies help to change the typically traditional, wasteful behavior of occupants. These strategies do not have to be intrusive or even noticeable. Although when assessing upgrade options, project teams are encouraged to conduct life-cycle cost assessments for determining the best solution for their projects. For example, waterless urinals do not contribute to water costs, but the maintenance costs might be higher and outweigh the costs of a low-flow fixture.

Overall, most of the following strategies will not be noticeable, but they will substantially reduce water consumption:

WE Prerequisite 1: Water Use Reduction. The LEED EBOM rating system defines potable water use as an important component that green buildings need to address and, therefore, requires a reduction in consumption as a minimal performance feature. This importance is characterized by the means of a prerequisite within the WE category. As a result, project teams pursuing certification must reduce water consumption for water closets (see Figure 5.5), urinals, showerheads, and faucets (see Figure 5.6) equal to the baseline case to meet the requirements of the prerequisite. The strategy to achieve this prerequisite involves implementing water efficient flush and flow fixtures. As previously stated, project teams would need to calculate a baseline water consumption using the UPC or IPC values based on the occupancy fixture usage groups with a 1:1 male-to-female gender ratio. The declarant will then need to input the values specific to the fixtures installed at the facility to then compare the different demanded consumptions to prove the reduction is at least equal to the calculated baseline. These calculations are completed on the submittal template on LEED-Online. Remember, the built-in functionality of the submittal template determines compliance based on the data input. The template is configured to assume *the rule of three* to calculate consumption for both the baseline and design cases. The rule of three presupposes a female uses a water closet and a lavatory three times each per day, whereas a male only uses a water closet one time per day, a urinal two times per day, and a lavatory three times a day. Consumption is determined by multiplying water needs of each fixture type by gender based on the fixture usage groups.

WE Credit 2: Additional Indoor Plumbing Fixture and Fitting Efficiency. In order to comply with this credit, project teams will need to exceed the minimum threshold required by WE Prerequisite 1 (see Figure 5.7). Project teams can earn up to five points for achieving 10 percent,

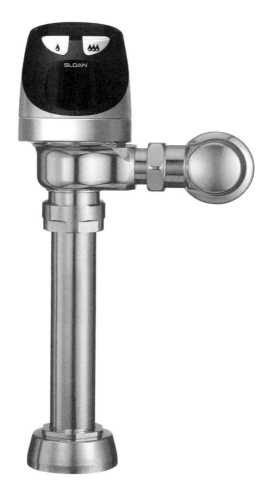

Figure 5.5 Using high-efficiency toilet (HET) fixtures and flushometers, which use 1.28 gpf or less, helps to achieve the water reduction prerequisite. *Photo courtesy of Sloan Valve Company*

15 percent, 20 percent, 25 percent, and 30 percent water reductions for indoor water use. They can pursue an exemplary performance opportunity to reducing water demand by 35 percent. To prove a 35 percent reduction, project teams are

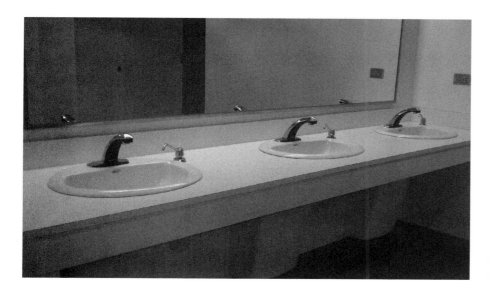

Figure 5.6 Implementing commercial bathroom lavatories with sensors help to reduce water consumption and could help to achieve WE Prerequisite 1. *Photo courtesy of Stephen Martorana, LEED AP BD+C*

Figure 5.7 The Armstrong World Industries corporate headquarters in Lancaster, Pennsylvania, implemented signage to help educate the occupants, a strategy that helped the project earn Platinum certification under the LEED for Existing Buildings rating system. *Photo courtesy of Armstrong Ceiling and Wall Systems*

 Create a flashcard to remember the two opportunities that address indoor water use.

permitted to include water-efficient dishwashers, laundry machines (see Figure 5.8), and other water-consuming fixtures in the water consumption calculations. Note these fixtures can only be used to achieve exemplary performance and are not to be incorporated in the calculations to prove compliance with the prerequisite or credit.

Figure 5.8 Water-efficient dishwashers or washing machines can help a team to pursue exemplary performance for WE Credit 2. *Photo courtesy of Gettys*

QUIZ TIME!

Q5.1. What is the year in which a percentage reduction is based to determine baseline water consumption level? (Choose one)

A. 1990

B. 1970

C. 1993

D. 1973

E. 1996

Q5.2. Which of the following products is not an example of a flow fixture? (Choose two)

A. Lavatory faucets

B. Toilets

C. Sprinkler heads

D. Aerators

E. Showerheads

F. Urinals

Q5.3. What is the threshold of reduced water consumption required in order to comply with WE Prerequisite 1: Water Use Reduction? (Choose one)

A. 10 percent better than the baseline

B. 15 percent better than the baseline

C. 20 percent better than the baseline

D. 25 percent better than the baseline

E. Equal to the baseline

Q5.4. Which of the following are permitted in the calculations to pursue Exemplary Performance for WE Credit 2: Water Use Reduction? (Choose two)

A. Dishwashers

B. Sprinkler heads

C. Hose bibs

D. Janitor sinks

E. Kitchen faucets

F. Washing machines

Q5.5. How would a team calculate the baseline water consumption if the facility underwent two renovations and, therefore, had two different substantial completion dates? (Choose one)

A. Calculate a 120 percent reduction of the UPC.

B. Calculate a 120 percent reduction of the IPC.

C. Calculate a 160 percent reduction of the UPC.

D. Calculate a 160 percent reduction of the IPC.

E. Determine a prorated average between 120 percent and 160 percent of the reference standard based on the whole building.

WATER CONSUMPTION MONITORING

Metering and monitoring water used for irrigating landscaping and indoor uses is a critical strategy of a holistic approach to sustainable building operations. The upfront cost to purchase and install meters and the ongoing labor cost for an operations and maintenance staff to document usage rates, along with the cost to maintain the devices, should be offset by the operational savings captured. Installing meters and monitoring consumption allows one to detect deficiencies and locate leaks to remedy, while also understanding consumption patterns (see Figure 5.9). This detection will help to preserve the amount of water required from local water bodies and reduce the burden on municipalities.

Water Consumption Monitoring in Relation to LEED Compliance

Project teams will have only one credit, but not one point, to pursue should they install metering for a facility, although the strategy relates to the prerequisite and each of the other credits contained within the WE category of the EBOM rating system.

WE Credit 1: Water Performance Measurement. Project teams can pursue one point for installing permanent metering equipment to measure the total potable water consumption for the entire building and property contained within the LEED boundary. If the facility also incorporates permanent submetering,

Figure 5.9 Metering potable water consumption will help existing building projects to earn WE Credit 1. *Photo courtesy of Michael R. Costello, P.E., LEED Green Associate*

they can pursue another point. At a minimum, one of the following uses must be submetered to capture at least 80 percent of the water consumed specifically for that use in order to comply with this additional point opportunity:

- Irrigation
- Indoor plumbing fixtures and fittings
- Cooling towers
- Domestic hot water
- Other process water uses

In order to achieve this credit, meters must be read at least once a week and documented in monthly and annual consumption surveys (depending on the length of the performance period). Should the facility submeter more than one use listed previously, the team can pursue an Exemplary Performance credit.

 Create a flashcard to remember the five uses that can be submetered in order to achieve WE Credit 1.

QUIZ TIME!

Q5.6. Which of the following submetering opportunities would not comply with the requirements of WE Credit 1: Water Performance Measurement, Option 2? (Choose one)

A. Dishwashers

B. Cooling towers

C. High-efficiency irrigation system

D. Low-flow toilets

E. Hose bibs

Q5.7. How much of the water consumption use needs to be captured by the submetering equipment in order to comply with WE Credit 1: Water Performance Measurement, Option 2? (Choose one)

A. 50 percent

B. 60 percent

C. 70 percent

D. 80 percent

E. 90 percent

Q5.8. What needs to be metered in order to achieve WE Credit 1: Water Performance Measurement, Option 1? (Choose one)

A. 80 percent of the facility

B. 80 percent of the facility and associated grounds within the LEED boundary

C. The entire building and associated grounds within the LEED boundary

D. All indoor plumbing fixtures and fittings

E. All process water

F. The water consumed and included on the utility bill, even if it is not included in the LEED boundary

Q5.9. How often does the meter equipment need to be checked in order to comply with WE Credit 1: Water Performance Measurement? (Choose one)

A. One time during the performance period

B. Annually

C. Monthly

D. Weekly

E. At least two times during the performance period

Q5.10. Which of the following are benefits associated to complying with WE Credit 1: Water Performance Measurement? (Choose three)

A. Detect leaks

B. Reduce usage

C. Installation costs

D. Find deficiencies

E. Labor costs

OUTDOOR WATER USE FOR IRRIGATION

 Remember, both composting and mulching optimize soil conditions to add to the efficiencies of native and adaptive plantings and high-efficiency irrigation systems.

Water used for irrigating landscaped areas accounts for the primary use of outdoor water and is, therefore. a component to be addressed and reduced by projects seeking LEED certification. Remembering the concepts discussed in the previous chapter, site design, including native and adaptive plants (see Figure 5.10), can drastically reduce the amount of water required for irrigation, if not eliminate the need for irrigation all together. If irrigation is required, implementing a high-efficiency system can also substantially reduce the amount of water required over conventional designs. Green building projects might also implement another sustainable option, including capturing rainwater to use for irrigation and indoor water flush functions (see Figure 5.11).

Chapter 4 introduced the heat island effect and explained how it is responsible for an overall temperature increase of an area. Combining the effects of greenhouse gas emissions, the heat island effect, and increased impervious surfaces from sprawling developments, water is evaporating at quicker rates and not getting delivered to plants and vegetation. Project teams need to be aware of these conditions and plan accordingly, efficiently, and sustainably.

Outdoor Water Use in Relation to LEED Compliance

Pulling together the concepts and strategies from the Sustainable Sites category, such as native planting and xeriscaping (see Figure 5.12), project teams could seek to achieve the following outdoor water use strategy when pursuing EBOM certification:

WE Credit 3: Water Efficient Landscaping. Project teams have an opportunity to earn up to five points within this credit. If the site uses 50 percent less potable water for irrigation purposes as compared to conventional needs, the project can earn one point and for every 12.5 percent reduction thereafter.

Figure 5.10 Native and noninvasive plantings do not require irrigation or fertilizers.

Reducing the demand can be achieved by replacing the existing conventional system with a high-efficiency irrigation system that includes moisture sensors. These irrigation systems include surface drip, underground, and bubbler systems. A team could also reduce the potable water demand by replacing invasive vegetation with native and adaptive plantings. A sustainable solution encompasses a decision about both vegetation and system types balanced by the triple bottom line goals of a project.

Project teams can choose from one of the three provided calculation methods to document compliance. Option 1 is available to teams with irrigation water consumption that is submetered. If the team pursues WE Credit 1 and installs submetering equipment to track the potable water demand for irrigation, the project team would submit the actual water use during the performance

 The amount of water delivered by sprinkler heads is measured in gallons per minute (gpm). Do you remember what other water fixtures are measured similarly?

 Native and noninvasive plant selections can reduce or possibly eliminate the need for potable water for irrigation and can also reduce the need for fertilizers, protecting the quality of water.

Figure 5.11 A salvaged train tanker car (food-grade, originally used for milk) collects 10,000 gallons of roof rainwater, which is then used for irrigation of the permaculture garden and to flush toilets at the EcoDorm project at Warren Wilson College. *Photo courtesy of Samsel Architects*

 TIP In order to be eligible to pursue this credit, at least 5 percent of the total site area in the LEED boundary must include landscaped areas, any nonvegetated yet ecologically appropriate features, gardens, and/ or planters.

TIP Each of the calculations required to document compliance with this credit is based on irrigation needs during the month of July.

period to be compared against the midsummer (July) baseline usage. Option 2 is available to teams that do not have the ability to track actual consumption, and they will then need to calculate both the design and baseline cases. Option 3 is "independent irrigation performance and ranking tools are available from local, regional, state or national sources, use such tools to demonstrate reductions in potable water or other natural surface or subsurface resource for irrigation purposes."[1]

Depending on the compliance path option the team pursues, a number of calculations could be required to document compliance for this credit. For the purposes of the exam, it is important to know the components of the calculations and not necessarily how to complete the calculations. Typically, a team will need to compute a baseline case (if historical data is not available) in which to compare calculated or actual consumption rates to. The first step requires the landscape area to be determined, as it will be the same for both design and baseline cases. Next, the **evapotranspiration rate** is calculated for each landscape area, followed by the amount of water actually delivered to vegetation by the proposed irrigation system and not blown away or evaporated. In order to do this, the declarant first determines the **irrigation efficiency** of the proposed type of system. The O&M reference guide indicates a traditional irrigation system has a 0.625 efficiency default value, whereas a drip system has a 0.90 irrigation efficiency default value. These values together with the controller efficiency value from the system's manufacturer will help to determine the total water usage for the design case. To create the baseline case, the conventional default values are used instead of project specific values.

If the team is pursuing Option 2, the **landscape coefficient** is calculated based on the vegetation type's **species factor** (water needs), **density factor** (spacing), and **microclimate factor** (environmental conditions such as humidity, temperature, and wind). The reference guide provides default values for each of these three components for different vegetation types such as trees, shrubs, and turfgrass for

Figure 5.12 Xeriscaping helps to reduce the demand for potable water with the help of high-efficiency irrigation systems and soil improvements for native plantings.

project teams to use. These default values do not need to be memorized for the purposes of the exam, just remember the three factors of the landscape coefficient calculation.

Project teams can look to a few different strategies in which to pursue this credit. Teams can replace invasive plantings with vegetation that requires less water. They can also look to use graywater to irrigate with. They can obtain **graywater** by collecting "cooling tower bleed-down water, condensation from air-conditioning systems, or other building activities that do not involve human waste or food processing,"[2] such as sink waste water. Teams can also collect rainwater to store on site and reuse for irrigation. Remember, stormwater collection was introduced in the previous chapter to reduce the runoff quantities for the site. Therefore, because there are multiple benefits of capturing stormwater,

If a project team is required to use potable water for irrigation for public health reasons, the mandate does not hinder achieving this credit, as those areas can be excluded from the calculations. An example might include irrigating near a swimming pool.

Create a flashcard to remember the definition of **graywater:** wastewater from showers, bathtubs, lavatories, and washing machines. This water has not come into contact with toilet waste according to the International Plumbing Code (IPC).

Figure 5.13 Stormwater is collected for reuse to reduce the need for potable water at the Natural Resources Defense Council's Robert Redford Building in Santa Monica, California. *Photo courtesy of Grey Crawford*

 TIP Wastewater from toilets and urinals is considered **blackwater**. Kitchen sink, shower, and bathtub wastewater is also considered a source of blackwater. Remember, it's not the source that matters, but what could be in it! For example, washing machine wastewater could be considered blackwater, as washing machines are used to wash cloth diapers.

it is important to understand how a project team would design to collect and reuse the water. Project teams need to evaluate different options to determine the appropriate collection systems for their specific project and how much water they can collect to determine how to best reuse it. Systems can range from small barrels to large cisterns (see Figures 5.13 and 5.14). Regardless of the system desired, project teams are encouraged to evaluate the following:

- *Water budget.* How much precipitation is expected versus how much water is needed for the purpose the water is intended?

Figure 5.14 Stormwater is collected on-site and stored in cisterns at the Utah Botanical Center's Wetland Discovery Point building and used to flush toilets, as well as irrigate the site, thereby reducing the need to use potable water. *Photo courtesy of Gary Neuenswander, Utah Agricultural Experiment Station*

■ *Drawdown.* How much water is needed in between rainfalls?

■ *Drainage area.* How will the water be collected to store onsite? Will it be a permeable surface? If so, what is the size of the surface to determine how much water can be collected?

■ *Conveyance system.* Different pipes will be needed as stormwater and graywater pipes are not allowed to be connected to potable water lines.

■ *Pretreatment.* Screen and/or filters will be needed to remove debris from runoff.

■ *Pressurization.* A pump maybe required depending on the system.

If a project team eliminates the need for potable water by the means of reusing water or by specifying native and adaptive plantings, they can earn five points. This opportunity is available under WE Credit 1 and not as Exemplary Performance credit under the Innovations in Operations (IO) category.

 Water efficiency strategies incorporated into site design, such as collecting rainwater onsite, can help to reduce the demand for indoor water for flush fixtures.

 TIP Collected stormwater can be used for irrigation, fire suppression, flush fixtures, and custodial purposes.

 Remember the strategies discussed in the previous chapter. Proper site design will help to reduce water consumption for landscaping needs. Reducing water demands affects both the SS and WE categories.

QUIZ TIME!

Q5.11. Which of the following strategies might contribute to WE Credit 3: Water Efficient Landscaping? (Choose three)

A. Planting of hardwood trees to provide shade

B. Planting native or adapted plant species

C. Installing turf grass

D. Reducing amount of pervious surface area

E. Combining vegetated swales and cisterns to capture rainwater

Q5.12. An existing and operating facility is undergoing a major site renovation. The plans include avoiding undeveloped areas and planting more than half of the site area with native and adapted vegetation. Retention ponds and bioswales will also be implemented with native vegetation. To which of the following LEED concepts might these design strategies contribute? (Choose four)

A. Heat island effect

B. Stormwater runoff reduction

C. Site disturbance

D. Water-efficient landscaping

E. Increase density

Q5.13. A four-story, 40,000-square-foot building in Florida includes repaving existing parking areas along the entire length of the south and west facades of the building. The building and parking areas compose the entire site to its boundaries, not leaving any green space. The common afternoon rain showers have led the design team to select open-grid paving with vegetated cells equivalent to 50 percent of its surface in lieu of a lower first cost solution, such as black asphalt. Based on the information provided, which of the following benefits and LEED strategies might the open-grid paving strategy contribute? (Choose three)

A. Reduced site disturbance

B. Water-efficient landscaping

C. Heat island effect

D. Stormwater management

E. Optimizing energy performance

F. Water use reduction

Q5.14. Which of the following would not reduce potable water used for irrigation? (Choose one)

A. Surface drip irrigation system

B. Sprinkler irrigation systems

C. Underground irrigation system

D. Bubbler irrigation systems

E. Installing native vegetation

PROCESS WATER

TIP "A cooling tower uses water to absorb heat from air-conditioning systems and regulate air temperature in a facility."[3]

The types of water use reduction strategies previously described may be more obvious for green buildings to pursue as opposed to the third type: process water. Water used for building systems, such as heating and cooling air, is considered process water. **Process water** is used for industrial purposes, such as chillers, cooling towers, and boilers, and also includes water used for operations, such as washing machines, ice machines, and dishwashers. Typically, it is easier to remember the industrial purposes of process water than the operational aspects. To help remember these other types of process water think of restaurants, schools, or hotels, and the need for water as part of business operations. For the purposes of the O+M exam, it is critical to connect process water use reduction with cooling towers, as the EBOM rating system only addresses process water use by the means of cooling tower water management.

Facility managers and owners should be aware where process water is required and how much is consumed at those specific locations. Green building design teams know efficient building systems require less water. Taking advantage of closed-loop systems allows for buildings to extend the use of water in a contaminant-free environment (see Figure 5.15). Installing meters to understand the demands of water for building systems and how much is consumed could help economically, specifically in terms of cooling tower makeup water. This water is evaporated during the operation of a cooling tower and, if metered, could be an opportunity for credit from the utility company, as it does not enter the sewer system, where it would then need to be treated and inflict a cost on municipalities.

Figure 5.15 Potable water can be reduced for a cooling tower by a closed-loop system. *Photo courtesy of SmithGroup, Inc*

Process Water Use in Relation to LEED Compliance

Teams working on projects seeking LEED EBOM certification can pursue the following credit if process potable water is reduced for cooling towers:

WE Credit 4: Cooling Tower Water Management. Project teams have two options to pursue in order to earn up to two points for this credit. Option 1 is available to teams that develop and implement a cooling tower water management plan that "addresses chemical treatment, bleed-off, biological control and staff training as it relates to cooling tower maintenance."[4] A conductivity meter will also need to be implemented with automatic controls to adjust the bleed rate to maintain the proper concentration at all times to prevent water loss in order for

 Create a flashcard to remember the nonpotable sources as defined by the O&M reference guide: "harvested rainwater, harvested stormwater, air-conditioner condensate, swimming pool filter backwash water, cooling tower blowdown, pass-through (once-through) cooling water, recycled treated wastewater from toilet and urinal flushing, foundation drain water, municipally reclaimed water or any other appropriate on-site water source that is not naturally occurring groundwater or surface water."[5]

Create a flashcard to remember the disease associated with poor cooling tower management.

 Create a flashcard to remember the two point opportunities to comply with WE Credit 4.

the point to be awarded under option 1. Not only is it important for the team to maintain proper concentration, but also they are encouraged to control corrosion to increase system efficiency and prohibit microbial growth. Option 2 requires the team to implement meters to document at least 50 percent of the makeup water is composed of nonpotable water sources. If nonpotable water sources are used, teams must ensure biocides are incorporated to control biological contamination, as poorly managed cooling towers can increase health risks, such as exposure to Legionnaires' disease. Should the team comply, the project will earn one point. The team has the option to pursue both options and collect two points. If the team exceeds 95 percent nonpotable makeup water use, the project could be eligible to pursue an Exemplary Performance credit under the IO category.

QUIZ TIME!

Q5.15. Which of the following are types of process water uses? (Choose three)

A. Cooling towers

B. Boilers

C. Washing machines

D. Cisterns

E. Toilets

Q5.16. Which of the following are potential sources of nonpotable water? (Choose three)

A. Blackwater

B. Municipally supplied reclaimed water

C. Captured rainwater

D. Wastewater from a toilet

E. Graywater

Q5.17. Which of the following uses are suitable for nonpotable water? (Choose two)

A. Drinking water

B. Irrigation

C. Clothes washing

D. Process water

E. Dishwashing

F. Showers

Q5.18. Which of the following applications can collected stormwater be used for? (Choose four)

A. Landscape irrigation

B. Fire suppression

C. Flush fixtures

D. Drinking water

E. Custodial uses

F. Shower water

Q5.19. Which of the following credits would not be applicable if a team were to install a stormwater collection system? (Choose one)

A. WE Credit 2: Additional Indoor Plumbing Fixture and Fitting Efficiency

B. SS Credit 6: Stormwater Quantity Control

C. WE Credit 1: Water Performance Measurement

D. WE Credit 4: Cooling Tower Water Management

E. WE Credit 3: Water-Efficient Landscaping

Q5.20. Which of the following would not contribute to water loss in a cooling tower? (Choose one)

A. Evaporation

B. Discharged water to control mineral buildup

C. Drift loss

D. Leaks, spills, or overflows

E. Evapotranspiration

Q5.21. Which of the following is not a benefit associated with pursuing WE Credit 4: Cooling Tower Water Management and submetering cooling tower makeup water? (Choose one)

A. Performance measurements

B. Could help to earn points for WE Credit 2: Additional Indoor Plumbing Fixture and Fitting Efficiency

C. Water-loss measurements

D. Could help to earn points for WE Credit 1: Water Performance Measurement

Q5.22. What is the minimum amount of nonpotable makeup water required in order to comply with the requirements of WE Credit 4: Cooling Tower Water Management? (Choose one)

A. 10 percent

B. 20 percent

C. 40 percent

D. 50 percent

E. 95 percent

Q5.23. Which of the following roof surface materials would not be an appropriate choice if rainwater is to be collected from the roof? (Choose one)

A. Metal

B. Clay

C. Asphalt

D. Concrete

Q5.24. Which of the following are not benefits associated with an increase in efficiency of indoor plumbing fixtures and fittings? (Choose two)

A. Decreased total amount of potable water withdrawn from nearby water bodies, including underground aquifers

B. Reduced chemical inputs for water treatment

C. Increased chemical inputs for water treatment

D. Reduced greenhouse gas emissions

E. Decreased building operating costs

F. Increased building operating costs

G. Upgrade paybacks

Q5.25. What is the purpose of controlling a cooling tower's bleed rate? (Choose one)

A. To control mineral build up and solubility

B. To prevent condensation

C. To control evapotranspiration

D. To prevent evaporation

AUDIT	WE Prerequisite 1:
	Minimum Indoor Plumbing Fixture & Fitting Efficiency

PERFORMANCE PERIOD/ CERTIFICATION	WE Credit 2:
	Additional Indoor Plumbing Fixture & Fitting Efficiency

PURPOSE

To ensure a reduction on the _____ of the potable water supply and _____ systems by _____ water _____ within buildings.

REQUIREMENTS

Determine _____ completion date for building's indoor plumbing system to determine _____ of consumption:

If prior to 1993, the baseline is _____ **percent** of the plumbing code

If completed in 1993 or later, the baseline is _____ **percent** of the plumbing code

Prerequisite requires project to meet baseline, whereas credit requires consumption to be at least 10 percent less than the code for shower heads, _____ closets, _____ and faucets.

POINT DISTRIBUTION

10%		15%		20%		25%		30%		35%
•1 point		•2 points		•3 points		•4 points		•5 points		•1 EP point

REFERENCED STANDARDS

The _____ Plumbing Code, 2006

International _____ Code, 2006

1–5 pts. for credit	**RESPONSIBLE PARTY:**
	BUILDING ENGINEER

WE Prerequisite 1:
Minimum Indoor Plumbing Fixture & Fitting Efficiency

WE Credit 2:
Additional Indoor Plumbing Fixture & Fitting Efficiency

ANSWER KEY

PURPOSE

To ensure a reduction on the **burden** of the potable water supply and **wastewater** systems by increasing water **efficiency** within buildings.

REQUIREMENTS

Determine **substantial** completion date for building's indoor plumbing system to determine **baseline** of consumption:

If prior to 1993, the baseline is **160 percent** of the plumbing code

If completed in 1993 or later, the baseline is **120 percent** of the plumbing code

Prerequisite requires project to meet baseline, whereas credit requires consumption to be at least 10 percent less than the code for shower heads, **water** closets, **urinals**, and faucets.

POINT DISTRIBUTION

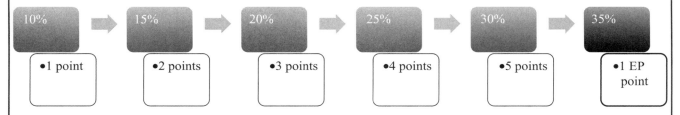

10%	15%	20%	25%	30%	35%
•1 point	•2 points	•3 points	•4 points	•5 points	•1 EP point

REFERENCED STANDARDS

The **Uniform** Plumbing Code, 2006

International **Plumbing** Code, 2006

PERFORMANCE PERIOD/CERTIFICATION

WE Credit 1:
Water Performance Management

PURPOSE

To identify water-saving opportunities and track _____ patterns by measuring building and _____ water performance.

REQUIREMENTS

For 1 point, install _____ metering to measure the total potable water consumed by the building and the site. Meters must be read _____ for results to be included in monthly and annual reports.

For 2 points, install submetering for at least _____ **percent** of one of the following :

_____

Indoor plumbing fixtures and fittings

Cooling towers

_____ hot water

Other _____ water

Exemplary Performance can be achieved if 80 percent of _____ or more of the above are metered.

1–2 pts.

RESPONSIBLE PARTY:

BUILDING ENGINEER

WE Credit 1:

Water Performance Management

ANSWER KEY

PURPOSE

To identify water-saving opportunities and track **consumption** patterns by measuring building and **subsystem** water performance.

REQUIREMENTS

For 1 point, install **permanent** metering to measure the total potable water consumed by the building and the site. Meters must be read **weekly** for results to be included in monthly and annual reports.

For 2 points, install submetering for at least **80 percent** of one of the following :

Irrigation

Indoor plumbing fixtures and fittings

Cooling towers

Domestic hot water

Other **process** water

Exemplary Performance can be achieved if 80 percent of **2** or more of the above are metered.

PERFORMANCE PERIOD/CERTIFICATION

PURPOSE

To reduce or eliminate the need for _____ water for landscape _____.

REQUIREMENTS

Option 1:

Reduce the need for potable water for irrigation by at least _____ percent.

Option 2:

Use stormwater or graywater to irrigate or plant drought-tolerant vegetation that does not require any watering. Temporary irrigation is allowed for up to _____ year.

STRATEGIES

Use native and _____ vegetation that can survive on natural rainfall

Use _____-efficiency irrigation systems

Use _____ stormwater and recycled wastewater for irrigation

Use municipally supplied _____ water

CALCULATIONS

Calculate water demand based meter readings or by theoretical calculations based on the following factors:

Square footage of landscaped area

Square footage for each type of vegetation

_____ factor, _____ factor, and _____ factor for each planting type

Evapotranspiration rate for climate region

If irrigation system is to be used, type and controller efficiency

POINT DISTRIBUTION

50% → 62.5% → 75% → 87.5% → 100%

- 1 point
- 2 points
- 3 points
- 4 points
- 5 points

1–5 pts.

	WE Credit 3:
	Water Efficient Landscaping

ANSWER KEY

PURPOSE

To reduce or eliminate the need for **potable** water for landscape **irrigation.**

REQUIREMENTS

Option 1:

Reduce the need for potable water for irrigation by at least **50** percent.

Option 2:

Use stormwater or graywater to irrigate or plant drought-tolerant vegetation that does not require any watering. Temporary irrigation is allowed for up to **one** year.

STRATEGIES

Use native and **adaptive** vegetation that can survive on natural rainfall

Use **high**-efficiency irrigation systems

Use **captured** stormwater and recycled wastewater for irrigation

Use municipally supplied **nonpotable** water

CALCULATIONS

Calculate water demand based meter readings or by theoretical calculations based on the following factors:

Square footage of landscaped area

Square footage for each type of vegetation

Species factor, **density** factor, and **microclimate** factor for each planting type

Evapotranspiration rate for climate region

If irrigation system is to be used, type and controller efficiency

POINT DISTRIBUTION

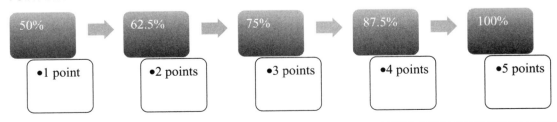

50%	62.5%	75%	87.5%	100%
•1 point	•2 points	•3 points	•4 points	•5 points

PROGRAM DEVELOPMENT

PURPOSE

To ensure a reduction on the burden of the municipal water supply by _____ water efficiency and/or using _____ sources within buildings for cooling tower equipment.

REQUIREMENTS

Pursue one or both of either of the following:

Option 1:

Install _____ meter with automatic controls to maintain the _____ rate

Develop and implement a cooling tower water _____ plan

Option 2:

Use _____ **percent** nonpotable makeup water for cooling towers

Measure makeup water to verify nonpotable _____ and _____

EXEMPLARY PERFORMANCE

Use _____ **percent** nonpotable makeup water for cooling towers

1–2 pts.

RESPONSIBLE PARTY:

OPERATIONS MANAGER

	WE Credit 4:
	Cooling Tower Water Management

ANSWER KEY

PURPOSE

To ensure a reduction on the burden of the municipal water supply by **maximizing** water efficiency and/or using **nonpotable** sources within buildings for cooling tower equipment.

REQUIREMENTS

Pursue one or both of either of the following:

Option 1:

Install **conductivity** meter with automatic controls to maintain the **bleed** rate

Develop and implement a cooling tower water **management** plan

Option 2:

Use **50 percent** nonpotable makeup water for cooling towers

Measure makeup water to verify nonpotable **sources** and **quantities**

EXEMPLARY PERFORMANCE

Use **95 percent** nonpotable makeup water for cooling towers

CHAPTER **6**

ENERGY AND ATMOSPHERE

THIS CHAPTER FOCUSES ON THE STRATEGIES and technologies to address energy use and consumption as described in the Energy & Atmosphere (EA) category of the Leadership in Energy and Environmental Design (LEED®) for Existing Buildings: Operations & Maintenance™ (EBOM) rating system.

Remember from Chapter 2 that conventionally designed and built facilities account for 39 percent of primary energy use, 72 percent of electricity consumption, and 38 percent of carbon dioxide (CO_2) emissions, according to the U.S. Green Building Council (USGBC®) website.[1] Therefore, the LEED EBOM rating system addresses means to reduce consumption and promote cleaner energy sources. The rating system puts the most emphasis on the EA category by offering the largest opportunity to earn points, but teams typically find many synergies within the Indoor Environmental Quality (EQ) category, as building occupants can affect the reduction in consumption and corresponding CO_2 emissions of certified buildings. At the same time, they may find some trade-offs to consider, as providing a healthy indoor environment can require additional energy, such as air exchanges. For the purposes of the exam, it is important to recognize both the synergies and trade-offs of any green building strategy.

With the help of the media, we all understand the environmental impacts of using fossil fuels to generate electricity. Each step of the electricity production process harms the environment and ecosystem in one way or another. For example, the burning of coal releases harmful pollutants and greenhouse gases that contribute to global warming and climate change, reducing air quality on a global scale. Therefore, not only is it important for green buildings to address energy consumption reduction strategies, but it is also pertinent to incorporate clean energy systems. As a result, project teams are encouraged to focus on the following three components in order to address the goals and intentions of the EA category to help reduce greenhouse gas emissions[2]:

1. Monitoring and improving building energy performance
2. Eliminating chlorofluorocarbons (CFCs)
3. Renewable energy

Each of these strategies is referred to in the prerequisites and credits of the category, as shown in Table 6.1. Note that Credit 1 offers the most opportunities to earn points, followed by Credit 4. Notice also Credits 1, 4, and 6 are approached during the performance period, while the rest are addressed during the audit or program development stages. Do not worry about remembering the exact credit name and number, but it is important to know which are credits versus prerequisites and, therefore, which ones are worth points and which ones are not.

It's time to pick a different color for flashcards created for EA category topics.

TIP Burning coal releases harmful pollutants into the atmosphere, such as carbon dioxide, sulfur dioxide, nitrogen oxide, and mercury.

Create a flashcard to remember the three components of the EA category.

Table 6.1 The Energy & Atmosphere Category

Timeframe	Prereq/ Credit	Title	Points
Program Development	Prereq 1	Energy Efficiency Best Management Practices	R
Audit	Prereq 2	Minimum Energy Efficiency Performance	R
Audit	Prereq 3	Fundamental Refrigerant Management	R
Performance Period/ Certification	Credit 1	Optimize Energy Efficiency Performance	1–18
Program Development	Credit 2.1	Existing Building Commissioning: Investigation and Analysis	2
Program Development	Credit 2.2	Existing Building Commissioning: Implementation	2
Program Development	Credit 2.3	Existing Building Commissioning: Ongoing Commissioning	2
Audit	Credit 3.1	Performance Measurement: Building Automation System	1
Audit	Credit 3.2	Performance Measurement: System-Level Metering	1-2
Performance Period/ Certification	Credit 4	On-Site and Off-Site Renewable Energy	1-6
Program Development	Credit 5	Enhanced Refrigerant Management	1
Performance Period/ Certification	Credit 6	Emissions Reduction Reporting	1

MONITORING AND IMPROVING BUILDING ENERGY PERFORMANCE

Assessing an existing building's energy profile helps to establish a starting point to reduce consumption. Understanding the energy related-building components that are typically audited lays the groundwork for discovering areas to be monitored, addressed, and improved. As part of the auditing process, patterns can be determined to find inefficiencies and determine preventative measures for the future. Once inefficiencies are determined and reduction goals are set, possible improvement strategies can be evaluated based on existing conditions, established energy performance and goals, demands, prevention, and operating and maintenance requirements. The auditing process will be detailed later, but for now it is important to understand the areas and strategies that can increase efficiencies and optimize energy performance, such as:

■ Improving site conditions, such as reducing the heat island effect, can reduce energy demand, as equipment will not need to compensate for heat gain from surrounding and adjacent areas (see Figure 6.1). Project teams will need to evaluate the triple bottom line benefits of product and material replacement.

■ How is the building oriented? Orientation can affect the amount of energy needed for artificial heating, cooling, and lighting by taking advantage of free energy by means of passive design strategies, such as daylighting and natural ventilation (see Figure 6.2). If a building's orientation was not addressed during design, the facility may require more energy because of poor design. For example, too much sun on the south façade can lead to heat gain, making the building occupants uncomfortable and causing the mechanical systems

Figure 6.1 The EcoDorm at Warren Wilson College in Swannanoa, North Carolina, earned its Platinum-level certification under the EBOM rating system for addressing site conditions with strategies in compliance with the Sustainable Sites (SS) category, which also reduced energy demand to help the team to earn points under the EA category. *Photo courtesy of Samsel Architects, Photography by John Warner Photography*

Patient Rooms ▲

Figure 6.2 This daylighting strategy at Concord Hospital helps to optimize natural light delivery to interior spaces to reduce the need for artificial lighting. *Image courtesy of Shepley Bulfinch*

TIP Minimize solar gain in the summer and maximize it in the winter with the help of passive design strategies! Passive designs capitalize on the four natural thermal processes: radiation, conduction, absorption, and convection.

to overcompensate. Maybe orientation was not addressed during the original building design, but analysis may reveal there may be some efficiencies to capture by the means of renovation.

■ How much water needs to be heated or cooled? If building system equipment and fixtures require less water, less energy is required. If all of the building equipment is sized appropriately and works efficiently, then less energy is demanded (see Figures 6.3 and 6.4).

■ Shifting loads to off-peak periods can help to reduce demand. Using thermal energy storage to take advantage of the temperature fluctuations associated

Figure 6.3 High-efficiency boilers can help to achieve energy performance and savings goals. *Photo courtesy of SmithGroup, Inc.*

Figure 6.4 Installing high-efficiency chillers can help to achieve energy performance and savings goals. *Photo courtesy of SmithGroup, Inc.*

with the day time versus the night, allows project teams to refuse heat at night to provide cooling during the day in the summer and capture heat during the day to use at night in the winter (see Figure 6.5).

Figure 6.5 Ice ball thermal energy storage helps to provide cooling during the day from ice generated at night to reduce energy demands. *Photo courtesy of Cryogel*

TIP Remember, SRI is the acronym for **solar reflectance index** and is synonymous with *albedo.* Do you remember the scale used for SRI? Is it better to have a higher or lower score?

■ Roof design can impact how much energy is required for heating and cooling by implementing a green roof or a roof with a high solar reflectance index (SRI) value (see Figure 6.6).

■ Building envelope thermal performance, including window selections, can reduce mechanical system sizing and energy demands by ensuring a thermal break between the interior and exterior environments. Insulating a building envelope can help to reduce the size of heating, ventilation, and air-conditioning (HVAC) systems, and thus help to use less energy (see Figure 6.7).

■ Choosing appropriate light fixtures and the lamps/bulbs they require can reduce energy use by providing more light per square foot while using fewer kilowatts per hour and thus optimize **lighting power density (LPD),** or the amount of lighting power installed per unit area.

 TIP Energy audits have proven that lighting is typically the largest energy consumer and, therefore, offers the largest opportunity to reduce demand.

■ **Building automation system (BAS)** technologies monitor and track consumption for building subsystems, such as lighting, equipment timing and scheduling, and alarm reporting. Implementing tracking and monitoring strategies is essential within the EA category, especially as a means of prevention.

■ Educating the operations and maintenance staff and building occupants can also help to reduce consumption by teaching them how to properly use a BAS, helping to reap the benefits of installing one! Providing the staff with a schedule for repair and replacement of equipment and fixtures also helps to bring efficiencies to a facility. Reminding staff members to turn off the lights, computers, and equipment can help to reduce energy consumption rates.

■ **Commissioning (Cx), recommissioning,** and **retro-commissioning (RCx)** can help to discover the operational efficiencies of building systems as they were designed and intended to operate. **Commissioning** is the process by which a commissioning agent (CxA) verifies the installation, calibration, and performance of a building's energy-related systems are in accordance with the owner's project requirements. **Recommissioning** applies projects that have been commissioned in the past and **retro-commissioning** is applicable

Figure 6.6 White roofs can reduce the energy demands of mechanical systems by increasing the thermal barrier. *Photo courtesy of Duro-Last Roofing, Inc.*

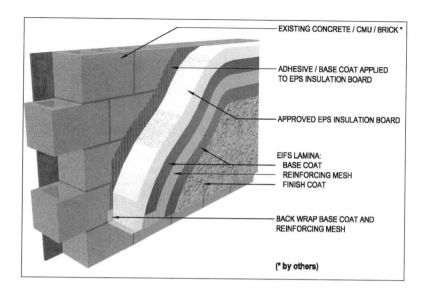

EXISTING CONCRETE / CMU / BRICK *

ADHESIVE / BASE COAT APPLIED
TO EPS INSULATION BOARD

APPROVED EPS INSULATION BOARD

EIFS LAMINA:
BASE COAT
REINFORCING MESH
FINISH COAT

BACK WRAP BASE COAT AND
REINFORCING MESH

(* by others)

Figure 6.7 Retrofitting an existing building with added insulation helps to optimize energy use. *Image courtesy of BASF Corporation — Wall Systems*

when a project has never been commissioned but is operational. **Ongoing commissioning** is the plan to continue to commission a facility. For example, a large office complex in South Florida was experiencing an unbalanced thermal environment. Exasperated by occupant complaints, the facilities team decided to launch an RCx exercise. To their surprise, they discovered someone had placed 2x4s in the variable air volume (VAV) units to override the controls! The team has since addressed the building's heat gain problem and balanced the mechanical system. Not only did this improve the occupant's comfort and productivity, but the building owner is also saving money, as there is a lower energy demand because of the RCx exercise.

Assessing Performance

The preceding bullet points offer strategies to reduce the amount of energy required for operations, allowing for the opportunity to optimize performance by the means of maintenance and monitoring. In order to determine which strategies are appropriate to implement or address, project teams are encouraged to begin with an **energy audit** to capture an energy profile of a facility to learn about consumption patterns and, thus, determine inefficient areas and components. American Society of Heating, Refrigerating, and Air-Conditioning Engineers (ASHRAE) offers three levels of audits, which are referenced in the *Green Building Operations & Maintenance Reference Guide*. The first option for the auditing process, **ASHRAE Level I, Walk-Through Analysis**, is an assessment of utility bills and a brief visual evaluation of the building to determine easy, low-cost efficiency and performance improvement measures, as well as other long-term capital improvement opportunities. The referenced standard offers two resources to aid project teams conducting Level I audits: *ASHRAE Procedures for Commercial Building Audits* and the *2007 ASHRAE Handbook*. This type of audit can be completed by the building operations staff and does not require an independent, third party. The second auditing option, **ASHRAE Level II, Energy Audit, Energy Survey and Analysis**, "considers the building's operations and

Both of these strategies also contribute to whole-building life-cycle cost assessments to determine trade-offs between up-front capital improvement costs and long-term savings.

Create a flashcard to remember the different levels of ASHRAE audits.

maintenance practices, constraints, and economic criteria."[3] This level of an audit must include the following eight tasks:[4]

1. *Summary Energy Use (by major end use).* Show calculation or description of software used.
2. *Building Systems Description.* Include an inventory of major energy-using equipment.
3. *Rejected Energy Efficiency Measures.* List measures considered, but not deemed practical.
4. *Recommended Energy Efficiency Measures.* For each measure, identify cause of excess energy use. Describe each measure and its impact: repairs needed, impact on occupant operations, impact on O&M procedures and costs, equipment life expectancy issues, impact on operating staff skills, and calculations used (or name of software).
5. *Table of Estimated Costs.* Show the value and estimated accuracy of the estimate.
6. *Overall Project Economic Evaluation.* Indicate the total value if all measures are adopted.
7. *Recommended Measurement & Verification Methods.* Identify the appropriate measurement and verification option for verification of projected savings.
8. *Potential Capital Improvements for Level III Analysis.* Identify capital-intensive measures that may be feasible.

 Create a flashcard to remember the eight tasks of a Level II energy audit.

Comparing Performance

LEED not only promotes strategies to assess and evaluate performance, but also a means to track and compare a facility's performance with another. To conduct this comparison, most project teams are required to take advantage of ENERGY STAR® Portfolio Manager online software to study and evaluate how their specific project compares against like project types in similar regions (see Figure 6.8). This benchmarking process requires whole-building energy metering at the very least. Data entered into the software provides a benchmark score for the project against the baseline information provided by Commercial Buildings Energy Consumption Survey (CBECS) gathered every four years by the Energy Information Administration of the U.S. Department of Energy. The software generates a performance rating for buildings ranging from 1 to 100, where a higher rating indicates a higher efficiency.

Create a flashcard to remember ENERGY STAR Portfolio Manager as the tool in which to compare building performance. Average building performance is noted with a score of 50, as the ratings range from 1 to 100. A higher value is better, just as with SRI and later you will learn the same about minimum efficiency reporting value (MERV) filters. The software can be found at www.energystar.gov.

Figure 6.8 Facility managers and owners are encouraged to use the Environmental Protection Agency's (EPA's) ENERGY STAR Portfolio Manager tool to benchmark a building's performance. *Image courtesy of U.S. EPA*

MONITORING AND IMPROVING BUILDING ENERGY PERFORMANCE IN RELATION TO LEED COMPLIANCE

The EBOM rating system addresses tracking and optimizing energy performance by assigning prerequisites and credits in order to require a minimum level of documentation and efficiency, with the ultimate goal of reducing the energy demand of green buildings, helping to save energy and, thus, reducing greenhouse gas emissions and saving money.

EA Prerequisite 1: Energy Efficiency Best Management Practices – Planning, Documentation, and Opportunity Assessment. Project teams will need to complete three tasks during the performance period in order to comply with this prerequisite. The first two tasks require documentation to be generated, although some buildings might already have established the assessments. In this case, the existing documentation might have to be modified and adjusted to reference the specific performance period. The amount of detail required for the documentation is dependent on the complexity and size of the project. Smaller buildings typically have less complex systems, as they utilize packaged equipment; whereas larger facilities usually implement more complex and customized systems.

If one has not been completed already, the first task requires the team to conduct an **energy use analysis** of the facility to determine the energy end uses and the energy use index. This analysis will help to generate the following four required pieces of documentation:

1. The **building operating plan**, also known as the owner's operating requirements, should include a description of the energy-related systems and how they should operate and what required goals the systems need to meet. These goals must be determined for each of the different spaces within the facility and are based on occupancy, the use of the space, whether the building is occupied or unoccupied, if it is day or night, and the different seasons. The goals can relate to such factors as CO_2 levels, air temperature, and relative humidity but can also go further to dictate the duct static pressure or room pressurization.

2. The **systems narrative** should include a description the site equipment, "space heating, space cooling, ventilation, domestic water heating, humidification, dehumidification, and lighting"[5] systems installed within the facility, as well as the controls for the systems.

3. The **sequence of operations** should address each building system in terms of system start-up and shutdown, and the different operating phases in between.

4. The **preventative maintenance plan** should address each of the systems included in the systems narrative and the measures implemented during the performance period. The teams should be sure to include the frequency in which the equipment inspection, cleaning, and repair measures were conducted to detect and prevent equipment failure.

The second task to be completed in order to comply with this prerequisite includes the completion of an ASHRAE Level I, Walk-Through Analysis, as described previously. This task is also completed during the performance period after the energy use analysis. As part of this analysis, project teams will need to gather utility bills for the facility for the last 1 to 3 years.

 Studies have found that implementing energy-efficient operating plans can save between 5 and 20 percent on energy bills without major significant capital investments.

 Create a flashcard to remember the four components required to complete the energy use analysis documentation as part of EA Prerequisite 1.

 Create a flashcard to remember the typical major energy-consuming systems to be analyzed during a walk-through: site equipment, air distribution systems, chilled and/or heating water systems, domestic hot water systems, HVAC controls, and lighting.

Create a flashcard to remember the three types of calculations needed to comply with EA Prerequisite 1.

TIP Remember, prerequisites are absolutely required, do not contribute to earning points, and ensure that certified buildings meet minimum performance criteria.

Create a flashcard to remember the minimum amount of utility data required to comply with EA Prerequisite 2.

TIP Remember, ENERGY STAR utilizes CBECS data to determine its baseline.

Create a flashcard to remember the minimum percentile rankings for the energy efficiency performance prerequisite and credit.

Finally, calculating the energy use intensity (EUI), energy cost index, and utility cost index will complete the requirements of this prerequisite. EUI measures energy consumption relative to the total output. These calculations will help to provide a benchmark in which to measure and track energy use during the performance period. The calculation details are provided in the prerequisite's reference standard, ASHRAE's Procedures for Commercial Building Energy Audits (RP-669, SP-56). For the purposes of the exam, do not worry about completing the calculations, but instead remember the three types required to comply.

EA Prerequisite 2: Minimum Energy Efficiency Performance. Each of the LEED rating systems requires buildings to perform to a minimum energy standard. During the auditing phase, EBOM project teams will need to refer to ENERGY STAR Portfolio Manager to determine eligibility to receive an environmental performance rating. If the project is of an eligible type (e.g., a supermarket, data center, office, hotel, or warehouse), the team can pursue Case 1. Case 2 is available to teams who are working with a special project ineligible to use the software, such as movie theaters, museums, or a manufacturing space. In either case, whole-building energy meters are required to be installed in and calibrated to manufacturer's recommendations in order to qualify the project. Any renewable clean energy that is generated on site is excluded from the compliance calculations.

Case 1. Project teams enter in 12 full months of utility data into the Portfolio Manager software in hopes of earning a rating of at least 69 to comply with this prerequisite. Portfolio Manager will assess the project's EUI to determine the percentile ranking.

Case 2. Projects ineligible to receive a Portfolio Manager performance rating have two options from which to choose:

- Option 1: Provide documentation to prove the facility performs at least 19 percent more efficiently than the average similar type of building. Publicly available information, such as CBECS, is used to compare performance.

- Option 2: If information is not publicly available in which to use for comparison, the team will need utilize an adjusted benchmark score or an alternative score in which to measure performance.

EA Credit 1: Optimize Energy Efficiency Performance. Whichever compliance path a project team pursues for EA Prerequisite 2, the same strategy is utilized to show compliance for this credit. The concept is to establish a performance level in the prerequisite and use the performance period in which to increase efficiency. This is not meant to insinuate a facility must have a score of 69 prior to the performance period but instead that in order to pursue certification, a facility must meet the prerequisite by the end of the performance period prior to submitting for certification review.

For Case 1, project teams will need to obtain an ENERGY STAR rating of at least 71 in order to earn one point. Project teams can earn up to 18 points by achieving a rating of at least 95. If they achieve a minimum of 97, the team can pursue an Exemplary Performance credit under the Innovation in Operations (IO) category. For teams not eligible to participate with Portfolio Manager software, they will pursue one of the following two options under Case 2:

- *Option 1:* Provide documentation to prove the facility performs at least 21 percent more efficiently than the average similar type of building in order to earn 1 point. Project teams can earn up to 18 points if they are able to prove a minimum of 45 percent efficiency. Project teams that can prove the project is at least in the 47th percentile above the national median, the project team can pursue an Exemplary Performance credit under IO Credit 1: Innovation in Operations.

- *Option 2:* If information is not publicly available to use for comparison, the team will need to utilize an adjusted benchmark score or an alternative score with which to measure performance (just as with the prerequisite). Teams utilizing the latter compliance path have three options from which to choose: streamlined baseline for a maximum of 2 points; energy baseline, including historical data, for a maximum of 7 points; or energy baseline, including historical data plus comparable buildings, for a maximum of 18 points. As you can see, the rating system does not penalize projects that are not able to obtain a performance rating from ENERGY STAR.

Project teams are able to achieve these demand reductions by implementing the strategies presented earlier, such as installing high-performance mechanical systems, including heat exchange systems (see Figure 6.9).

 Site energy is the amount of energy reflected in a project's utility bills, whereas **source energy** is the "total amount of raw fuel required to operate a building; it incorporates all transmission, delivery, and production losses for a complete assessment of a building's energy use."[6]

 Earning a rating of 75 or more awards a project the ENERGY STAR label, although it is not required to comply with the prerequisite or the credit.

Figure 6.9 Utilizing a heat exchange system can help to reduce energy demands and save an owner operating costs. *Photo courtesy of SmithGroup, Inc.*

Create a flashcard to remember the different compliance path teams can choose from in order to comply with EA Credit 1.

Remember, space heating and lighting consume the majority of a building's energy; therefore, both should be addressed to increase the efficiency and reduce the demand required.

The main differences between an ASHRAE Level I and an ASHRAE Level II audit is an investigation of costs associated with implementing energy-efficiency measures (EEMs), and a Level I energy audit does not require an independent, third-party auditor.

RCx has an average simple payback of 0.7 years and typically costs about $0.27 per square foot, according to a study conducted by Lawrence Berkeley National Laboratory. Project teams have experienced a 15 percent whole building energy savings as a result of the effort.[8]

Create a flashcard to remember the four tasks required for EA Credit 2.2.

As depicted earlier, Cx efforts can help to bring efficiencies to a project and reduce energy demands. Project teams have three opportunities to address Cx endeavors. Regardless of the credit pursued, they are each worth two points each.

EA Credit 2.1: Existing Building Commissioning – Investigation and Analysis. Project teams will look to taking the efforts pursued for EA Prerequisite 1: Energy Efficiency Best Management Practices and build upon them in order to address this credit. They have two compliance path options from which to choose to comply: Option 1 includes Cx (see Figure 6.10), while option 2 requires an ASHRAE Level II Energy Audit; both are worth two points. For teams pursuing option 1, the Cx process must include the five components, as shown in Table 6.2. For option 2, although the components of the energy audit were presented earlier, project teams will need to break down the energy uses in the building, conduct a savings and cost analysis for each measure and its impact on operation and maintenance strategies, and provide a list of the capital improvements and their associated costs and benefits.

EA Credit 2.2: Existing Building Commissioning – Implementation. In order to comply, project teams will need to complete the following four tasks, as listed in the reference guide:

Task 1. Implement no-cost operational changes or low-cost repairs or upgrades and develop a capital plan for any major improvements and/or **retrofits** (with 50 percent of improvements to be completed by the end of the performance period).

Task 2. Conduct training for management staff (recommended time is 24 hours per staff member per year).

Task 3. Document the financial impacts of improvements by the means of the **simple payback** period, return on investment (ROI), and cost-benefit ratio calculations.

Task 4. Update the building operating plan as appropriate.

EA Credit 2.3: Existing Building Commissioning – Ongoing Commissioning. In order to pursue this 2-point credit, project teams will need to complete four tasks, just as with the previous credit.

Table 6.2 The Commissioning Process[7]

1.	Develop a retro-commissioning, recommissioning, or ongoing commissioning plan for the building's major energy-using systems.
2.	Conduct the investigation and analysis phase. Site assessment Energy use breakdown Diagnostic monitoring and functional testing Master list of findings
3.	Document the breakdown of energy use in the building.
4.	List the operating problems that affect occupants' comfort and energy use, and develop potential operational changes that will solve them.
5.	List the identified capital improvements that will provide cost-effective energy savings and document the cost-benefit analysis associated with each.

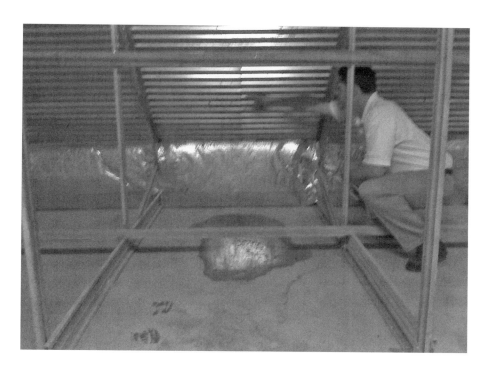

Figure 6.10 Inspecting building systems and educating the operations and maintenance staff on how the systems are intended to operate helps to ensure that a building performs the way it was designed to. *Photo courtesy of ENERActive Solutions*

Task 1. Execute an ongoing Cx plan and a summary of the overall Cx cycle. Assuming a RCx activity occurred, a typical ongoing Cx plan includes the following eight components:

1. Overview of organization's facilities included in the ongoing commissioning program
2. Ongoing Cx team
3. Building systems included in the program
4. Ongoing Cx cycle and schedule
5. Monitoring, testing, and performance verification plan
6. Sensors and test equipment calibration plan
7. Issue identification and response protocols
8. Ongoing Cx annual report

Task 2. Develop a summary of the overall Cx cycle (maximum 24 months) characterized by equipment or by building system group. The "plan must include a building equipment list, performance measurement frequency for each equipment item and steps to respond to deviation from expected performance parameters."[9]

Task 3. Implement or finish at least half of the work included within the first Cx cycle.

Task 4. Update the building operating plan as appropriate.

EA Credit 3.1: Performance Measurement – Building Automation System. Facilities with a computer-based BAS that monitors and controls HVAC and lighting, at a minimum, will be able to pursue this one-point credit. A typical BAS includes sensors, controllers, and controlled devices (see Figure 6.11). Just as with the equipment and systems the BAS controls, the system itself needs to be properly maintained and calibrated.

Create a flashcard to remember the four tasks required for EA Credit 2.3.

Create a flashcard to remember the three credits that address existing building commissioning.

Create a flashcard to remember that a BAS must address both lighting and HVAC at minimum.

Figure 6.11 Implementing a BAS helps to ensure that a building's energy-related systems are performing as intended, a strategy that promotes energy savings. *Photo courtesy of Samsel Architects*

A BAS is required to control the lighting system for a facility, thus providing EA Credit 3.1 a direct correlation with SS Credit 8: Light Pollution Reduction. Later you will learn of the synergy the credit has with EQ Credit 2.2: Controllability of Systems, Lighting. Knowing these types of synergies is critical for success on the O+M exam.

TIP Did you recognize that the previous three credits all require four tasks?

TIP Energy uses that do not contribute to at least 10 percent of the building's total energy consumption should not be submetered.

Create a flashcard to remember the two credits that address performance measurement.

EA Credit 3.2: Performance Measurement – System-Level Metering. Project teams will need to complete four tasks to comply with this credit offering up to 2 points. Regardless of the compliance path of Task 3, all metering must be permanent, continuous, electronic, automatic, and calibrated to meet the manufacturer's recommendation.

Task 1. Determine the major energy uses for the facility either by EA Credit 2.1, EA Credit 2.2, or metering efforts (see Figure 6.12).

Task 2. "Based on the energy-use breakdown, employ system-level metering covering at least 40 percent or 80 percent of the total expected annual energy consumption of the building. Permanent metering and recording are required. All types of submetering are permitted."[10]

Task 3. If pursuing the 40 percent compliance path, at least one of the two largest energy use categories must be 80 percent submetered, whereas teams pursuing two points must provide system-level metering for 80 percent of at least two of the three largest energy use categories.

Task 4. Document compliance proving 80 percent of the largest energy use categories are metered.

EA Credit 6: Emissions Reduction Reporting. Project teams that track, record, and report reduction in emissions can pursue this one-point credit. Teams

Figure 6.12 Metering utilities to monitor consumption helps building owners and facility managers ensure that the building is functioning properly. *Photo courtesy of Stephen Martorana, LEED AP BD+C*

can include reductions earned from the purchase of **renewable energy credits** (RECs). Reporting to a third-party voluntary program is required. Documentation is streamlined for projects that utilize ENERGY STAR Portfolio Manager software. Teams are not required to prove emission reductions in order to earn this credit.

 Create a flashcard to remember the prerequisites and credits LEED utilizes to address the monitoring and tracking of energy consumption.

QUIZ TIME!

Q6.1. Which of the following strategies would help to reduce the energy demand of an existing facility? (Choose two)

A. Insulating the envelope

B. Utilizing BIM software

C. Using ENERGY STAR Portfolio Manager

D. Recovering waste heat

E. Recycling stormwater

Q6.2. What is the minimum amount of months a project team must track a facility's performance in order to pursue EA Credit 1: Optimize Energy Efficiency Performance? (Choose one)

A. 10 months

B. 3 months

C. 12 months

D. 24 months

E. 6 months

Q6.3. What are the minimum percentages required in order to meet the EA energy efficiency performance prerequisite and credit for projects not eligible for a Portfolio Manager rating? (Choose one)

A. 69 and 71 percent

B. 19 and 21 percent

C. 19 and 23 percent

D. 69 and 75 percent

E. 61 and 71 percent

Q6.4. When must a ASHRAE Level 1 Walk-Through Analysis be completed in order to comply with EA Prerequisite 1: Energy Efficiency Best Management Practices – Planning, Documentation, and Opportunity Assessment? (Choose one)

A. Before registering the project with GBCI

B. Before the performance period

C. During the performance period

D. After the performance period

E. 3 months after the performance period began

Q6.5. What is CO_2e? (Choose one)

A. CO_2 emissions

B. Carbon equivalents

C. CO_2 energy

D. CO_2 emissivity

Q6.6. Which of the following are not part of the commissioning (Cx) process as detailed in the requirements of EA Credit 2.1: Existing Building Commissioning, Investigation & Analysis? (Choose two)

A. Develop an ongoing Cx plan

B. Conduct a life-cycle analysis on HVAC system replacement

C. Meter 80 percent of the top two largest energy use consumers

D. Document the breakdown of energy use

E. List the operating problems that affect occupants' comfort and energy use

Q6.7. What is the maximum length of a commissioning (Cx) cycle? (Choose one)

A. 2 years

B. 5 years

C. 1 year

D. 3 years

E. 4 years

Q6.8. Which of the following are not required components of a ASHRAE Level II, Energy Survey and Analysis Report? (Choose two)

A. Metering equipment and installation fees

B. Building systems description

C. Potential capital improvements for ASHRAE Level III Analysis.

D. Certification fees

E. Breakdown of energy use by major end use

Q6.9. Which of the following is not required to be completed prior to the ASHRAE Level I Walk Through Analysis? (Choose one)

A. Building operating plan

B. ASHRAE Level II

C. Systems narrative

D. Sequence of operations

E. Preventative maintenance plan

Q6.10. If a project is not eligible for a performance rating by ENERGY STAR Portfolio Manager, what are the three compliance path options from which project teams can choose to comply? (Choose three)

A. CBECS

B. ASHRAE Advanced Energy Design Guide

C. Adjusted benchmark score

D. Alternative score

E. Retro-commissioning (RCx)

ELIMINATING CHLOROFLUOROCARBONS

Beside the Cx and minimum energy performance prerequisites, the LEED rating system also requires buildings to manage refrigerants appropriately. Refrigerants enable the transfer of thermal energy and are, therefore, a critical component of air conditioning and refrigeration equipment for their ability to reject heat at high temperatures. Although they are cost-effective, refrigerants have environmental trade-offs, as they contribute to ozone depletion and global warming. Therefore, project teams need to be mindful of the **ozone-depleting potential** (ODP) and **global warming potential** (GWP) of each refrigerant to determine the impact of the trade-offs, as an environmentally perfect refrigerant does not yet exist.

Eliminating Chlorofluorocarbons in Relation to LEED Compliance

EA Prerequisite 3: Fundamental Refrigerant Management. To comply with this prerequisite, teams should refer to the Montreal Protocol when determining

 TIP It is assumed to be unfeasible to replace a system if the simple payback period is more than 10 years. Make a note on your cheat sheet.

Make a flashcard to remember the EPA Clean Air Act, Title VI, Rule 608, Refrigerant Recycling Rules for refrigerant management, reporting, and maintaining acceptable leakage rates for CFCs.

TIP Notice all the 5s for this prerequisite! Make a note to remember 5 percent leakage rate maximum, 0.5 lbs threshold for inclusion in calculations, and a 5-year maximum phase-out plan.

TIP If the building relies on a central plant for energy (chilled or heated water) the central plant must comply with the prerequisite and credit.

Create a flashcard to remember the two strategies that address eliminating chlorofluorocarbons.

which refrigerants to use for their projects. The Montreal Protocol bans **chlorofluorocarbons** (CFCs), as they have the biggest impact on ozone depletion. HVAC&R systems that use more than 0.5 pounds of refrigerant are required to comply. For projects using CFC refrigerants where an economic analysis determines it unfeasible to retrofit, conversion, or replacing the existing system, project teams are required to reduce the annual leakage to less than 5 percent, using EPA Clean Air Act, Title VI, Rule 608 procedures AND commit to phasing out the refrigerant within five years.

EA Credit 5: Enhanced Refrigerant Management. This credit takes the requirements beyond the prerequisite to restrict the use of any refrigerants in HVAC&R systems. If refrigerants are used, project teams will need to document that they have minimal ODP and GWP by using the calculations provided within the reference guide. Just as with the prerequisite, equipment that uses less than a half-pound of refrigerants is exempt from compliance, as well as refrigerators and small water coolers. The credit also requires replacement fire suppression systems to avoid CFCs, hydrofluorocarbons (HCFCs), and halons.

QUIZ TIME!

Q6.11. In order to be included in the calculation for EA Credit 5: Enhanced Refrigerant Management, what is the minimum pound of refrigerant required? (Choose one)

A. 0.25 pounds

B. .025 pounds

C. .5 pounds

D. 1 pound

Q6.12. Which of the following refrigerants is not allowed in order to comply with EA Prerequisite 3: Fundamental Refrigerant Management? (Choose one)

A. CFCs

B. HCFCs

C. HFCs

D. NH_3

E. Halons

Q6.13. Which of the following are not subject to compliance with EA Prerequisite 3: Fundamental Refrigerant Management? (Choose three)

A. Equipment that uses less than 0.5 pounds of refrigerant

B. Equipment that uses more than 0.5 pounds of refrigerant

C. Chillers

D. Refrigerators

E. Water coolers

Q6.14. When addressing refrigerants for a project and to comply with EA Prerequisite 3: Fundamental Refrigerant Management, which of the following should be considered? (Choose three)

    A. Fan motors and variable-frequency drives for ventilation air handlers

    B. Base building air-conditioning systems

    C. Boilers for heating systems

    D. Reuse of existing HVAC&R systems

    E. Elimination of substances with high ODP from use in air-conditioning and refrigeration systems

Q6.15. Which of the following leakage rates are in accordance with EPA Clean Air Act, Title VI, Rule 608? (Choose two)

    A. 1 percent

    B. 10 percent

    C. 4 percent

    D. 20 percent

    E. 25 percent

RENEWABLE ENERGY

Keeping with the same goals previously discussed, implementing clean, renewable energy technologies into a green building project can reduce the need to produce and consume coal, nuclear power, and oil and natural gases for energy, therefore reducing pollutants and emissions, as well as increasing air quality. For the purposes of LEED compliance, eligible renewable energy sources include solar thermal, photovoltaic systems, wind, wave, some biomass systems, geothermal (heating and electric) power, and low-impact hydropower systems (see Figure 6.13). The O&M Reference Guide provides the following strategy to incorporate renewable energy and reduce the use of fossil fuels for projects seeking LEED certification:

EA Credit 4: On-site and Off-site Renewable Energy. Project teams are encouraged to evaluate the triple bottom line benefits of each of the eligible renewable energy sources to find the proper solution for the project (see Figure 6.14). In order to comply, project teams can implement an on-site renewable energy system, purchase green power from off-site, or pursue a combination of both strategies during the performance period. Project teams will need to determine how much energy the on-site system can provide in million Btus (MBtus) in proportion to the total amount of energy required for the project in MBtus to determine compliance and how many points can be earned. They can earn one point for implementing an on-site system that provides 3 percent of annual energy for the facility and up to six points for quadrupling the system's capacity. The O&M rating system offers an exemplary performance opportunity for projects that surpass 13.5 percent applicable percentage threshold for on-site renewable energy.

 Create a flashcard to remember the types of qualifying renewable energy sources. Ineligible systems include any architectural features, passive solar strategies, daylighting strategies, and geo-exchange systems using a ground-source heat pump. These heat pumps require electricity to operate and, therefore, are an ineligible renewable energy source. If it cannot be metered or uses electricity to operate, it cannot contribute to earning the credit.

 TIP Project teams that implement an on-site renewable energy system and sell the power to the grid are not eligible to pursue the on-site renewable energy compliance path of EA Credit 4.

Figure 6.13 Sherman Hospital in Elgin, Illinois, utilizes geothermal energy to minimize energy demands from the grid. *Image courtesy of Shepley Bulfinch*

 TIP The Green-e program was developed "by the Center of Resource Solutions to promote green electricity products and provide consumers with a rigorous and nationally recognized method to identify those products."[11]

 Create a flashcard to remember the two strategies and the percentage requirements of each to earn Credit 4: On-site and Off-site Renewable Energy for LEED project teams to pursue.

In order to comply with the off-site renewable energy compliance path of this credit, project owners would need to purchase energy from a Green-e certified provider or **renewable energy certificates (RECs)** from a Green-e eligible source. The renewable energy associated with this credit is generated at a different location than the project site seeking LEED certification (see Figure 6.15). Project owners would need to purchase at least 25 percent of the project's estimated energy demand for at least two years based on quantity, not the cost of energy, to comply. They can earn up to six points for purchasing 100 percent of the building's energy demand. If the team is pursuing on-site renewable strategies as well, the team can only earn six points under this credit for the combination approach.

Figure 6.14 Stoller Vineyards in Dayton, Oregon, generates electricity on site by the means of photovoltaic panels mounted on the roof. *Photo courtesy of Mike Haverkate, Stoller Vineyards*

Figure 6.15 Cedar Creek Wind Farm in Colorado helps to produce clean, renewable energy. *Photo courtesy of Brian Stanback, Renewable Choice Energy*

QUIZ TIME!

Q6.16. Which of the following calculations are required by EA Prerequisite 1: Energy Efficiency Best Management Practices – Planning, Documentation, and Opportunity Assessment? (Choose three)

A. Simple payback period

B. Energy use intensity

C. Emissions reduction

D. Energy cost index

E. Utility cost index

F. Annual leakage rate

Q6.17. If the project team is pursuing the off-site renewable energy compliance path for EA Credit 4, how long must the contract be in place to purchased RECs? (Choose one)

A. 6 months

B. The length of the performance period

C. 1 year

D. 2 years

E. 3 years

F. 5 years

Q6.18. Which of the following could contribute to earning the on-site renewable energy compliance path for EA Credit 4: On-site and Off-site Renewable Energy? (Choose three)

A. Passive solar design concept that captures winter heat from the sun

    B. Photovoltaic panels that provide electricity to the building

    C. A wind farm located within 500 miles of the project and operated by the local utility company

    D. A ground-source heat pump that takes heat from the ground

    E. Solar hot water system

    F. An on-site electric generator powered by geothermal energy

    G. A solar farm adjacent to the project site providing clean power to the grid

Q6.19. What is the primary intent of EA Credit 4: On-site and Off-site Renewable Energy? (Choose one)

    A. To comply with the Montreal Protocol

    B. To encourage more solar farms in the United States and avoid carbon trading

    C. To reduce environmental and economic impacts associated with fossil fuel energy use

    D. To minimize production of greenhouse gases by generating on-site renewable energy

Q6.20. The engineer working on an existing corporate building project seeking LEED EBOM certification has proposed a cogeneration system that provides electricity, cooling, heating, hot water, and dehumidification of outside air. The waste heat from the gas turbine–powered electric generator exhaust is designed and intended to drive an absorption chiller for cooling the building, thus not using any CFCs or HCFCs. To which of the following LEED credits might these strategies contribute? (Choose two)

    A. Enhanced Commissioning

    B. On-Site Renewable Energy

    C. Enhanced Refrigerant Management

    D. Green Power

    E. Optimize Energy Performance

    F. Measurement and Verification

Q6.21. Which of the following credits utilize ENERGY STAR Portfolio Manager software? (Choose three)

    A. EA Credit 6: Emissions Reduction Reporting

    B. WE Prerequisite 1: Minimum Indoor Plumbing Fixture and Fitting Efficiency

    C. EA Prerequisite 2: Minimum Energy Efficiency Performance

    D. EA Credit 1: Optimize Energy Efficiency Performance

    E. SS Credit 6: Stormwater Quantity Control

    F. EA Credit 3.1: Performance Measurement, Building Automation System

Q6.22. Which of the following systems are typically controlled and monitored by a BAS? (Choose three)

A. Lighting

B. Printing stations

C. Breakroom appliances

D. Variable frequency drives (VFDs)

E. Employee turnover

F. Zone temperature

Q6.23. Which of the following credits are related to EA Credit 4: On-site and Off-site Renewable Energy? (Choose three)

A. EA Prerequisite 1: Energy Efficiency Best Management Practices – Planning, Documentation, and Opportunity Assessment

B. SS Credit 7.2: Heat Island Effect, Roof

C. SS Credit 8: Light Pollution Reduction

D. EA Credit 2: Existing Building Commissioning

E. EA Credit 1: Optimize Energy Efficiency Performance

Q6.24. Which of the following are examples of a third-party voluntary reporting or certification program to report emission reduction to comply with EA Credit 6: Emissions Reduction Reporting? (Choose three)

A. U.S. Environmental Protection Agency (EPA) Climate Leaders

B. ENERGY STAR

C. ASHRAE

D. World Resources Institute/World Business Council for Sustainable Development (WRI/WBCSD)

E. ACEEE

F. USGBC

Q6.25. Every _____ years energy consumption data is gathered by the EIA of the U.S. Department of Energy. (Choose one)

A. 2

B. 4

C. 5

D. 6

E. 10

Q6.26. Which of the following team members is involved in every EA prerequisite and credit except for EA Credit 6: Emissions Reduction Reporting? (Choose one)

A. Building engineer

B. Property manager

C. Facility manager

D. Architect

E. Groundskeeper

F. Tenant(s)

Q6.27. Which of the following is exempt from the calculations for EA Credit 1: Optimize Energy Efficiency Performance? (Choose one)

A. Diesel fuel

B. Natural gas

C. Electricity

D. On-site renewable energy

E. District chilled water

F. Propane

Q6.28. Which of the following refrigerants is permitted to comply with EA Credit 5: Enhanced Refrigerant Management? (Choose three)

A. Ammonia (NH_3)

B. Water (H_2O)

C. CFCs

D. Carbon dioxide (CO_2)

Q6.29. Which of the following are eligible sources of an off-site renewable energy to comply with EA Credit 4: On-site and Off-site Renewable Energy? (Choose four)

A. A power provider

B. A geoexchange system servicing the facility

C. A utility program

D. RECs

E. Carbon offsets

F. Daylighting strategies

G. Passive solar strategies

Program Development

PURPOSE

To provide a groundwork for training and system _____ to promote energy-efficient _____ strategies are maintained.

REQUIREMENTS

Complete an ASHRAE Level _____ Walk-_____ Analysis to include an energy use breakdown and energy use index

Develop the following documents:

- Building _____ plan
- _____ narrative
- Sequence of _____
- _____ maintenance plan

CALCULATIONS

Energy _____ intensity

Energy _____ index

_____ cost index

REFERENCED STANDARD

_____ Level I, Walk-Through Analysis

Required

RESPONSIBLE PARTY:

BUILDING ENGINEER/FACILTITY MANAGER

	EA Prerequisite 1:
	Energy Efficiency Best Management Practices, Planning, Documentation, and Opportunity Assessment

ANSWER KEY

PURPOSE

To provide a groundwork for training and system **analysis** to promote energy-efficient **operating** strategies are maintained.

REQUIREMENTS

Complete an ASHRAE Level **I** Walk-**Through** Analysis to include an energy use breakdown and energy use index

Develop the following documents:

- Building **operating** plan
- **Systems** narrative
- Sequence of **operations**
- **Preventative** maintenance plan

CALCULATIONS

Energy **use** intensity

Energy **cost** index

Utility cost index

REFERENCED STANDARD

ASHRAE Level I, Walk-Through Analysis

Audit	EA Prerequisite 2:
	Minimum Energy Efficiency Performance

Performance Period/Certification	EA Credit 1:
	Optimize Energy Efficiency Performance

PURPOSE

To ensure a minimum level of performance to increase efficiency and to reduce the _____ and _____ impacts from _____ energy demand.

REQUIREMENTS

Install _____-building energy _____ and track performance for at least _____

For ENERGY STAR Portfolio Manager Eligible Projects:

Prerequisite: Use EPA's ENERGY _____ Portfolio Manager rating tool to establish at least a score of

_____

Credit: Use EPA's ENERGY STAR _____ Manager rating tool to establish at least a score of _____

For projects not eligible to use Portfolio Manager:

Use adjusted _____ score

Use alternative score, such as _____ (with similar use and climate zone) or historical data

REFERENCED STANDARD

_____ STAR Portfolio Manager

EXEMPLARY PERFORMANCE

Use EPA's ENERGY STAR Portfolio Manager rating tool to establish at least a score of _____ or higher

1-18 pts. for credit	RESPONSIBLE PARTY:
	BUILDING ENGINEER

EA Prerequisite 2:

Minimum Energy Efficiency Performance

EA Credit 1:

Optimize Energy Efficiency Performance

ANSWER KEY

PURPOSE

To ensure a minimum level of performance to increase efficiency and to reduce the **environmental** and **economic** impacts from **excessive** energy demand.

REQUIREMENTS

Install **whole**-building energy **meters** and track performance for at least **1 year**

For ENERGY STAR Portfolio Manager Eligible Projects:

Prerequisite: Use EPA's ENERGY **STAR** Portfolio Manager rating tool to establish at least a score of **69**

Credit: Use EPA's ENERGY STAR **Portfolio** Manager rating tool to establish at least a score of **71**

For projects not eligible to use Portfolio Manager:

Use adjusted **benchmark** score

Use alternative score, such as **CBECS** (with similar use and climate zone) or historical data

REFERENCED STANDARD

ENERGY STAR Portfolio Manager

EXEMPLARY PERFORMANCE

Use EPA's ENERGY STAR Portfolio Manager rating tool to establish at least a score of **97** or higher

Audit	**EA Prerequisite 3:**
	Fundamental Refrigerant Management

Program Development	**EA Credit 5:**
	Enhanced Refrigerant Management

PURPOSE

Prerequisite:

To reduce the depletion of the _____.

Credit:

To encourage compliance with the _____ Protocol and reduce ozone depletion to minimize _____ change contributions.

REQUIREMENTS

Prerequisite

The use of _____-based refrigerants is prohibited unless a third party indicates it is not economically _____ for a return on investment within _____ years.

Credit:

All projects must not use ozone depleting chemicals, such as CFCs, HCFCs, or halons, within the _____ suppression _____.

Option 1: Do not use _____ refrigerants in HVAC&R equipment.

Option 2: Evaluate the _____ depleting potential (ODP) and global _____ potential (GWP) of refrigerants to be used for HVAC&R equipment to ensure concentrations do not exceed maximum threshold allowed.

CALCULATIONS

Prerequisite:

If CFCs are used, calculate _____ rate and submit along with _____ analysis or a _____ year maximum _____-out plan.

Credit 1: Option 2:

Small equipment, such as HVAC units that use less than _____ pounds of refrigerant, refrigerators and small water coolers, are excluded from complying with this credit.

To determine _____ and _____ annual and end-of-life leakage rate concentrations, calculate the following factors:

– For HVAC&R equipment - Refrigerant _____, _____ types, and _____ types

– Equipment _____ (provided default value)

– _____ rate (provided default value)

– End-of-life refrigerant _____ (provided default value)

REFERENCED STANDARD

_____ Clean _____ Act, Title VI, Rule 608, Refrigerant Recycling Rules

1 pt. for credit	**RESPONSIBLE PARTY:**
	BUILDING ENGINEER

| | **EA Prerequisite 3:** |
| | **Fundamental Refrigerant Management** |

| | **EA Credit 5:** |
| | **Enhanced Refrigerant Management** |

ANSWER KEY

PURPOSE

Prerequisite:

To reduce the depletion of the **stratosphere.**

Credit:

To encourage compliance with the **Montreal** Protocol and reduce ozone depletion to minimize **climate** change contributions.

REQUIREMENTS

Prerequisite:

The use of **CFC**-based refrigerants is prohibited unless a third party indicates it is not economically **unfeasible** for a return on investment within **10** years.

Credit:

All projects must not use ozone depleting chemicals, such as CFCs, HCFCs, or halons, within the **fire** suppression **systems.**

Option 1: Do not use **any** refrigerants in HVAC&R equipment.

Option 2: Evaluate the **ozone** depleting potential (ODP) and global **warming** potential (GWP) of refrigerants to be used for HVAC&R equipment to ensure concentrations do not exceed maximum threshold allowed.

CALCULATIONS

Prerequisite:

If CFCs are used, calculate **leakage** rate and submit along with **economic** analysis or a **5** year maximum **phase**-out plan.

Credit 1: Option 2:

Small equipment, such as HVAC units that use less than **0.5** pounds of refrigerant, refrigerators and small water coolers, are excluded from complying with this credit.

To determine **ODP** and **GWP** annual and end-of-life leakage rate concentrations, calculate the following factors:

- For HVAC&R equipment - Refrigerant **charge, refrigerant** types, and **equipment** types
- Equipment **life** (provided default value)
- **Leakage** rate (provided default value)
- End-of-life refrigerant **loss** (provided default value)

REFERENCED STANDARD

EPA Clean **Air** Act, Title VI, Rule 608, Refrigerant Recycling Rules

Program Development	**EA Credit 2.1:**
	Existing Building Commissioning Investigation & Analysis

PURPOSE

To develop an understanding of the building's major energy _____ systems' operations, _____ to optimize energy _____, and a plan to achieve energy savings by the means of a _____ process.

REQUIREMENTS

Choose from the commissioning process or an ASHRAE Level II energy audit.

If pursuing the commissioning process:

1. Develop a _____, recommissioning, or _____commissioning plan for the building's major energy-using systems.

2. Conduct the investigation and analysis phase.

    o _____ assessment

    o Energy _____ breakdown

    o Diagnostic _____ and _____ testing

    o Master list of _____

3. Document the breakdown of energy use in the building.

4. List the _____ problems that affect occupants' _____ and _____use, and develop potential operational changes that will solve them.

5. List the identified capital _____ that will provide cost-effective energy savings and document the cost-benefit analysis associated with each.

If pursuing the Level _____ Energy Audit:

o Breakdown the energy _____ in the building

o Conduct a savings and cost _____ for each measure and their impact on _____ and _____ strategies

o Provide a list of the capital _____ and their associated costs and_____.

REFERENCED STANDARD

_____ Level_____, Energy _____, Energy Survey and _____

2 pts.	**RESPONSIBLE PARTY:**
	BUILDING ENGINEER

EA Credit 2.1:

Existing Building Commissioning Investigation & Analysis

ANSWER KEY

PURPOSE

To develop an understanding of the building's major energy **consuming** systems' operations, **strategies** to optimize energy **performance**, and a plan to achieve energy savings by the means of a **systematic** process.

REQUIREMENTS

Choose from the commissioning process or an ASHRAE Level II energy audit.

If pursuing the commissioning process:

1. Develop a **retro-commissioning,** recommissioning, or **ongoing** commissioning plan for the building's major energy-using systems.

2. Conduct the investigation and analysis phase.

    o **Site** assessment

    o Energy **use** breakdown

    o Diagnostic **monitoring** and **functional** testing

    o Master list of **findings**

3. Document the breakdown of energy use in the building.

4. List the **operating** problems that affect occupants' **comfort** and **energy** use, and develop potential operational changes that will solve them.

5. List the identified capital **improvements** that will provide cost-effective energy savings and document the cost-benefit analysis associated with each.

If pursuing the Level II Energy Audit:

o Breakdown the energy **uses** in the building

o Conduct a savings and cost **analysis** for each measure and their impact on **operation** and **maintenance** strategies

o Provide a list of the capital **improvements** and their associated costs and **benefits.**

REFERENCED STANDARD

ASHRAE Level **II**, Energy **Audit**, Energy Survey and **Analysis**

Program Development

PURPOSE

To ensure the building's major energy-use systems are _____, _____ , and _____ to _____ energy performance by implementing _____ improvements and _____ capital projects.

REQUIREMENTS

o Implement no or low-cost operational improvements

   No-cost examples include _____ or _____ changes and adjustments to equipment run time or _____

   Low-cost examples include _____ equipment _____ or upgrades and staff _____

o Create a capital plan for _____ or upgrades

o Provide _____ for management staff

o Prove observed and anticipated economic _____ and _____ of improvements

o Update the building _____ plan as necessary

CALCULATION

Simple _____ Period

$$SPB\ (Yrs) = \frac{Project\ Cost\ (\$)}{Annual\ Operating\ Savings\ (\$)}$$

2 pts.

RESPONSIBLE PARTY:

BUILDING ENGINEER

EA Credit 2.2:

Existing Building Commissioning Implementation

ANSWER KEY

PURPOSE

To ensure the building's major energy-use systems are **repaired**, **operated**, and **maintained** to **optimize** energy performance by implementing **minor** improvements and **identify** capital projects.

REQUIREMENTS

o Implement no or low-cost operational improvements

> No-cost examples include **operational** or **procedural** changes and adjustments to equipment run-time or **setpoints**

> Low-cost examples include **minor** equipment **repairs** or upgrades and staff **training**

o Create a capital plan for **retrofits** or upgrades

o Provide **training** for management staff

o Prove observed and anticipated economic **costs** and **benefits** of improvements

o Update the building **operating** plan as necessary

CALCULATION

Simple **Payback** Period

$$\text{SPB (Yrs)} = \frac{\text{Project Cost (\$)}}{\text{Annual Operating Savings (\$)}}$$

Program Development

PURPOSE

Address changes in facility _____, use, _____ and repair by the means of _____ and make _____ adjustments and reviews of building operating systems and procedures to _____ energy performance.

REQUIREMENTS

o Summarize the overall commissioning cycle by the means of a _____ plan. The cycle must not exceed _____ months and _____ must be completed within the _____ period.

   All applicable _____ must be listed within the schedule

   The plan must include the _____ of performance _____ for each type of equipment or component.

o Update the building _____ plan as necessary

2 pts.

RESPONSIBLE PARTY:

BUILDING ENGINEER

	EA Credit 2.3:
	Existing Building Commissioning Ongoing Commissioning

ANSWER KEY

PURPOSE

Address changes in facility **occupancy**, use, **maintenance** and repair by the means of **commissioning** and make **periodic** adjustments and reviews of building operating systems and procedures to **optimize** energy performance.

REQUIREMENTS

o Summarize the overall commissioning cycle by the means of a **written** plan. The cycle must not exceed **24** months and **50%** must be completed within the **performance** period.

  All applicable **equipment** must be listed within the schedule

  The plan must include the **frequency** of performance **test** for each type of equipment or component.

o Update the building **operating** plan as necessary

Audit	EA Credit 3.1:
	Performance Measurement Building Automation System

PURPOSE

To identify opportunities for additional energy-_____ investments and to increase energy _____.

REQUIREMENTS

Implement a building _____ system (BAS) and preventative maintenance plan for the _____ and _____ systems.

Lighting can be separated but HVAC should be on the _____ BAS.

BAS for HVAC should monitor _____ and_____, scheduling and setpoints.

BAS for lighting should schedule lights to turn off _____ hours.

1 pt.

RESPONSIBLE PARTY:

BUILDING ENGINEER

ANSWER KEY

PURPOSE

To identify opportunities for additional energy-**saving** investments and to increase energy **performance**.

REQUIREMENTS

Implement a building **automation** system (BAS) and preventative maintenance plan for the **HVAC** and **lighting** systems.

Lighting can be separated, but HVAC should be on the **same** BAS.

BAS for HVAC should monitor **sensors** and **controls**, scheduling, and setpoints.

BAS for lighting should schedule lights to turn off **after** hours.

Audit	**EA Credit 3.2:**
	Performance Measurement System-Level Metering

PURPOSE

To support energy_____ and identify opportunities for _____ energy-saving strategies by providing energy use information.

REQUIREMENTS

Implement_____-level _____ that covers either _____ (1 point) or _____ (2 points) of the _____ expected annual energy consumption of the building, based on the energy-_____ breakdown.

Should coordinate with EA Credit _____: Existing Building Commissioning – Investigation & Analysis efforts

Subsystems that contribute to more than _____ of the total consumption of the facility shall be included.

Metering must be _____, continuous, _____, and electronic.

1-2 pts.

RESPONSIBLE PARTY:

BUILDING ENGINEER

	EA Credit 3.2:
	Performance Measurement System-Level Metering

ANSWER KEY

PURPOSE

To support energy **management** and identify opportunities for **additional** energy-saving strategies by providing energy use information.

REQUIREMENTS

Implement **system**-level **metering** that covers either **40%** (1 point) or **80%** (2 points) of the **total** expected annual energy consumption of the building, based on the energy-**use** breakdown.

Should coordinate with EA Credit **2.1:** Existing Building Commissioning - Investigation & Analysis efforts

Subsystems that contribute to more than **10%** of the total consumption of the facility shall be included.

Metering must be **permanent**, continuous, **automatic**, and electronic.

Performance Period/Certification

PURPOSE

To reduce the _____ and _____ impact of _____ fuel energy use by encouraging and recognizing increasing levels of _____-site and _____-site renewable energy systems.

REQUIREMENTS & POINT DISTRIBUTION

Install an on-site renewable energy system and/or purchase qualifying off-site renewable energy to meet the following percentage thresholds:

On-Site Renewable Energy		Off-Site Renewable Energy	Points
3.0%	or	25.0%	1
4.50%	or	37.50%	2
6.0%	or	50.0%	3
7.50%	or	62.50%	4
9.0%	or	75.0%	5
12.0%	or	100%	6

CALCULATION

Off-site equivalency for on-site renewable energy:

$$\text{Percentage of off-site equivalency} \quad \text{Percentage of on-site renewable energy} \times \frac{25\ (\%)}{3(\%)}$$

EXEMPLARY PERFORMANCE

Install an on-site renewable energy system that delivers at least _____ of the building's energy needs.

REFERENCED STANDARD

_____ for Resource Solutions, _____ Energy Certification Program

1-6 pts.

	EA Credit 4:
	On-Site and Off-Site Renewable Energy

ANSWER KEY

PURPOSE

To reduce the **environmental** and **economic** impact of **fossil** fuel energy use by encouraging and recognizing increasing levels of **on**-site and **off**-site renewable energy systems.

REQUIREMENTS & POINT DISTRIBUTION

Install an on-site renewable energy system and/or purchase qualifying off-site renewable energy to meet the following percentage thresholds:

On-Site Renewable Energy		Off-Site Renewable Energy	Points
3.0%	or	25.0%	1
4.50%	or	37.50%	2
6.0%	or	50.0%	3
7.50%	or	62.50%	4
9.0%	or	75.0%	5
12.0%	or	100%	6

CALCULATION

Off-site equivalency for on-site renewable energy:

$$\text{Percentage of off-site equivalency} = \text{Percentage of on-site renewable energy} \times \frac{25\ (\%)}{3(\%)}$$

EXEMPLARY PERFORMANCE

Install an on-site renewable energy system that delivers at least **13.5%** of the building's energy needs.

REFERENCED STANDARD

Center for Resource Solutions, **Green-e** Energy Certification Program

Performance Period/Certification	EA Credit 6:
	Emissions Reduction Reporting

PURPOSE

To prove the benefits of _____ reductions by_____ building efficiency.

REQUIREMENTS

_____, document, and _____ emission reductions as a result of improvements of energy efficiency and the implementation of renewable energy sources for building operational systems.

Must include emissions from the use of on-site _____and emissions from _____ electricity

1 pt.	RESPONSIBLE PARTY:
	OWNER

ANSWER KEY

PURPOSE

To prove the benefits of **emission** reductions by **improving** building efficiency.

REQUIREMENTS

Monitor, document, and **report** emission reductions as a result of improvements of energy efficiency and the implementation of renewable energy sources for building operational systems.

Must include emissions from the use of on-site **fuel** and emissions from **purchased** electricity

CHAPTER **7**

MATERIALS AND RESOURCES

Figure 7.1 Procuring green materials, such as these 3Form® panels with recycled content, is a strategy to reduce the detrimental impacts of the built environment and the need for virgin materials. *Photo courtesy of Skylar Nielson, 3Form*

AS THE PREVIOUS CHAPTERS POINTED OUT, the built environment can take quite a toll on the natural environment. This book has so far presented means of minimizing impacts from the project site and reducing water and energy demands, while this chapter details strategies to minimize the environmental impacts of building materials as depicted in the Materials & Resources (MR) category in the Leadership in Energy and Environmental Design (LEED®) for Existing Buildings: Operations and Maintenance™ (EBOM) rating system. This chapter details how to properly select materials and what to do with them after their useful life is over (see Figure 7.1). These

It's time to pick a different color for flashcards created for MR topics.

are two critical elements for the environment and the building industry, as buildings are a large consumer of natural resources and also contribute to the amount of solid waste generated operationally. If facilities focused more effort toward recycling, the demand for natural resources would be lower. With the U.S. Environmental Protection Agency (EPA) reporting a 65 percent increase in waste generation from residents, businesses, and institutions since 1980, this is a major concern environmentally.[1]

From an economic standpoint, waste reduction strategies can reduce operational costs. If packaging strategies are evaluated to find more efficient means, packaging can be reduced, therefore lowering the costs of products and materials. If less packaging is used, there will be less waste, therefore lowering the cost for collection and disposal.

As a result of the increase in waste, green building project team members are advised to evaluate the environmental impact of their materials and product specifications and how to address waste during construction and operations. The EPA recommends source reduction, reuse, and recycling as a means to waste reduction.[2] Think about what is coming into the facility and what is going out.

Teams working on sustainable projects seeking certification may find themselves asking, "What kinds of materials are used to make green building products? How far did the raw material for these products have to travel to the manufacturing plant? How far is the manufacturing plant from the facility? How can we choose products to reduce environmental consequences, such as pollution and depleting natural resources? What happens to the waste after it leaves our site? What are the social and health impacts related to procurement decisions?" To help answer these types of questions, this chapter addresses two components for consideration as related to material and resource selection and disposal:

1. Sustainable purchasing

2. Solid waste management

These strategies are referred to in the prerequisites and credits of the category, as seen in Table 7.1. Note the two prerequisites and Credit 6 are the only ones

 Create a flashcard to remember the two components to address within the MR category.

Table 7.1 The Materials & Resources Category

Timeframe	Prereq/ Credit	Title	Points
Program Development	Prereq 1	Sustainable Purchasing Policy	R
Program Development	Prereq 2	Solid Waste Management Policy	R
Performance Period/ Certification	Credit 1	Sustainable Purchasing — Ongoing Consumables	1
Performance Period/ Certification	Credit 2	Sustainable Purchasing — Durable Goods	1-2
Performance Period/ Certification	Credit 3	Sustainable Purchasing — Facility Alterations and Additions	1
Performance Period/ Certification	Credit 4	Sustainable Purchasing — Reduced Mercury in Lamps	1
Performance Period/ Certification	Credit 5	Sustainable Purchasing — Food	1
Program Development	Credit 6	Solid Waste Management — Waste Stream Audit	1
Performance Period/ Certification	Credit 7	Solid Waste Management — Ongoing Consumables	1
Performance Period/ Certification	Credit 8	Solid Waste Management — Durable Goods	1
Performance Period/ Certification	Credit 9	Solid Waste Management — Facility Alterations and Additions	1

addressed in the program development stage, while the rest are measured during the performance period/certification. Credit 2 is the only credit that offers more than one-point opportunity. It also might be helpful to think of the two prerequisites as setting the stage with policy development and implementation as the credits measure actual performance. As you read through the chapter, you will learn the prerequisites and credits in this category are not related to any other prerequisites or credits in the rating system but instead related to each other. This type of information is summarized in Appendix D.

Facilities Alterations and Additions

MR Credits 3 and 9 (and to be discussed in the next chapter, Indoor Environmental Quality [EQ] Credit 1.5) all refer to facility alterations and additions. For the purposes of the exam, it is important to know there is a defined minimum and maximum limit for eligibility for an existing facility to pursue certification under the EBOM rating system. Simply said, if the scope of work exceeds the maximum threshold, the team should pursue certification under a different rating system, such as LEED for New Construction and Major Renovations™. Should the scope of work fall shy of the minimum requirements, the team cannot pursue points under these three credits, for those efforts as they are considered repairs. The limitations are defined as:

■ *Maximum.* The scope of work cannot impact more than 50 percent of floor area or require 50 percent or more of the building occupants to be relocated.

■ *Minimum.* The scope of work must impact more than 5 percent of the floor area.

SUSTAINABLE PURCHASING

Implementing sustainable building materials impacts a project's triple bottom line, just as with site selection and energy and water demands. As introduced in Chapter 2, project teams should perform **life-cycle assessments (LCAs)** of building materials, prior to specification, to evaluate the "cradle-to-grave" cycle of each material, especially as related to the environmental components of pollution and the demand of natural resources. The cradle-to-grave cycle includes the embodied energy, such as the extraction location of raw materials, the manufacturing process and location, the impact on construction workers and building occupants, the expectancy term of use during operations, the disposal options available, and the energy contained within the product itself.

 Remember, the most sustainable approach to operating and maintaining a building is to select materials with multiple environmental benefits, allowing a holistic strategy.

Material selection should begin with the development and implementation of a sustainable purchasing policy "to reduce the environmental impacts of materials acquired for use in the operations, maintenance and upgrades of buildings."[3] The policy should address **ongoing consumables**, such as printer paper, batteries, and printing cartridges and **durable goods**, such as furniture, appliances, and equipment. For the purposes of LEED compliance, ongoing consumables and durable goods are evaluated based on sustainable criteria, such as:

 Create a flashcard to remember the examples of ongoing consumables and durable goods.

Recycled Content. It is important to remember that this refers to the purchasing of materials with recycled content (see Figure 7.2), not the actual recycling of materials, as that process will be addressed later. Table 7.2 defines the difference between the two types of recycled content and also provides examples of each. Try to think of the different processes to help remember the difference between postindustrial/preconsumer and

Figure 7.2 Permeable pavers made with recycled content not only help to recharge the groundwater but also help to reduce the need for virgin materials. *Photo courtesy of Vast Enterprises, LLC*

Create a flashcard to remember that regional materials must be extracted, processed, *and* manufactured within 500 miles of the project site to comply.

postconsumer. For example, postindustrial refers to material reentering the manufacturing process without ever being sold as an end product, such as scraps. Therefore, postconsumer products, such as furniture, metal, and concrete, refer to items that are at the end of their useful life.

Regional Materials. Purchasing products from vendors nearby reduces transportation impacts, such as pollution, and also preserves the local economy (see Figure 7.3). But what is considered local? This component requires a project team to track not only the location from which a product was sold or distributed but also the extraction points of the materials used

Figure 7.3 Purchasing materials that were extracted, processed, and manufactured within 500 miles reduced the transportation impacts associated with building materials for the EcoDorm at Warren Wilson College in Swannanoa, North Carolina. The strategy helped the college to earn Platinum certification under the LEED® for Existing Buildings rating system. *Photo courtesy of Samsel Architects, Photography by John Warner Photography*

to make the product, where those materials were processed, and where the final product was manufactured and assembled. To comply, all of these processes must take place within 500 miles of the project site.

Rapidly Renewable Materials. Rapidly renewable materials are "agricultural products, both fiber and animal, that take 10 years or less to grow or raise and can be harvested in a sustainable fashion"[4] and, thus preserve natural resource materials for future generations. Be sure to refer to Table 7.2 for examples of rapidly renewable materials, and note that both animal and fiber types are included.

Certified Wood. Wood certified by the **Forest Stewardship Council (FSC)** proves compliance for responsible forest management, preserving materials for future generations and habitats, as well as maintaining biodiversity (see Figure 7.4). For ongoing consumables, teams are required to look to FSC-certified paper products for compliance, while durable goods include wood products, such as furniture. Teams must collect the vendor or manufacturer's **chain-of-custody (COC)** certification documentation to prove compliance for all stages of processing, manufacturing, and distribution. It can include different types of FSC-certified products, such as FSC Pure, FSC Mixed Credit, and FSC Mixed (NN) percent. For the purposes of calculating compliance, the FSC Pure and FSC Mixed Credit are valued at 100 percent of their cost, while the FSC Mixed (NN) percent shall only have a value of its percentage of the FSC product. For example, wood that is certified FSC Mixed (35) percent can contribute only 35 percent of its value toward compliance. FSC Recycled certified products do not qualify as FSC, but they can be included in the recycled content product calculations.

Salvaged/Reused Materials. Materials that are salvaged from off-site or outside the organization comply with the intentions of this criterion. Materials can also be salvaged from on-site, through an internal organization materials and equipment reuse program in order to be eligible for calculation inclusion for compliance.

 Create a flashcard to remember that rapidly renewable fiber or animal materials must be grown or raised in 10 years or less, and some examples, such as cotton and bamboo.

 Create a flashcard to remember that FSC wood requires chain-of-custody (COC) documentation.

 TIP Remember ongoing consumables as low-cost products that are typically ordered often as a means to support business and facility operations, whereas durable goods typically cost more and have a useful life of at least two years.

Figure 7.4 Purchasing wood from sustainable and responsible forests helps to ensure resources for future generations. *Photo courtesy of Armstrong Ceiling and Wall Systems*

Table 7.2 Green Building Products

Characteristic		Description	Examples
Materials with recycled content		Products manufactured with material previously used	Masonry, concrete, carpet, acoustic ceiling tile, tile, rubber flooring, insulation, metal, and gypsum wallboard
	Postindustrial waste	Material left over from the manufacturing process and introduced to a different manufacturing process	Fly ash, sawdust, walnut shells, sunflower seed hulls, obsolete inventories, shavings, and trimmings
	Postconsumer waste	Manufactured products at the end of their useful life	Any products that were consumed (such as metals, plastics, paper, cardboard, glass), and demolition and construction debris
Regional materials		Products that are extracted, processed, and manufactured close to a project site	Materials obtained within 500 miles of the project site
Rapidly renewable materials		Animal or fiber materials that grow or can be raised in less than 10 years	Bamboo flooring and plywood, cotton batt insulation, linoleum flooring, sunflower seed board panels, wheatboard cabinetry, wool carpeting, cork flooring, bio-based paints, geotextile fabrics, soy-based insulation, and straw bales
FSC-certified materials		Sustainably managed forest resources	Contractors are required to show chain-of-custody (COC) documentation

Create a flashcard to remember the difference between preconsumer/postindustrial and postconsumer recycled contents.

Facility alterations and additions that impact usable space in the building should also be addressed in the sustainability purchasing policy, as proper material selection is key to environmental success. Construction products and materials should be evaluated not only as durable goods and ongoing consumables, but also for volatile organic compound (VOC) content and included salvaged/reused materials (see Figure 7.5). A sustainable approach to purchasing lamps

Figure 7.5 The ebony oak wood for the reception desk at the LEED certified One Haworth Center in Holland, Michigan, was recovered from the Great Lakes and other waterways to avoid depleting old-growth forests. *Photo courtesy of Haworth Inc.*

should also be included in the policy to ensure a reduction in mercury in the facility's solid waste stream, thus reducing the facility's contribution to air, land, and water pollution. The procurement of food is another area in which one can reduce the environmental impact of the facility. Although for the purposes of LEED compliance, the sustainable purchasing policy is not required to include all of these components, except ongoing consumables, it is encouraged.

Sustainable Purchasing in Relation to LEED Compliance

MR Prerequisite 1: Sustainable Purchasing Policy. As noted previously, the first step in addressing material selection is the development and implementation of an **environmentally preferable policy** (EPP) to reduce the environmental impact of what is coming into the facility. The team will need to make sure MR Credit 1: Sustainable Purchasing – Ongoing Consumables is addressed in the EPP, as well as at least one of the following other MR credits:

MR Credit 2: Sustainable Purchasing – Durable Goods

MR Credit 3: Sustainable Purchasing – Facility Alterations and Additions

MR Credit 4: Sustainable Purchasing – Reduced Mercury in Lamps

Although it is not required, teams are encouraged to refer to the **EPA's Environmentally Preferable Purchasing (EPP) Program** guidelines, as the policy should address the triple bottom line impacts of the components implemented. This could include resource and pollution reductions, and employee health and safety, as well as the economic benefits or purchasing goals by the means of **life-cycle cost** analysis.

MR Credit 1: Sustainable Purchasing – Ongoing Consumables. During the performance period, project teams will need to track the ongoing consumables purchased to determine if 60 percent (by cost) comply with the at least one of the following criteria:[5]

- Contains at least 10 percent postconsumer and/or 20 percent postindustrial material (see Figure 7.6)

- Contains at least 50 percent rapidly renewable materials

- Contains at least 50 percent materials harvested and processed or extracted and processed within 500 miles of the project

- Consists of at least 50 percent FSC–certified paper products

- Uses batteries that are rechargeable

Project teams can pursue an exemplary performance point under the Innovation in Operations (IO) category if they purchase at least 95 percent of ongoing consumables in compliance with at least one sustainable characteristic defined by the credit.

MR Credit 2: Sustainable Purchasing – Durable Goods. Project teams are presented with three options to comply with this credit, offering up to two points for compliance. During the performance period, project teams will need to track the purchase of electric-powered equipment and/or furniture to determine if 40 percent of purchases are in compliance. For teams pursuing option 1 for electric powered equipment, they must prove 40 percent of the equipment is either ENERGY STAR® qualified or replaces conventional gas-powered equipment. If the project team is pursuing option 2 for furniture, they must prove 40 percent of the performance period purchases comply with at least one of the following criteria:[5]

- Contains at least 10 percent postconsumer and/or 20 percent postindustrial material

TIP Life-cycle costing looks not only at the initial investment but also at operating costs, maintenance expenditures, and replacement fees.

Create a flashcard to remember the EPA's EPP guidelines as a resource for creating a sustainable purchasing policy.

TIP Notice Prerequisite 1 does not require any performance measurements but only a policy. MR Credits 1 through 5 are designed to track the performance after the policy has been implemented.

Multiple tenant buildings are allowed to exclude up to 10 percent of the project's floor area from the compliance calculations for MR Credits 1 through 5.

Create a flashcard to remember the five sustainable characteristics of ongoing consumables.

Figure 7.6 Specifying cradle-to-cradle (C2C) certified surfaces made of recycled content with low to no volatile organic compounds (VOCs) helps to reduce the need of virgin materials, as well as improve the indoor environment. *Photo courtesy of Icestone, LLC, and Green Team*

Create a flashcard to remember the six sustainable criteria to comply with option 2 for furniture.

TIP Project teams may be challenged by whether to assign products as ongoing consumables or durable goods. In this case, they have the option to choose, as long it is done consistently and they do not apply the goods to both credit calculations. No double-dipping!

- Contains at least 70 percent material salvaged from off-site or outside the organization
- Contains at least 70 percent material salvaged from on-site, through an internal organization materials and equipment reuse program
- Contains at least 50 percent rapidly renewable materials
- Consists of at least 50 percent FSC–certified wood products
- Contains at least 50 percent materials harvested and processed or extracted and processed within 500 miles of the project

For option 3, project teams can earn two points should they purchase durable goods in compliance with both the electric-powered equipment and the furniture compliance path options. Should they purchase at least 80 percent of durable goods in compliance with either option 1 or 2, they can pursue an Exemplary Performance point under the IO category.

MR Credit 3: Sustainable Purchasing – Facility Alterations and Additions. During the performance period, project teams will need to track the materials purchased for renovations to determine if 50 percent (by cost) comply with the at least one of the following criteria:[6]

- Contains at least 10 percent postconsumer and/or 20 percent postindustrial material

- Contains at least 70 percent material salvaged from off-site or outside the organization

- Contains at least 70 percent material salvaged from on-site, through an internal organization materials and equipment reuse program

- Contains at least 50 percent rapidly renewable materials

- Consists of at least 50 percent FSC–certified wood products

- Contains at least 50 percent materials harvested and processed or extracted and processed within 500 miles of the project

- Adhesives and sealants have a VOC content less than the current VOC content limits of South Coast Air Quality Management District (SCAQMD) Rule #1168, or sealants used as fillers meet or exceed the requirements of the Bay Area Air Quality Management District Regulation 8, Rule 51

- Paints and coatings with VOC emissions not exceeding the VOC and chemical component limits of Green Seal's Standard GS-11 requirements (see Figure 7.7)

 Create a flashcard to remember the three compliance path options for MR Credit 2.

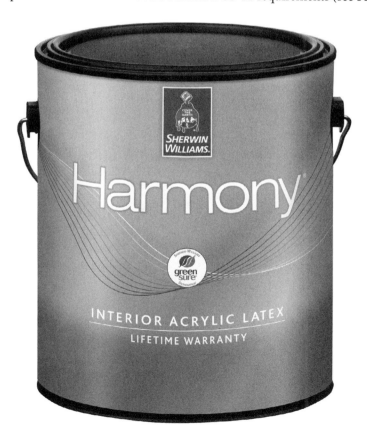

Figure 7.7 Using a low-VOC paint provides a better indoor environment for the occupants, including the Operations and Maintenance (O&M) staff. *Photo courtesy of Sherwin-Williams*

- Noncarpet finished flooring is FloorScore certified and constitutes a minimum of 25 percent of the finished floor area
- Carpet meets the requirements of the CRI Green Label Plus Carpet Testing Program (see Figure 7.8)
- Carpet cushion meets the requirements of the CRI Green Label Testing Program

Project teams are not to include furniture, fixtures, or equipment (FF&E), or any mechanical, electrical, or plumbing (MEP) components in the calculations for compliance. They can pursue an Exemplary Performance point under the IO category if they purchase at least 95 percent of materials in compliance with at least one of the defined sustainable characteristics.

Create flashcards to remember the reference standards listed for the different sustainable criteria of MR Credit 3.

Remember, products must be kept separate for calculation purposes, as items can only be included in one of the MR Credits 1, 2, or 3 spreadsheets.

Calculating Compliance for MR Credits 1, 2, and 3

The three previous credit opportunities describe compliance as a percentage of cost. How does a team document the total cost of materials purchased during the performance period? Teams will need to track all applicable materials purchased during the performance materials by creating a chart with the date of purchase, purchasing entity (internal department, tenant, individual, etc.), type of item, cost (not including labor or equipment), quantity, and any complying sustainable criteria, such as recycled content. Teams must also note the documentation method proving compliance with a sustainable criterion. Therefore, if a team is pursuing each of the three credits, there should be three unique spreadsheets or charts with different items listed on each. No two spreadsheets should contain the same line items.

What if a product has two or more sustainable qualities? For example, it is not uncommon to find a product that meets the definition of a regional material and has recycled content as well. In this case, the declarant would proceed with a weighted average for calculation purposes. For every sustainable quality, the item's contribution multiplies for calculation purposes. For example, if a spreadsheet were compiled for MR Credit 1 and included $400 worth of FSC-certified

Figure 7.8 Installing CRI Green Label Plus Program carpet tiles helps to avoid contaminating the indoor air. *Photo courtesy of Beaulieu Commercial*

paper products that were locally extracted, processed, and manufactured, the products' weighted value would be $800, since the spreadsheet had two qualifying sustainable attributes. If the products were to comply with three sustainable criteria, the weighted value would be $1,200.

MR Credit 4: Sustainable Purchasing – Reduced Mercury in Lamps. Project teams will need to first develop a purchasing plan to address the procurement of lamps for the outdoor and indoor environments, focusing on the following three characteristics:

1. Mercury content (mg/lamp)
2. **Lamp life** (hours)
3. Light output (lumens)

During the performance period, project teams will then need to track all lamps purchased for the site and inside the facility to verify at least 90 percent of the lamps purchased have a maximum mercury content level of 90 **pictograms** per **lumen**-hour or less. Project teams typically meet the intentions of this credit if they purchase lamps with low mercury content, those with a long lamp life, and when light output is highest the strategy meets the intentions of the credit earning the team a point. Light-emitting diode (LED) lamps may be included in the calculations to help with compliance, but only if the lamps have an energy efficiency equal to or better than comparable mercury-containing lamps. "Screw-based, integral compact fluorescent lamps (CFLs) may be excluded from both the plan and the performance calculation if they comply with the voluntary industry guidelines for maximum mercury content published by the National Electrical Manufacturers Association (NEMA)."[7] Therefore, if the CFLs do not comply, they must be included in the calculations.

Project teams can pursue an exemplary performance point under the IO category if at least 90 percent of the lamps purchased during the performance period have a maximum mercury content level of 70 **pictograms** per **lumen**-hour or less.

MR Credit 5: Sustainable Purchasing – Food. During the performance period, project teams will need to track the food and beverages purchased for renovations to determine if 25 percent (by cost) comply with the at least one of the following criteria:[9]

USDA Organic (see Figure 7.9a)

Food Alliance certified (see Figure 7.9b)

Rainforest Alliance certified

 Create a flashcard to remember the three factors with which to measure performance for a lamp purchasing plan.

 Create two flashcards to remember a **pictogram** is a trillionth of a gram and a **lumen** is a "unit of luminous flux equal to the light emitted in a unit solid angle by a uniform point source of 1 candle intensity."[8]

TIP Project teams must include lamps for hardwired and portable fixtures that are located inside and outside the facility in the calculations.

 Create a flashcard to remember NEMA guidelines as a reference standard depicting CFL compliance for calculations purposes.

 Create a flashcard to remember the six different types of labels in compliance with MR Credit 5.

 Create a flashcard to remember the minimum percentage thresholds for MR Credits 1, 2, 3, and 5 and the exemplary performance opportunities for each.

a   b

Figures 7.9a and 7.9b Purchasing food certified by any of the 6 qualifying organizations helps project teams to pursue MR Credit 5 under the EBOM rating system. *Images courtesy of U.S. Department of Agriculture and Food Alliance*

Create a flashcard to remember the six strategies to address sustainable purchasing, including MR Prerequisite 1.

Protected Harvest certified

Fair Trade certified

Marine Stewardship Council's Blue Eco-Label

Project teams will need to ensure the products are purchased from within a 100-mile radius of the project site to comply, although any items purchased for vending machines are to be excluded from the calculations. The team can pursue an Exemplary Performance point under the IO category if they purchase at least 50 percent of food and beverages in compliance with at least one of the defined sustainable labels.

QUIZ TIME!

Q7.1. Which of the following sustainable characteristics are to be considered for compliance with MR Credit 1: Ongoing Consumables? (Choose three)

   A. Recycled content

   B. Regional materials

   C. Salvaged materials from on site

   D. FSC-certified wood

   E. FSC-certified paper products

   F. Salvaged materials from outside of organization

Q7.2. Which of the following credits is eligible for more than one point? (Choose one)

   A. MR Credit 1: Sustainable Purchasing – Ongoing Consumables

   B. MR Credit 2: Sustainable Purchasing – Durable Goods

   C. MR Credit 3: Sustainable Purchasing – Facility Alterations and Additions

   D. MR Credit 4: Sustainable Purchasing – Reduced Mercury in Lamps

   E. MR Credit 5: Sustainable Purchasing – Food

Q7.3. How would a project team show proof of compliance for FSC-certified wood products? (Choose one)

   A. Submit a spreadsheet documenting that all of the wood was purchased within 500 miles of the project site

   B. Upload receipts of FSC wood purchased to LEED-Online

   C. Upload chain-of-custody documentation to LEED-Online

   D. Complete a LEED credit template and upload it to LEED-Online, including the chain-of-custody numbers and invoice amounts

   E. Mail all documentation to USGBC

Q7.4. Which of the following should be documented for compliance with MR Credits 1 through 3? (Choose four)

   A. Date of purchase

   B. Cost (including labor)

C. Material cost

D. Quantity

E. Sustainable criterion met

Q7.5. Which of the following statements are true regarding MR Credit 3: Sustainable Purchasing – Facility Alterations and Additions? (Choose three)

A. Compliance is based on spaces in the building affected by renovation work.

B. Mechanical, electrical, and plumbing components must be included in the calculations for compliance.

C. Mechanical, electrical, and plumbing components cannot be included in the calculations for compliance.

D. Compliance is based on spaces in the building *not* affected by renovation work.

E. Furniture, fixtures, and furnishings are to be included in the calculations, as they are part of the base building.

F. Furniture, fixtures, and furnishings are *not* to be included in the calculations, as they are not part of the base building.

Q7.6. Which of the following materials could comply with the definition of recycled content, as preconsumer recycled content? (Choose three)

A. Metal stud manufacturing scrap sent back into the same manufacturing process

B. Paper towels manufactured from cardboard used for packaging

C. Medium-density fiberboard panels manufactured with sawdust generated by the manufacturing of structural insulated panels

D. Concrete made with fly ash collected from coal-burning power plants

E. Carpet padding manufactured with waste fiber collected from textile manufacturing plants

Q7.7. Which of the following components must be included in the lighting purchasing plan and tracked during the performance period to comply with the requirements of MR Credit 4: Sustainable Purchasing – Reduced Mercury in Lamps? (Choose three)

A. Lamp life

B. Cost

C. Type of lamp replaced

D. Light output in lumens

E. Mercury content per lamp

Q7.8. Which of the following is not an example of rapidly renewable materials? (Choose one)

A. Strawboard

B. Oak wood flooring

C. Cotton insulation

D. Cork flooring

E. Wheatboard

Q7.9. Which of the following are not acceptable labels to comply with MR Credit 5: Sustainable Purchasing – Food? (Choose four)

A. NEMA

B. EPA EPP

C. USDA Organic

D. EPEAT

E. Fair Trade Certified

F. Protected Harvest

G. FSC-certified

Q7.10. What are the compliance path options for MR Credit 2: Sustainable Purchasing – Durable Goods, Option 1, Electric-Powered Equipment? (Choose two)

A. FSC-certified

B. ENERGY STAR qualified

C. Local products obtained within 500 miles

D. Replaces gas-powered equipment

E. Replaces electric-powered equipment

Q7.11. What is the maximum distance in which food and beverage products can be purchase from and still comply with Credit 5: Sustainable Purchasing – Food? (Choose one)

A. 100 miles

B. 200 miles

C. 50 miles

D. 500 miles

E. 1,000 miles

F. 1,500 miles

Q7.12. What is the maximum floor area exclusion percentage allowed for multiple-tenant buildings for compliance with MR Credits 1 through 5? (Choose one)

A. 5 percent

B. 10 percent

C. 15 percent

D. 20 percent

E. 25 percent

Q7.13. Which MR Credit is required to be addressed in the sustainable purchasing policy for compliance with MR Prerequisite 1: Sustainable Purchasing Policy? (Choose one)

A. MR Credit 1: Sustainable Purchasing – Ongoing Consumables

B. MR Credit 2: Sustainable Purchasing – Durable Goods

C. MR Credit 3: Sustainable Purchasing – Facility Alterations and Additions

D. MR Credit 4: Sustainable Purchasing – Reduced Mercury in Lamps

E. MR Credit 5: Sustainable Purchasing – Food

Q7.14. A pictogram is:

A. 1 millionth of a gram

B. 1 billionth of a gram

C. 1 trillionth of a gram

D. 1 thousandth of a gram

E. 1 tenth of a gram

Q7.15. Which of the following are not an example of an ongoing consumable product? (Choose two)

A. Notepads

B. Dishwashers

C. Monitors

D. Batteries

E. Toner cartridges

SOLID WASTE MANAGEMENT

Construction processes and building operations should be addressed to minimize environmental impacts from disposal and waste. In the United States, building operations account for 300 tons of waste per year for a building with 1,500 employees.[10] With an emphasis on recycling and diversion strategies, contamination risks are reduced, landfill space is preserved, and the command for raw material shrinks.

 TIP Landfills require sunlight, moisture, and oxygen in order to decompose material—quite a challenging feat for a dark, enclosed environment, don't you think?

When waste is collected and hauled from a construction site or an existing facility, it is typically brought to a landfill or an incineration facility, both of which contribute to greenhouse gas emissions. Landfills produce and then leak methane, and incineration facility processes produce carbon dioxide. As another environmental detriment, think about the potential for landfills to contaminate groundwater sources with toxic elements. Toxic items, such as batteries and fluorescent lamps, can be removed from the **waste stream** with recycling efforts, thus helping to reduce air and groundwater contamination.

 Create a flashcard to remember a waste stream "is the overall flow of waste from the building to a landfill, incinerator, or other disposal site."[11]

Create a flashcard to remember the 3R's of waste management: reduce, reuse, and recycle. Remember them in that order as a hierarchal approach for policies.

If project teams are not able to reduce waste from entering a facility, they are encouraged to reuse or recycle the materials. Not only does this save on collection and disposal fees, but it also preserves landfill space. Reusing and recycling efforts also help to reduce the need for virgin materials, thus preserving resources for future generations. These materials typically include steel, plastic, and wood, but should also include construction, demolition, and land-clearing (CDL) debris. Consider the extraction, processing, and transportation impacts these materials have on the triple bottom line.

To help reach these waste stream, raw material demands, and contamination risk reduction goals, the EBOM rating system requires teams to implement waste management policies and offers point opportunities for diverting waste by reuse and recycling.

Solid Waste Management in Relation to LEED Compliance

MR Prerequisite 2: Solid Waste Management Policy. Project teams are required to develop a solid waste management policy for the building and site that addresses the following components to divert from landfills and incineration facilities:

- Ongoing consumables
- Durable goods
- Facility alterations and additions
- Mercury in lamps

The policy should include strategies to reduce waste at its source, reuse, recycling, waste monitoring, and resource reduction. Locations for collection and storage should be identified, as well as the responsible parties for developing and implementing the policy. MR credits 7, 8, and 9 will address tracking the performance of the policy during the performance period, as this prerequisite only requires the team to develop and implement a policy for the facility.

MR Credit 6: Solid Waste Management – Waste Stream Audit. During the performance period, project teams will need to complete the following six steps for the ongoing consumables waste stream in order to earn this one-point credit. The audit will establish a baseline performance of consumption patterns and how waste is disposed of for the facility to improve upon.[12]

Step 1. Determine the appropriate unit for the waste stream audit, either volume or weight, and use it consistently throughout.

Step 2. Determine the appropriate waste categories for the audit.

Step 3. Establish a time interval for the audit that is representative of the building's waste stream and reflects a normal business and collection cycle.

Step 4. Determine the volume or weight of the waste that is disposed of in landfills or incinerated and the waste that is recycled, reused, composted, or otherwise diverted from conventional disposal.

Step 5. For each category of waste, sort the major types and determine their volume or weight (see Figure 7.10).

Step 6. For each waste category, add the volume or weight of conventionally disposed waste to the volume or weight of the alternatively disposed waste to identify the total volume or weight of that waste category for the audit period.

Figure 7.10 Conducting a waste stream audit can help a project team earn a point under MR Credit 6. *Photo courtesy of Stiles Property Management*

MR Credit 7: Solid Waste Management – Ongoing Consumables. Project teams will need to divert at least 50 percent of the waste stream generated from ongoing consumables by the means of source reduction, reuse, and recycling strategies during the performance period. They should address at a minimum, products such as "paper, toner cartridges, glass, plastics, cardboard and old corrugated cardboard, food waste, and metals."[13] Battery recycling should also be implemented with a goal of diverting at least 80 percent from landfill sites. Project teams are eligible to pursue an Exemplary Performance credit under the IO category should they divert at least 95 percent of the facility's ongoing consumables from landfills and/or incineration facilities.

MR Credit 8: Solid Waste Management – Durable Goods. During the performance period, project teams will need to divert at least 75 percent of the waste

 Notice that this credit did not require durable goods or construction waste for facility additions and alterations to be included in the waste stream audit for compliance.

 Waste can be calculated in volume or weight (tons), as long as this is done consistently.

Figure 7.11 Diverting construction waste from facilities alterations and addition can help to reduce the command for virgin materials and preserve landfill space. *Photo courtesy of SmithGroup, Inc.*

Figure 7.12 Separating waste on site is one method to comply with the solid waste management strategies to avoid landfills and incineration facilities. *Photo courtesy of Auld & White Constructors, LLC*

 Did you notice none of the solid waste management strategies has a reference standard to remember?

 Create a flashcard to remember the five strategies used to address solid waste management.

stream generated from durable goods by the means of reuse, recycling, or donation strategies. This should include computer and audiovisual equipment and adapters, monitors, and appliances. Documentation will need to verify diversion by weight, volume, or replacement value.

MR Credit 9: Solid Waste Management - Facility Alterations and Additions. This credit is addressed during the performance period during demolition, renovation, retrofits, and new construction addition activities encompassing base building components that are permanently or semi-permanently attached to the building (see Figure 7.11). Hazardous materials should be excluded, and just as with MR Credit 3 for renovation work, FF&E and MEP components are not to be included in the calculations proving compliance either. **Alternative daily cover** material may be included in calculations, as it helps to control fires and odors, and it also helps to reduce air pollution and scavenging at the top of a landfill. In order to earn this one-point credit, teams will need to prove at least 70 percent of the waste generated from the alteration and/or addition was reused, recycled, or diverted away from landfills and incineration facilities (Figure 7.12). The team can pursue an exemplary performance opportunity for recycling 95 percent. The percentage of waste diverted must be calculated based on volume.

QUIZ TIME!

Q7.16. Which of the following greenhouse gases is a by-product of landfills? (Choose one)

A. Carbon monoxide
B. Methane
C. Sulfur dioxide
D. Nitrous oxide

Q7.17. Which of the following statements are *not* true about green building materials? (Choose two)

    A. Rapidly renewable materials are harvested within 10 years.

    B. Cradle-to-grave materials can be recycled.

    C. Products with postconsumer recycled content comply with the recycled content requirements, whereas products with preconsumer recycled content do not.

    D. Cotton insulation can be considered a type of rapidly renewable material.

Q7.18. How is waste hauled from a construction site calculated for the purposes of LEED? (Choose one)

    A. As a percentage of total material cost of a project

    B. As a percentage of the total material volume or weight

    C. As a percentage of total cost of a project

    D. In tons

Q7.19. Which of the following are not required for collection to comply with MR Credit 7 1: Solid Waste Management – Ongoing Consumables? (Choose two)

    A. Glass

    B. Plastics

    C. Wood

    D. Rubber

    E. Corrugated cardboard

    F. Metal

    G. Food waste

Q7.20. Which of the following must a solid waste management policy address to be in compliance with MR Prerequisite 1: Solid Waste Management Policy? (Choose three)

    A. Printer paper

    B. Computer equipment

    C. Waste stream audit

    D. Batteries

    E. Construction waste

Q7.21. Which of the following credits offer exemplary performance opportunities? (Choose three)

    A. WE Credit 4: Cooling Tower Management

    B. MR Credit 6: Solid Waste Management – Waste Stream Audit

    C. EA Credit 2.1: Existing Building Commissioning, Investigation & Analysis

    D. MR Credit 8: Solid Waste Management – Durable Goods

    E. SS Credit 4: Alternative Commuting Transportation

    F. MR Credit 2: Sustainable Purchasing – Durable Goods

Q7.22. Which of the following is not addressed during the performance period? (Choose two)

A. MR Prerequisite 1: Sustainable Purchasing Policy

B. MR Credit 2: Sustainable Purchasing – Durable Goods

C. MR Credit 8: Solid Waste Management – Durable Goods

D. MR Credit 4: Sustainable Purchasing – Reduced Mercury in Lamps

E. MR Credit 6: Solid Waste Management – Waste Stream Audit

Q7.23. What is the minimum percentage threshold for diverting batteries from landfills and incineration facilities to comply with MR Credit 7: Solid Waste Management – Ongoing Consumables? (Choose one)

A. 20 percent

B. 40 percent

C. 50 percent

D. 75 percent

E. 80 percent

F. 95 percent

Q7.24. What is the maximum pictograms per lumen-hour allowed to comply with MR Credit 4: Sustainable Purchasing – Reduced Mercury in Lamps? (Choose one)

A. 10

B. 25

C. 50

D. 75

E. 90

Q7.25. An existing facility is pursuing MR Credit 2: Sustainable Purchasing – Durable Goods and has documented 41.6 percent of their electric-powered equipment is ENERGY STAR qualified and 83.1 percent of their furniture purchases during the performance had at least one qualifying sustainable characteristic. How many points is the team eligible to pursue? (Choose one)

A. 1

B. 2

C. 3

D. 4

E. None

Q7.26. Which of the following are eligible tasks to be considered a facility alteration and/or addition project? (Choose three)

A. Air filter changes

B. Installing carpeting common areas

C. Installing aerators for bathroom lavatories

D. Workstation upgrades

E. Replacing the flooring in the cafeteria

F. Increasing the R-value of the building envelope

G. Renovation work impacting 65 percent of the building occupants

Q7.27. What is the rule to adhere to for maximum VOC limits for adhesives and sealants to be in compliance with MR Credit 3: Sustainable Purchasing – Facility Alterations and Additions? (Choose one)

A. EPEAT

B. SCAQMD Rule 1168

C. Green Seal GS-11

D. Green Label Plus

Q7.28. A purchasing manager is looking to evaluate, compare, and select computer equipment based on environmental performance. What resource should they refer to? (Choose one)

A. EPA EPP

B. EPEAT

C. SCAQMD Rule 1168

D. Green Seal GS-11

E. Green Label Plus

Q7.29. A 38,000-sq-ft facility is replacing its carpet tiles and pursuing MR Credit 3: Sustainable Purchasing – Facility Alterations and Additions for 1 point. They have purchased CRI Green Label Plus carpet tiles made with 34 percent postconsumer and 16 percent postindustrial content that was processed and manufactured 235 miles from the project site in Charlotte, North Carolina, for $11,000. What is the sustainable weighted value of the tiles? (Choose one)

A. There is not enough information

B. $11,000

C. $22,000

D. $44,000

E. $33,000

Q7.30. Each of the MR prerequisites and credits are all addressed in which of the following phases of an EBOM project? (Choose two)

A. Audit

B. Plan

C. Program Development

D. Performance Period/Certification

E. Education/Recertification

Program Development	MR Prerequisite 1: Sustainable Purchasing Policy

PURPOSE

During the operations, _____, and alterations of buildings, reduce the _____ impacts of materials _____.

REQUIREMENTS

Create an environmentally _____ purchasing (EPP) policy that includes the requirements of MR _____ 1: Sustainable Purchasing Policy – Ongoing _____ and at least of the following credits:

> MR Credit 2: Sustainable Purchasing Policy – _____ Goods

> MR Credit 3: Sustainable Purchasing _____ – Facility Alterations & Additions

> MR Credit _____: Sustainable Purchasing Policy – Reduced _____ in Lamps

The policy _____ cover the product purchases that are _____ the building and site management's _____, at a minimum.

Required	RESPONSIBLE PARTY: OWNER

MR Prerequisite 1: **Sustainable Purchasing Policy**

ANSWER KEY

PURPOSE

During the operations, **maintenance**, and alterations of buildings, reduce the **environmental** impacts of materials **purchased**.

REQUIREMENTS

Create an environmentally **preferable** purchasing (EPP) policy that includes the requirements of MR **Credit** 1: Sustainable Purchasing Policy - Ongoing **Consumables** and at least of the following credits:

MR Credit 2: Sustainable Purchasing Policy — **Durable** Goods

MR Credit 3: Sustainable Purchasing **Policy** — Facility Alterations & Additions

MR Credit **4:** Sustainable Purchasing Policy — Reduced **Mercury** in Lamps

The policy **must** cover the product purchases that are **within** the building and site management's **control**, at a minimum.

Program Development	MR Prerequisite 2:
	Solid Waste Management Policy

PURPOSE

Divert building occupant waste from _____ and _____ facilities.

REQUIREMENTS

Create a _____ waste management policy that addresses the following:

            _____ consumables

            durable _____

            facility _____ and additions

            mercury-containing _____

The policy _____ cover the product purchases that are _____ the building and site management's _____, at a minimum.

Required	RESPONSIBLE PARTY:
	OWNER

	MR Prerequisite 2:
	Solid Waste Management Policy

ANSWER KEY

PURPOSE

Divert building occupant waste from **landfills** and **incineration** facilities.

REQUIREMENTS

Create a **solid** waste management policy that addresses the following:

> **ongoing** consumables
>
> durable **goods**
>
> facility **alterations** and additions
>
> mercury-containing **lamps**

The policy **must** cover the product purchases that are **within** the building and site management's **control**, at a minimum.

Performance Period/ Certification	MR Credit 1: Sustainable Purchasing Policy Ongoing Consumables

PURPOSE

During the _____ and maintenance of buildings, reduce the environmental impacts of _____ purchased.

REQUIREMENTS

Track the purchasing of ongoing consumables during the _____ period to meet at least _____ of the following sustainable criteria:

        o Purchases contain at least _____ postconsumer and/or _____ postindustrial material.

        o Purchases contain at least _____ rapidly renewable materials.

        o Purchases contain at least _____ materials harvested and processed or extracted and processed within _____ miles of the project.

        o Purchases consist of at least _____ Forest Stewardship Council (FSC)–certified _____ products.

        o Batteries are _____.

Credit is awarded if _____ of purchased ongoing consumables meet at least one of the listed criteria (based on _____ value of the total purchases).

EXEMPLARY PERFORMANCE

EP is awarded if _____ percent of purchased ongoing consumables meet at least one of the listed criteria (based on weighted value of the total purchases).

REFERENCED STANDARDS

Forest _____ Council (FSC)

_____ Environmentally _____ Purchasing (EPP) Program guidelines

1 pt.	RESPONSIBLE PARTY: PROPERTY MANAGER

	MR Credit 1:
	Sustainable Purchasing Policy Ongoing Consumables

ANSWER KEY

PURPOSE

During the **operations** and maintenance of buildings, reduce the environmental impacts of **materials** purchased.

REQUIREMENTS

Track the purchasing of ongoing consumables during the **performance** period to meet at least **one** of the following sustainable criteria:

- o Purchases contain at least **10 percent** postconsumer and/or **20 percent** postindustrial material.
- o Purchases contain at least **50 percent** rapidly renewable materials.
- o Purchases contain at least **50 percent** materials harvested and processed or extracted and processed within **500** miles of the project.
- o Purchases consist of at least **50 percent** Forest Stewardship Council (FSC)–certified **paper** products.
- o Batteries are **rechargeable**.

Credit is awarded if **60 percent** of purchased ongoing consumables meet at least one of the listed criteria (based on **weighted** value of the total purchases).

EXEMPLARY PERFORMANCE

EP is awarded if **95** percent of purchased ongoing consumables meet at least one of the listed criteria (based on weighted value of the total purchases).

REFERENCED STANDARDS

Forest **Stewardship** Council (FSC)

EPA's Environmentally **Preferable** Purchasing (EPP) Program guidelines

Performance Period/Certification	**MR Credit 2:**
	Sustainable Purchasing Policy Durable Goods

PURPOSE

During the operations and _____, reduce the _____ impacts of materials _____.

REQUIREMENTS

Option 1: Electric-powered equipment (1 point)

Track the purchasing of ongoing consumables during the _____ period to meet at least _____ of the following sustainable criteria:

      o Purchases are _____ STAR qualified

      o Purchases replace conventional _____-powered equipment

Credit is awarded if _____ of electric-powered equipment purchases qualify (based on _____ value of the total purchases).

Option 2: Furniture (1 point)

Track the purchasing of ongoing consumables during the _____ period to meet at least _____ of the following sustainable criteria:

      o Purchases contain at least _____ postconsumer and/or _____ postindustrial material.

      o Purchases contain at least _____ material salvaged from _____-site or outside the organization.

      o Purchases contain at least_____ material salvaged from _____ site, through an internal organization materials and equipment reuse program.

      o Purchases contain at least _____ rapidly renewable materials.

      o Purchases consist of at least _____ Forest _____ Council (FSC)–certified products.

      o Purchases contain at least _____ materials harvested and processed or extracted and processed within ___ miles of the project.

Credit is awarded if _____ of furniture purchases qualify (based on _____ value of the total purchases)

Option 3: Combination (2 points)

Credit is awarded if both Option 1 and Option 2 requirements are met.

EXEMPLARY PERFORMANCE

EP is awarded if _____ of purchases qualify under Option 1 or Option 2 (based on _____ value of the total purchases).

REFERENCED STANDARD

_____ STAR® _____ products

1-2 pts.	**RESPONSIBLE PARTY:**
	PROPERTY MANAGER

	MR Credit 2:
	Sustainable Purchasing Policy Durable Goods

ANSWER KEY

PURPOSE

During the operations and **maintenance**, reduce the **environmental** impacts of materials **purchased**.

REQUIREMENTS

Option 1: Electric-powered equipment (1 point)

Track the purchasing of ongoing consumables during the **performance** period to meet at least **one** of the following sustainable criteria:

o Purchases are **ENERGY** STAR qualified.

o Purchases replace conventional **gas**-powered equipment.

Credit is awarded if **40 percent** of electric-powered equipment purchases qualify (based on **weighted** value of the total purchases).

Option 2: Furniture (1 point)

Track the purchasing of ongoing consumables during the **performance** period to meet at least **one** of the following sustainable criteria:

o Purchases contain at least **10 percent** postconsumer and/or **20 percent** postindustrial material.

o Purchases contain at least **70 percent** material salvaged from **off** site or outside the organization.

o Purchases contain at least **70 percent** material salvaged from **on**-site, through an internal organization materials and equipment reuse program.

o Purchases contain at least **50 percent** rapidly renewable materials.

o Purchases consist of at least **50 percent** Forest **Stewardship** Council (FSC)–certified products.

o Purchases contain at least **50 percent** materials harvested and processed or extracted and processed within **500** miles of the project.

Credit is awarded if **40 percent** of furniture purchases qualify (based on **weighted** value of the total purchases).

Option 3: Combination (2 points)

Credit is awarded if both Option 1 and Option 2 requirements are met.

EXEMPLARY PERFORMANCE

EP is awarded if **80 percent** of purchases qualify under Option 1 or Option 2 (based on **weighted** value of the total purchases).

REFERENCED STANDARD

ENERGY STAR®–**qualified** products

Performance Period/ Certification	MR Credit 3:
	Sustainable Purchasing Policy Facility Alterations & Additions

PURPOSE

During the alterations of buildings, reduce the _____ impacts of materials _____.

REQUIREMENTS

Track the purchasing of ongoing consumables during the _____ period to meet at least ____ of the following sustainable criteria:

- o Purchases contain at least _____ postconsumer and/or _____ postindustrial material.
- o Purchases contain at least _____ material salvaged from _____ site or outside the organization.
- o Purchases contain at least _____ material salvaged from _____ site, through an internal organization materials and equipment reuse program.
- o Purchases contain at least _____ rapidly renewable materials
- o Purchases consist of at least _____ Forest Stewardship Council (FSC)–certified products.
- o Purchases contain at least _____ materials harvested and processed or extracted and processed within_____ miles of the project.
- o _____ and sealants have a VOC content less than South Coast Air Quality Management District (SCAQMD) Rule _____.
- o VOC levels of paints and coating do not exceed Green Seal's Standard GS-11 requirements.
- o At least _____ of the hardsurface finished floor area is _____-certified.
- o _____ meets the requirements of the CRI Green Label Plus Carpet Testing Program.
- o Carpet _____ meets the requirements of the CRI _____ Label Testing Program.
- o Composite panels and _____ products do not contain added _____-formaldehyde resins.

Credit is awarded if _____ of furniture purchases qualify (based on _____ value of the total purchases).

EXEMPLARY PERFORMANCE

Credit is awarded if _____ of furniture purchases qualify (based on _____ value of the total purchases).

REFERENCED STANDARDS

Forest _____ Council (FSC)

FloorScore

The _____ and Rug Institute (CRI) _____ Label Testing Program and Green Label _____ Testing Program

Green Seal GS-_____ Environmental Requirements for _____

_____ Area Air Quality Management District (BAAQMD)

South _____ Air Quality Management District (SCAQMD) Rule _____, Adhesive and _____ Applications

1 pt.

RESPONSIBLE PARTY:

PROPERTY MANAGER

MR Credit 3:

Sustainable Purchasing Policy Facility Alterations & Additions

ANSWER KEY

PURPOSE

During the alterations of buildings, reduce the **environmental** impacts of materials **purchased**.

REQUIREMENTS

Track the purchasing of ongoing consumables during the **performance** period to meet at least **one** of the following sustainable criteria:

- o Purchases contain at least **10 percent** postconsumer and/or **20 percent** postindustrial material.

- o Purchases contain at least **70 percent** material salvaged from **off**-site or outside the organization.

- o Purchases contain at least **70 percent** material salvaged from **on**-site, through an internal organization materials and equipment reuse program.

- o Purchases contain at least **50 percent** rapidly renewable materials.

- o Purchases consist of at least **50 percent** Forest Stewardship Council (FSC)–certified products.

- o Purchases contain at least **50 percent** materials harvested and processed or extracted and processed within **500** miles of the project.

- o **Adhesives** and sealants have a VOC content less than South Coast Air Quality Management District (SCAQMD) Rule **#1168.**

- o VOC levels of paints and coating do not exceed Green Seal's Standard GS-11 requirements.

- o At least **25 percent** of the hardsurface finished floor area is **FloorScore**-certified.

- o **Carpet** meets the requirements of the CRI Green Label Plus Carpet Testing Program.

- o Carpet **cushion** meets the requirements of the CRI **Green** Label Testing Program.

- o Composite panels and **agrifiber** products do not contain added **urea**-formaldehyde resins.

Credit is awarded if **50 percent** of furniture purchases qualify (based on **weighted** value of the total purchases).

EXEMPLARY PERFORMANCE

Credit is awarded if **95 percent** of furniture purchases qualify (based on **weighted** value of the total purchases).

REFERENCED STANDARDS

Forest **Stewardship** Council (FSC)

FloorScore

The **Carpet** and Rug Institute (CRI) **Green** Label Testing Program and Green Label **Plus** Testing Program

Green Seal GS-11 Environmental Requirements for **Paints**

Bay Area Air Quality Management District (BAAQMD)

South **Coast** Air Quality Management District (SCAQMD) Rule **1168**, Adhesive and **Sealants** Applications

Performance Period/Certification	MR Credit 4:
	Sustainable Purchasing Policy Reduced Mercury in Lamps

PURPOSE

Reduce the amount of _____ brought onto a building site through _____ purchases by implementing a _____ material source _____ program.

REQUIREMENTS

Develop and implement a lighting purchasing plan targeting a maximum _____ of 90 _____ per lumen-hour for mercury-containing lamps during the _____ period. When developing purchasing plan, use the following metrics:

  o _____ content (mg/lamp)

  o Mean _____ output (lumens)

  o _____ life (hours)

Credit is awarded if at least _____ of purchased lamps have an _____ maximum mercury content of _____ pictograms per lumen-hour.

EXEMPLARY PERFORMANCE

EP is awarded if at least _____ of purchased lamps have an average maximum mercury content of _____ pictograms per lumen-hour.

REFERENCED STANDARD

_____ Voluntary Commitment on _____ in Compact Fluorescent Lights

1 pt.

RESPONSIBLE PARTY:

FACILITY MANAGER

	MR Credit 4:
	Sustainable Purchasing Policy Reduced Mercury in Lamps

ANSWER KEY

PURPOSE

Reduce the amount of **mercury** brought onto a building site through **lamp** purchases by implementing a **toxic** material source **reduction** program.

REQUIREMENTS

Develop and implement a lighting purchasing plan targeting a maximum **average** of 90 **pictograms** per lumen-hour for mercury-containing lamps during the **performance** period. When developing purchasing plan, use the following metrics:

o **Mercury** content (mg/lamp)

o Mean **light** output (lumens)

o **Rated** life (hours)

Credit is awarded if at least **90 percent** of purchased lamps have an **average** maximum mercury content of **90** pictograms per lumen-hour.

EXEMPLARY PERFORMANCE

EP is awarded if at least **90 percent** of purchased lamps have an average maximum mercury content of **70** pictograms per lumen-hour.

REFERENCED STANDARD

NEMA's Voluntary Commitment on **Mercury** in Compact Fluorescent Lights

Performance Period/Certification

MR Credit 5:

Sustainable Purchasing Policy Food

PURPOSE

Reduce the detriments of food _____ and _____ as related to _____ and the environment.

REQUIREMENTS

Track the purchasing of _____ purchased during the _____ period to meet at least _____ of the following sustainable criteria:

- o _____ Organic
- o _____ Alliance certified
- o Rainforest _____ certified
- o _____Harvest certified
- o Fair Trade certified
- o Marine _____ Council's Blue _____-Label

Credit is awarded if _____ of food purchases qualify (based on _____ value of the total purchases) and are _____ within a 100-mile radius from the site.

EXEMPLARY PERFORMANCE

Credit is awarded if _____ of food purchases qualify (based on _____ value of the total purchases) and are produced within a_____-mile radius from the site.

REFERENCED STANDARDS

_____ Labeling Organizations International certification

Food _____ certification

_____ Stewardship Council (MSC)_____ Eco-Label

Protected _____ certification

_____ Alliance certification

U.S. Department of Agriculture _____ certification

---

1 pt.

RESPONSIBLE PARTY:

PROPERTY MANAGER

	MR Credit 5:
	Sustainable Purchasing Policy Food

ANSWER KEY

PURPOSE

Reduce the detriments of food **production** and **distribution** as related to **transportation** and the environment.

REQUIREMENTS

Track the purchasing of **food** purchased during the **performance** period to meet at least **one** of the following sustainable criteria:

- o **USDA** Organic
- o **Food** Alliance certified
- o Rainforest **Alliance** certified
- o **Protected** Harvest certified
- o Fair Trade certified
- o Marine **Stewardship** Council's Blue **Eco**-Label

Credit is awarded if **25 percent** of food purchases qualify (based on **weighted** value of the total purchases) and are **produced** within a 100-mile radius from the site.

EXEMPLARY PERFORMANCE

Credit is awarded if **50 percent** of food purchases qualify (based on **weighted** value of the total purchases) and are produced within a **100**-mile radius from the site.

REFERENCED STANDARDS

Fairtrade Labeling Organizations International certification

Food **Alliance** certification

Marine Stewardship Council (MSC) **Blue** Eco-Label

Protected **Harvest** certification

Rainforest Alliance certification

U.S. Department of Agriculture **Organic** certification

Program Development	MR Credit 6:
	Solid Waste Management Waste Stream Audit

PURPOSE

Reduce building occupant waste and toxins that is hauled to _____ and _____ facilities.

REQUIREMENTS

During the _____ period, conduct a _____stream _____ of the building's entire ongoing _____waste stream taking the following steps:

1. Determine the appropriate _____ for the waste stream audit, either _____ or _____, and use it _____ throughout the performance period.

2. Determine the appropriate waste _____ for the audit.

3. Establish a _____ interval for the audit that is representative of the building's waste stream and reflects a _____ business and collection cycle.

4. Determine the volume or weight of the waste that is _____ of in landfills or incinerated and the waste that is _____ from conventional disposal.

5. For each _____ of waste, sort the major types and determine their _____ or weight.

6. For each waste category, add the volume or weight of conventionally disposed waste to the volume or weight of the alternatively disposed waste to identify the total volume or weight of that waste category for the audit period.

Use the audit to establish a _____ identifying the types of waste within the waste stream to identify opportunities to _____recycling and waste diversion.

1 pt.

RESPONSIBLE PARTY:

TEAM/FACILITY MANAGER

	MR Credit 6:
	Solid Waste Management Waste Stream Audit

ANSWER KEY

PURPOSE

Reduce building occupant waste and toxins that is hauled to **landfills** and **incineration** facilities.

REQUIREMENTS

During the **performance** period, conduct a **waste** stream **audit** of the building's entire ongoing **consumables** waste stream taking the following steps:

1. Determine the appropriate **unit** for the waste stream audit, either **volume** or **weight**, and use it **consistently** throughout the performance period.

2. Determine the appropriate waste **categories** for the audit.

3. Establish a **time** interval for the audit that is representative of the building's waste stream and reflects a **normal** business and collection cycle.

4. Determine the volume or weight of the waste that is **disposed** of in landfills or incinerated and the waste that is **diverted** from conventional disposal.

5. For each **category** of waste, sort the major types and determine their **volume** or weight.

6. For each waste category, add the volume or weight of conventionally disposed waste to the volume or weight of the alternatively disposed waste to identify the total volume or weight of that waste category for the audit period.

Use the audit to establish a **baseline** identifying the types of waste within the waste stream to identify opportunities to **increase** recycling and waste diversion.

| **Performance Period/Certification** | **MR Credit 7:** |
| | **Solid Waste Management Ongoing Consumables** |

PURPOSE

Reduce building _____ and building _____ waste and _____ generated by ongoing _____ that is hauled to landfills and incineration facilities.

REQUIREMENTS

Divert _____ of the ongoing consumable waste stream from landfills or incineration facilities, including at least _____ of batteries. Verify diversion at least _____ a year.

The ongoing consumable material must include at a minimum: paper, _____ cartridges, glass, plastics, _____ and old corrugated cardboard, _____ waste, and _____.

EXEMPLARY PERFORMANCE

Divert at least _____ percent of the ongoing _____ waste stream from _____ or incineration facilities.

1 pt.

RESPONSIBLE PARTY:

FACILITY MANAGER

MR Credit 7:

Solid Waste Management Ongoing Consumables

ANSWER KEY

PURPOSE

Reduce building **occupant** and building **operation** waste and **toxins** generated by ongoing **consumables** that is hauled to landfills and incineration facilities.

REQUIREMENTS

Divert **50 percent** of the ongoing consumable waste stream from landfills or incineration facilities, including at least **80 percent** of batteries. Verify diversion at least **once** a year.

The ongoing consumable material must include at a minimum: paper, **toner** cartridges, glass, plastics, **cardboard** and old corrugated cardboard, **food** waste, and **metals**.

EXEMPLARY PERFORMANCE

Divert at least **95 percent** of the ongoing **consumable** waste stream from **landfills** or incineration facilities.

Performance Period/Certification	MR Credit 8:
	Solid Waste Management Durable Goods

PURPOSE

Reduce building _____ and building _____ waste and _____ generated by durable _____ that is hauled to landfills and incineration facilities.

REQUIREMENTS

Divert _____ of the _____ goods waste stream from landfills or incineration facilities (by weight, volume, or _____ value) during the _____ period.

Office _____, appliances, external _____ adapters, televisions, and _____ equipment should be considered.

1 pt.

RESPONSIBLE PARTY:

FACILITY MANAGER

	MR Credit 8:
	Solid Waste Management Durable Goods

ANSWER KEY

PURPOSE

Reduce building **occupant** and building **operation** waste and **toxins** generated by durable **goods** that is hauled to landfills and incineration facilities.

REQUIREMENTS

Divert **75 percent** of the **durable** goods waste stream from landfills or incineration facilities (by weight, volume, or **replacement** value) during the **performance** period.

Office **equipment**, appliances, external **power** adapters, televisions, and **audiovisual** equipment should be considered.

Performance Period/Certification	MR Credit 9: Solid Waste Management Facility Alterations and Additions

PURPOSE

Divert _____ and _____ waste from landfills and incineration facilities and redirect the _____ material back into the _____ process or appropriate sites.

REQUIREMENTS

Divert _____ of facility alteration waste from landfills or incineration facilities (by _____) during the _____ period.

EXEMPLARY PERFORMANCE

Divert _____ of facility alteration waste from landfills or incineration facilities (by volume) during the _____ period.

1 pt.	RESPONSIBLE PARTY: FACILITY MANAGER

	MR Credit 9:
	Solid Waste Management Facility Alterations and Additions

ANSWER KEY

PURPOSE

Divert **construction** and **demolition** waste from landfills and incineration facilities and redirect the **reusable** material back into the **manufacturing** process or appropriate sites.

REQUIREMENTS

Divert **70 percent** of facility alteration waste from landfills or incineration facilities (by **volume**) during the **performance** period.

EXEMPLARY PERFORMANCE

Divert **95 percent** of facility alteration waste from landfills or incineration facilities (by volume) during the **performance** period.

CHAPTER 8

INDOOR ENVIRONMENTAL QUALITY

THIS CHAPTER FOCUSES ON THE ELEMENTS INVOLVED to improve the indoor environment as detailed in the Indoor Environmental Quality (EQ) category of the Leadership in Energy and Environmental Design (LEED®) for Existing Buildings: Operations & Maintenance™ (EBOM) rating system. Remember that Chapter 2 introduced the importance of interior spaces, since Americans typically spend about 90 percent of their time indoors, according to the Environmental Protection Agency (EPA). The EPA also reports conventionally designed, constructed, and maintained indoor environments have significantly higher levels of pollutants than the outdoors.[1] However, studies have shown that green buildings with an improved interior environmental quality "have the potential to enhance the lives of building occupants, increase their resale value of the building, and reduce the liability for building owners."[2] Because employee salaries and benefits are the biggest cost for a business, larger than operating costs for facilities, such as utilities, the satisfaction and health of the occupants should be a high priority. Retaining employees in order to avoid the additional costs of training new hires can help to add efficiencies to the economic bottom line for businesses. Reducing absenteeism because of health impacts increases productivity and reduces liability of inadequate indoor environmental quality. Businesses, such as Haworth, will enjoy a return on their investment for increasing their employee satisfaction by providing a comfortable work environment (see Figure 8.1).

It's time to pick a different color for flashcards created for EQ topics.

As a result, the LEED rating systems, through the EQ category, focus on the factors to improve occupant comfort and well-being that also benefit the environment, such as:[3]

■ Improve ventilation—to improve indoor air quality, and follow up with a survey of the occupants' satisfaction.

■ Manage air contaminants, such as environmental tobacco smoke (ETS), carbon dioxide (CO_2), and particulate matter.

■ Implement green cleaning—to improve water and air quality from the use of cleaning agents and pesticides.

■ Specify less harmful materials—watch those volatile organic compounds (VOC) levels for products such as paints, adhesives, composite wood products, carpets, and furniture.

■ Provide occupants with controls—to set their desired thermal comfort and lighting levels.

Figure 8.1 Addressing such factors as daylighting, views, and low-emitting materials, helps to bring value to the indoor environmental quality. *Photo courtesy of Haworth Inc.*

■ Provide occupants with daylight and views to the exterior environment to increase their productivity levels and reduce absenteeism and illness.

To help prepare for the exam, these concepts can be organized into the following three strategies:

1. Indoor air quality management

2. Occupant comfort

3. Green cleaning

Each of these strategies is referred to in the prerequisites and credits of the category, as shown in Table 8.1. Notice that all of the EQ credits are only worth

Create a flashcard to remember the three main strategies of the EQ category.

Table 8.1 The Indoor Environmental Quality Category

Timeframe	Prereq/ Credit	Title	Points
Plan	Prereq 1	Minimum Indoor Air Quality Performance	R
Program Development	Prereq 2	Environmental Tobacco Smoke (ETS) Control	R
Program Development	Prereq 3	Green Cleaning Policy	R
Program Development	Credit 1.1	Indoor Air Quality Best Management Practices – IAQ Management Program	1
Audit	Credit 1.2	Indoor Air Quality Best Management Practices – Outdoor Air Delivery Monitoring	1
Plan	Credit 1.3	Indoor Air Quality Best Management Practices – Increased Ventilation	1

Timeframe	Prereq/ Credit	Title	Points
Audit	Credit 1.4	Indoor Air Quality Best Management Practices – Reducing Particulates in Air Distribution	1
Plan	Credit 1.5	Indoor Air Quality Best Management Practices – IAQ Management for Facility Additions & Alterations	1
Performance Period / Certification	Credit 2.1	Occupant Comfort – Occupant Survey	1
Audit	Credit 2.2	Controllability of Systems – Lighting	1
Audit	Credit 2.3	Occupant Comfort – Thermal Comfort Monitoring	1
Audit	Credit 2.4	Daylight and Views	1
Program Development	Credit 3.1	Green Cleaning – High Performance Cleaning Program	1
Performance Period / Certification	Credit 3.2	Green Cleaning- Custodial Effectiveness Assessment	1
Performance Period / Certification	Credit 3.3	Green Cleaning – Purchase of Sustainable Cleaning Products and Materials	1
Performance Period / Certification	Credit 3.4	Green Cleaning– Sustainable Cleaning Equipment	1
Audit	Credit 3.5	Green Cleaning – Indoor Chemical and Pollutant Source Control	1
Performance Period / Certification	Credit 3.6	Green Cleaning – Indoor Integrated Pest Management	1

one point each and that Prerequisite 1 and Credit 1.5 are addressed during the planning stage, whereas most of the others are tackled during the performance period. Just as with the other categories, EQ provides opportunities to allow the team to set the pace with policy development and implementation and then pursue points for tracking their success during the performance period. Do not worry about remembering the exact credit name and number, but it is important to know which are credits versus prerequisites.

INDOOR AIR QUALITY MANAGEMENT

The *LEED Reference Guide for Green Building Operations & Maintenance* uses the American Society of Heating, Refrigerating, and Air-Conditioning Engineers' (ASHRAE's) definition for **indoor air quality** (IAQ) as it states it "is the nature of air inside the space that affects the health and well-being of building occupants."[4] Studies have shown that poor indoor air quality can lead to respiratory disease, allergies and asthma, and **sick building syndrome,** and can therefore impact the performance and productivity of employees. Assessing and managing indoor pollutants has become a major concern in the battle against sick building syndrome. If buildings are designed, operated, and maintained with the ability of providing a safe and healthy environment, building occupants will be more productive and have a greater sense of well-being.

Increasing ventilation may improve the overall IAQ, but it may increase the energy demand of heating, ventilation, and air-conditioning (HVAC) systems at the same time. Therefore, it is important to recognize that this category is about the occupants' well-being and not necessarily energy efficiency.

Project teams are encouraged to provide adequate ventilation for occupants without compromising energy use efficiencies, so as not to be a burden on the environment by contributing to the need for fossil fuels. Mechanical systems should work to thermally balance outdoor air with every air change; therefore, the key is to find the right balance. Too many air changes are wasteful and would impact economic and environmental bottom lines. However, too little ventilation can result in reduced quality of the indoor air, which would impact the health and satisfaction of occupants, thus also affecting the triple bottom line components. Existing buildings should also address any inefficiencies resulting from the lack of maintenance and repair. Teams should also look to heat recovery ventilation and/or economizing strategies to reduce a facility's energy demand.

The EBOM rating system addresses components from a triple bottom line perspective to improve air quality during alterations and operations to avoid effects on human health and to improve the quality of life. In order to achieve this, the rating system requires project teams to address IAQ in terms of ventilation rates, construction practices, and minimizing exposure of contaminants by prevention and segregation. These strategies are grouped together for discussion purposes and will not necessarily follow the order of the LEED scorecard.

IAQ Management Strategies in Relation to LEED Compliance

TIP Any time you see ASHRAE 62, think IAQ! Say it out loud IAQ 62, 62 IAQ! Whenever you see a prerequisite or a credit with IAQ in the title, most likely ASHRAE 62 will be the reference standard.

Project teams designing green buildings use the industry standard, **ASHRAE Standard 62.1, Ventilation for Acceptable for Indoor Air Quality**, to adequately and appropriately size mechanical systems that will deliver the proper amounts of outside air while balancing energy demands. ASHRAE 62 describes proper **ventilation rates,** or the "amount of air circulated through a space, measured in air changes per hour."[5]

EQ Prerequisite 1: Minimum Indoor Air Quality Performance. Just as with all the previous prerequisites described, this one sets a minimum level of performance required of all projects seeking LEED certification. The building engineer should refer to ASHRAE 62.1-2007 to establish the outdoor air ventilation rate to learn how the facility's outdoor air intakes, supply air fan, and/or ventilation needs to be modified to meet the referenced standards requirements. Each of the air-handling units will need to comply, with compliance proven by measurements. If the facility cannot meet the referenced standard's requirements, the facility will need to supply at least 10 cubic feet per minute (cfm) of outside air per person. In either case, the facility's exhaust systems, such as bathroom, shower, kitchen and parking locations will need to be tested for proper functioning of the fan's speed, voltage, control sequences, and set points. An HVAC maintenance program will also need to be developed and implemented to include the following:[6]

- Visual inspections of outdoor air vents and dampers to remove obstructions and contaminants

- Regularly scheduled replacement or cleaning of air filters

- Regular cleaning

- Cooling tower management

- Testing and balancing

Create a flashcard to remember the five components of an HVAC maintenance program.

If the building has natural ventilation strategies, the building engineer would consult paragraph 5.1 of ASHRAE 62.1 in order to determine the compliance requirements (see Figure 8.2). "All naturally ventilated spaces must be within 25 feet of (and permanently open to) operable wall or roof openings to the outdoors; the openable area also must be at least 4 percent of the space's net occupiable floor area."[7] Should any interior spaces not have access to outdoor openings, these spaces can comply if they are ventilated through an adjoining room by the means of an unobstructed opening and at least 8 percent or 25 square feet of the area is free.

EQ Credit 1.3: Indoor Air Quality Management Practices - Increased Ventilation. Building off of EQ Prerequisite 1, project teams with mechanical or mixed-mode ventilation systems must increase the outdoor air supply to exceed ASHRAE 62.1, the referenced standard, by at least 30 percent in order to meet the intentions of this credit. For naturally ventilated project types, the teams are directed to comply with the Carbon Trust's "Good Practice Guide 237." They will also need to complete the air flow diagram process of Figure 1.18 as detailed in the Chartered Institution of Building Services Engineers (CIBSE) Applications Manual 10:2005, Natural Ventilation in Nondomestic Buildings. The building engineer has two compliance paths from which to choose. Option 1 requires diagrams and calculations to prove the strategy's effectiveness and compliance with the referenced standards, while option 2 requires an analytic model proving compliance with ASHRAE 62.1-2007, Chapter 6, for at least 90 percent of the occupied spaces. For the purposes of the exam, be sure to know how to comply for each ventilation type, but not necessarily the details required to prove compliance, such as the details of the diagrams and calculations of CIBSE and the Good Practice Guide 237 for naturally ventilated buildings.

 Create a flashcard to remember the three referenced standards for EQ Credit 1.3.

EQ Prerequisite 2: Environmental Tobacco Smoke (ETS) Control. Commercial project teams have a couple of options from which to choose in order to comply with this prerequisite, depending on the use of the project. Compliance with option 1 requires smoking to be prohibited in the building, and if smoking will be allowed on site, an area must be designated that is at least 25 feet away from any building

Figure 8.2 Providing operable windows offers building occupants access to means of adequate ventilation. *Photo courtesy of Gary Neuenswander, Utah Agricultural Experiment Station*

entrances, outdoor air intakes, and operable windows. Option 2 allows teams to permit smoking within the building, but only in designated areas. These areas must be separately exhausted to the outdoors, so they do not contaminate other areas in the building. Although periodic testing is required, the designated areas must be able to contain, capture, and remove ETS. The rooms shall be enclosed with impermeable deck-to-deck partitions. Just as with option 1, if smoking will be allowed on site, an area must be designated that is at least 25 feet away from any building entrances, outdoor air intakes, and operable windows.

Residential and mixed-use projects must prohibit smoking in all common areas within the building and provide periodic air testing. All exterior doors and operable windows must be weather-stripped. All penetrations between units and vertical chases must be sealed to minimize contamination. Blower door tests must be conducted in accordance with ANSI/ASTM E779-03, Standard Test Method for Determining Air Leakage Rate by Fan Pressurization for residential units to prove successful sealing. Teams must follow the California Residential Alternative Calculation Method Approval Manual for the progressive sampling methodology to demonstrate the residential units have less than 1.25 square inches of leakage area per 100 square feet of enclosure area. Continuing with the requirements mentioned for options 1 and 2, where smoking will be allowed outdoors, an area must be designated that is at least 25 feet away from any building entrances, outdoor air intakes, and operable windows.

EQ Credit 1.1: Indoor Air Quality Best Management Practices – Indoor Air Quality Management Program. Project teams will need to develop an IAQ management program based on the EPA's **Indoor [air quality] Building Education and Assessment Model (I-BEAM).** This program will need to be implemented on an ongoing basis. An IAQ manager will need to conduct an IAQ audit to determine the building's status, including the basic conditions, using I-BEAM to diagnose and correct common IAQ problems, such as remodeling and renovations, painting, pest control, and shipping and receiving for vehicle contaminants. The program should also address how to log occupant complaints for effective communication and correction.

EQ Credit 1.2: Indoor Air Quality Best Management Practices – Outdoor Air Delivery Monitoring. The building engineer will need to develop a strategy to include carbon dioxide (CO_2) sensors to ensure that minimum requirements are maintained to help promote occupant comfort and well-being. The strategy must include outdoor airflow measurement devices capable of determining the minimum outdoor airflow rate under all operating conditions. Mechanically ventilated buildings should have permanently installed monitors in at least 80 percent of the building's total outdoor air intake flow to detect a 15 percent variation from the design minimum outdoor air rate as required by ASHRAE Standard 62.1. Should the mechanical system predominately serve **densely occupied spaces** (25 people per 1,000 square feet), each of these spaces will need a CO_2 sensor to compare the results with the outdoor ambient CO_2 concentrations. Naturally ventilated facilities will need to locate CO_2 sensors in every densely occupied room and within every naturally ventilated space. The sensors will need to generate an alarm (visual or audible) if the CO_2 levels are greater than 530 ppm (or 1,000 ppm absolute) above outdoor CO_2 levels. For either project type, all monitors shall be calibrated to meet the manufacturer's recommendations.

Note this is the only prerequisite or credit that does *not* permit a 10 percent floor area exemption for multi-tenant buildings, even if they are under separate management.

Create a flashcard to remember the referenced standard for EQ Credit 1.1.

Be sure to remember that CO_2 sensors must be located between 3 and 6 feet above the floor in the **breathing zone.** CO_2 concentrations greater than 530 parts per million (ppm) as compared to exterior environments indicate inadequate ventilation and are typically harmful to occupants.

EQ Credit 1.4: Indoor Air Quality Best Management Practices – Reducing Particulates in Air Distribution. The building will need to employ **Minimum Efficiency Reporting Value (MERV) filters** at each outside air intake and inside air recirculation returns. The rating of MERV filters ranges from 1 (lowest) to 16 (highest), where this LEED credit requires a minimum of MERV 13 filters to be implemented and maintained for compliance (see Figure 8.3).

EQ Credit 1.5: Indoor Air Quality Best Management Practices – Indoor Air Quality Management for Facility and Alterations. The team will need to create and execute an IAQ management plan for facility alterations (including tenant improvements) and additions to address the construction and occupancy phases. An accredited professional or organization is required to oversee the construction IAQ management plan. A professional could include a certified industrial hygienist, professional engineer, or environmental consultant, whereas a qualifying organization would need to be ISO 9001 or ISO 17075 certified.

During facility additions and alterations, an IAQ management plan must be implemented to detail how the construction team will address the SMACNA guidelines during renovations, including tenant improvements. The plan must include the strategies for the five **Sheet Metal and Air Conditioning Contractors' National Association (SMACNA)** aspects: heating, ventilation, and air-conditioning (HVAC) protection, source control, pathway interruption, housekeeping, and scheduling (see Figure 8.4). The plan will also need to require any air handlers that are used during the construction phase to have a minimum of a MERV 8 filter at each return air grille to protect the ductwork. The filtration media must be replaced after construction.

To address source control measures, contractors need to be mindful of reducing contaminants or blocking them from entering the indoor environment, including mechanical systems, to deliver an environment with better air quality. Contaminants include **volatile organic compounds (VOCs)**, carbon dioxide, particulates, and tobacco smoke. SMACNA guidelines include source control

 Create flashcard to remember MERV and 1–16 range of filters, where 16 allows the least amount of particulates to pass through.

 Create a flashcard to remember the the two different qualifying ISO certifications.

Figure 8.3 Installing MERV 13 filters or better will help to improve the indoor air quality by eliminating dust and particles. *Photo courtesy of Auld & White Constructors, LLC*

Figure 8.4 SMACNA-compliant practices include sealing off ductwork from dust and particulates.

 Create a flashcard to remember the 5 SMACNA control measures: HVAC protection, source control, pathway interruption, housekeeping, and scheduling.

 TIP Remember, Credit 1.4: IAQ Best Management Practices – Reducing Particulates in Air Distribution requires a minimum of a MERV 13 filter, and to comply with this credit, a MERV 8 filter must be installed during construction and prior to occupancy. If needed, make a flashcard to remember the minimum MERV filters required for which credit. It might help that Credit 1.5 requires a MERV filter with a value of 5 less than the previous credit.

 Create a flashcard to remember the two prerequisites and five credits that address IAQ improvement strategies.

measures that recommend VOCs from furniture, paints, adhesives, and carpets should be kept below defined maximum levels to avoid polluting the indoor environment. As discussed in the previous chapter, industry standards, such as Green Seal (for paints, coatings, adhesives, etc.), South Coast Air Quality Management District (SCAQMD) (for sealants), the Carpet and Rug Institute (CRI), and the FloorScore™ Program specify the maximum levels of VOCs, in grams per liter (g/L), not to be exceeded. Other standards, such as GREENGUARD and Scientific Certification Systems (SCS) Indoor Advantage, certify products, such as furniture, that do not off-gas harmful levels of pollutants.

The SMACNA guidelines also recommend good housekeeping practices during construction, to protect absorptive materials from moisture damage to later prevent the growth of toxic substances, such as mold. These materials, such as drywall, acoustic ceiling tiles, and carpet, should be stored in dry, elevated, and protected areas to avoid their coming into contact with liquids (see Figure 8.5).

The other requirement for teams to earn this point is that they must conduct a building **flush-out** to eliminate any pollutants in the air caused by construction processes and activities. The mechanical system is to be flushed out with 14,000 cubic feet of outside air per square foot to remove residual contaminants prior to occupancy. The key to comply is to maintain an internal temperature of at least 60° F and for the relative humidity not to exceed 60 percent within the building. If the schedule does not permit project teams to complete the latter or if occupancy is desired, they could also comply if at least 3,500 cubic feet of outside air per square foot is delivered prior to occupancy and then once the space is occupied, ventilation is started three hours prior to occupancy each day and is continued during occupancy at a rate of 0.30 cubic feet per minute (cfm) per square foot.

Figure 8.5 Elevating product storage protects against damage as suggested by SMACNA guidelines.

QUIZ TIME!

Q8.1. All naturally ventilated spaces must be within _____ feet of (and permanently open to) operable wall or roof openings to the outdoors; the openable area also must be at least _____ of the space's net occupiable floor area. (Choose one)

  A. 10 feet; 1 percent

  B. 25 feet; 4 percent

  C. 10 feet; 4 percent

  D. 25 feet; 1 percent

Q8.2. Which of the following statements are not true? (Choose two)

  A. All of the EQ credits are worth one point.

  B. There are two prerequisites within the EQ category.

  C. Although there are prerequisites within the EQ category, project teams only have to comply with at least one in order to pursue certification.

  D. EQ prerequisites and credits intend to improve occupant well-being and comfort and, therefore, productivity as well.

  E. EQ credits may compensate the energy efficiency of the project, but they will improve the indoor air quality.

Q8.3. What percentage above ASHRAE 62.1 must the mechanical engineer increase the ventilation rate in order to comply with

EQ Credit 1.3: Indoor Air Quality Best Management Practices – Increased Ventilation? (Choose one)

A. 5 percent

B. 10 percent

C. 20 percent

D. 30 percent

E. 0 percent, the team only has to meet the reference standard requirements

Q8.4. What is considered a densely occupied area? (Choose one)

A. At least 10 people per 100 square feet

B. At least 25 people per 1,000 square feet

C. At least 25 people per 10,000 square feet

D. At least 25 people per 500 square feet

E. At least 15 people per 1,000 square feet

Q8.5. In order to comply with EQ Credit 1.2: Indoor Air Quality Best Management Practices – Outdoor Air Delivery Monitoring, what should the alarm set points be set to? (Choose one)

A. +/– 1 percent

B. +/– 3 percent

C. +/– 5 percent

D. +/– 10 percent

E. +/– 15 percent

Q8.6. The range of MERV filters is which of the following? (Choose one)

A. 1–30

B. 0–50

C. 1–110

D. 1–16

E. 1–100

Q8.7. How many cubic feet of outdoor air per square foot of floor area must be delivered prior to occupancy to comply with the flush-out requirements of EQ Credit 1.5: Indoor Air Quality Management Best Management Practices – Indoor Air Quality Management for Facility Additions and Alterations? (Choose one)

A. 14,000

B. 10,000

C. 3,500

D. 500

E. 1,000

Q8.8. What is the maximum humidity level and minimum temperature to comply with the flush-out requirements of EQ

Credit 1.5: Indoor Air Quality Management Best Management Practices – Indoor Air Quality Management for Facility Additions and Alterations? (Choose one)

A. 60 percent humidity; 60°

B. 80 percent humidity; 20°

C. 20 percent humidity; 80°

D. 50 percent humidity; 50°

E. 40 percent humidity; 40°

Q8.9. At what rate must the space be ventilated in order for the newly renovated space to be occupied prior to the delivery of the required total outdoor air volume, to be in accordance with EQ Credit 1.5: Indoor Air Quality Management Best Management Practices – Indoor Air Quality Management for Facility Additions and Alterations? (Choose one)

A. 0.30 cfm per square foot of outdoor air

B. 1.30 cfm per square foot of outdoor air

C. 3.0 cfm per square foot of outdoor air

D. 30.0 cfm per square foot of outdoor air

Q8.10. Which of the following is not required by SMACNA standards? (Choose one)

A. Source control

B. Housekeeping

C. HVAC protection

D. Air quality testing

E. Scheduling

Q8.11. CO_2 concentrations above _____ ppm typically indicate inadequate ventilation? (Choose one)

A. 800

B. 1,000

C. 100

D. 530

E. 10,000

Q8.12. A project team has learned the facility will not be able to meet the requirements of ASHRAE 62.1 to be in compliance with EQ Prerequisite 1: Minimum Indoor Air Quality Performance because of the limitations of the current HVAC system. In order to still pursue certification, how much air must the ventilation system supply? (Choose one)

A. 10 cfm per person

B. 100 cfm per person

C. 30 percent more than the referenced standard

D. 20 percent more than the referenced standard

E. 30 cfm per person

Q8.13. Which of the following standards should teams refer to when developing an IAQ Management Program to comply with EQ Credit 1.1: IAQ Best Management Practices – IAQ Management Program? (Choose one)

A. GREENGUARD

B. ASHRAE 62.1

C. I-BEAM

D. SMACNA

E. ENERGY STAR

Q8.14. Which of the following qualifies to oversee a construction IAQ management plan to be in compliance with EQ Credit 1.5: Indoor Air Quality Management Best Management Practices – Indoor Air Quality Management for Facility Additions and Alterations? (Choose three)

A. ISO 9001 certified organization

B. Certified industrial hygienist

C. Licensed general contractor

D. LEED Accredited Professional

E. Professional engineer

F. LEED Green Associate

G. LEED Fellow

Q.8.15. If smoking is going to be allowed onsite, what is the minimum distance to designate smoking areas from building entrances, air intakes, and any operable windows in order to comply with EQ Prerequisite 2: ETS Control? (Choose one)

A. 10 feet

B. 15 feet

C. 20 feet

D. 25 feet

E. 50 feet

OCCUPANT COMFORT

As previously mentioned, improving the occupants' comfort can have a beneficial impact on the bottom line. Not only will their productivity levels increase, but the facility will also run more efficiently, resulting in an economic savings. For the purposes of LEED and the project's bottom line, facilities should address comfort in terms of controllability and access to daylight and views.

Occupant controls can be implemented for thermal comfort and/or lighting levels. In order to determine how a facility should address occupant controls for either of these components, the facility manager should conduct an occupant survey as the first step. A survey will help determine an areas for corrective action in which adding controls may resolve.

Although temperature settings should vary with the seasons, buildings should allow occupants to control their thermal conditions to optimize satisfaction and

> **TIP** Any time you see ASHRAE 55, think THERMAL COMFORT. What do you think of when you see ASHRAE 62?

comfort. Remember, occupants who are satisfied and comfortable tend to be more productive! The *Green Building and LEED Core Concepts Guide* defines **thermal comfort** as "the temperature, humidity, and airflow ranges within which the majority of people are most comfortable, as determined by **ASHRAE Standard 55-2004**."[8] ASHRAE 55 indicates that there are four environmental factors that impact thermal comfort determined by the building design: humidity, air speed, air temperature, and radiant temperature. For the purposes of LEED, occupants must be able to control one of the four components of thermal comfort in order to comply with the control strategy.

The EBOM rating system addresses lighting in terms of naturally available daylight and artificially supplied light. When debating whether to incorporate daylighting strategies, project teams are advised to conduct a life-cycle cost analysis to determine the up-front costs and operational savings. For example, when using daylighting strategies, sensors could be installed to trigger alternative light sources when needed, which would impact up-front costs, although the costs can be offset by the energy saved during operations since less artificial light would be required. Daylighting can also result in improved occupant satisfaction and health because access and connection to the exterior environment, also affecting the economic bottom line over time (see Figure 8.6).

Create a flashcard to remember the four environmental factors of thermal comfort defined by ASHRAE 55. Personal factors include metabolic rate, clothing, and preferences.

Besides daylighting, providing occupants with the ability to control their lighting needs can also benefit the triple bottom line. For example, occupant-controlled lighting contributes to employee satisfaction, as well as productivity as light levels can be altered for specific tasks, needs, and preferences (see Figure 8.7). Therefore, providing overall ambient light, as well as individual task lighting, is the best strategy to address lighting needs. Facilities can also see a reduction in energy usage for lighting needs by educating employees on the benefits of turning off fixtures after use.

Occupant Comfort in Relation to LEED Compliance

EQ Credit 2.1: Occupant Comfort – Occupant Survey. Facility managers will need to conduct an anonymous occupant survey at least once during the performance period to learn of the overall satisfaction of the occupant comfort levels of the majority of the occupants to determine areas for improvement. The survey should address thermal comfort, acoustics, IAQ, lighting levels, and building cleanliness and have a plan for corrective action. If 20 percent or more of the respondents are dissatisfied with the building conditions, corrective action is required. The survey should represent at least 30 percent of the regular building occupants as project teams can randomly select a representative sample. The survey shall provide a seven-point scale in which the respondents can select from to rate the 5 comfort criteria. Although one survey is required during the performance period, an ongoing surveying program is required to comply with this credit.

Create a flashcard to remember examples of corrective action: HVAC control adjustments (temperature, schedule modes), diffuser airflow adjustments, solar control, acoustical and lighting modifications, and investigation.

Create a flashcard to remember the five comfort criteria an occupant survey should address.

TIP What other credit refers to the calculation to determine a random sample size for surveys?

EQ Credit 2.2: Controllability of Systems – Lighting. Project teams will need to provide lighting controls for at least 50 percent of the building occupants for at least 50 percent of the individual workstations and for at least 50 percent of all shared multioccupant spaces (see Figure 8.8). Projects that employ 95 percent of building occupants with lighting controls in both individual workstations and multioccupant spaces could be eligible to pursue exemplary performance under the Innovation in Operations (IO) category. Teams should inform occupants

Figure 8.6 Daylighting strategies can help to improve occupant satisfaction and productivity, as long as glare control components, such as these interior roller shades, are implemented as well. *Photo courtesy of Lutron Electronics Co., Inc.*

 Create a flashcard to remember the definition of **relative humidity**: "the ratio of partial density of airborne water vapor to the saturation density of water vapor at the same temperature and total pressure."[9]

about the new controls and how to use them. Nonoccupied spaces, such as closets, are exempt from the calculations.

EQ Credit 2.3: Occupancy Comfort, Thermal Comfort Monitoring. In order to ensure thermal comfort criteria is in accordance with ASHRAE 55, the building engineer will need to implement a continuous and permanent monitoring system to examine air temperature and **relative humidity** every 15 minutes. At least one air temperature sensor is required within each HVAC zone and at least one humidity sensor is required within each humidity zone. Sensors must

Figure 8.7 Providing occupants with task lighting allows for more individual control of work environments to improve their satisfaction and productivity. *Photo courtesy of Skylar Nielson, 3Form*

be located between 4 and 72 inches above the finish floor to comply. Periodic testing of air speed and radiant temperature will also need to be conducted in occupied spaces using hand held meters or other monitoring equipment. Alarms are required to signify when the system is out of alignment with the thermal comfort criteria and needs adjustment and/or repair.

EQ Credit 2.4: Daylight and Views. Teams must provide at least 50 percent of regularly occupied areas with daylight illumination (see Figure 8.9) or they can provide a direct line of sight to the exterior environment from 45 percent of regularly occupied areas and still earn this point. Projects are eligible for an Exemplary Performance point under the IO category if they achieve 75 percent daylighting in regularly occupied areas *and* provide 90 percent of regularly occupied areas with a direct line of sight to the outdoors.

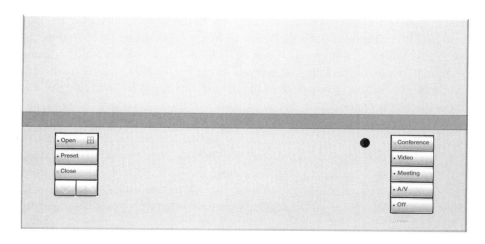

Figure 8.8 Lighting controls should not only include various lighting options to increase productivity but also incorporate daylighting and shading options. *Photo courtesy of Lutron Electronics Co., Inc.*

Figure 8.9 Providing interior environments with access to natural daylight not only improves the occupant's satisfaction and productivity levels but also helps to reduce the need for artificial lighting to reduce operating costs. *Photo courtesy of Steelcase, Inc.*

 Remember, building orientation and passive design strategies impact the opportunity to utilize daylighting as an ambient light source. There is a direct relationship between the amount of **vision glazing** (glazing between 30 and 90 inches above the floor) provided and the access to daylight and views.

 TIP Project teams should design the overall illumination light level to be about 40–60 footcandles on an office work surface.

TIP For private offices, all of the square footage may count toward credit compliance if 75 percent or more has a view to the exterior. This concept cannot be applied to multioccupant areas, as only the actual square footage compliant can be included in the calculations to achieve the minimum percentage threshold.

 Create a flashcard to remember the four credits that address occupant comfort.

The most important factor for teams to address is consistent across both compliance path options for this credit: **glare control**. This strategy is important to address because avoiding it can hinder the productivity and comfort of the building occupants. Solar heat gain is another factor for teams to consider and address as it directly impacts energy efficiency. Different types of glass perform in different ways depending on how much light is reflected, absorbed, and transmitted. **Transmitted light, or T_{vis},** and the amount of light absorbed impacts solar heat gain. For daylighting purposes, it is best to select glazing with a high T_{vis} to allow for the most amount of incident light to pass through the glazing. Therefore, project teams are challenged to find the balance between solar heat gain and T_{vis}.

Daylighting. Project teams can choose whether to pursue a performance-based or a prescriptive-based compliance path. The performance-based option includes a computer simulation demonstrating footcandle (fc) levels between 25 and 500 provided by daylight for the applicable spaces. The prescriptive path involves completing calculations to show compliance depending on top-lighting daylighting zones (using skylights) and side-lighting daylighting zones (using windows or glass doors). Top-lighting daylight strategies must include skylights with a minimum 0.5 **visible light transmittance (VLT)** for at least 3 to 6 percent of the roof area, and the distance between the skylights must not be more than 1.4 times the ceiling height. Only glazing areas 30 inches above the floor can be included in side-lighting daylight calculations. In this zone, the window-to-floor ratio (WFR) multiplied by the VLT must be between 0.150 and 0.180 in order to comply with the requirements of this option. A third option is available for teams wishing to measure the actual light levels in the applicable spaces and a fourth option can be pursued to show compliance with this credit by combining of any of the three other options.

Views. Project teams will need to provide 90 percent of the regularly occupied areas with views to the exterior by the means of vision glazing in order to meet the requirements of this credit (see Figure 8.10). Remember, **vision glazing** is the glass from 30 inches to 90 inches above the floor. Project teams will need to upload a plan view to show all of the perimeter glazing and a section view to depict the line of sight from the regularly occupied area to the perimeter glazing with the line of sight at 42 inches above the floor.

Figure 8.10 Connecting the interior and exterior environments helped the Nulhegan Administrative Building in Brunswick, Vermont, earn Silver certification under the LEED for Existing Buildings, version 2.0 rating system. *Photo courtesy of Liz Dawson of U.S. Fish and Wildlife Service*

QUIZ TIME!

Q8.16. When addressing thermal comfort, which two of the following are not addressed? (Choose two)

  A. Humidity

  B. Ventilation requirements

  C. Air movement

  D. Artificial light

  E. Average temperature

Q8.17. An Environmental Tobacco Smoke Control policy *best* addresses which of the following? (Choose one)

  A. Providing ventilation requirements to effectively remove tobacco smoke

  B. Providing dedicated smoking rooms 25 feet away from building entrances

  C. Preventing tobacco smoke from contaminating indoor environments

  D. Preventing tobacco smoke from entering the air occupied by nonsmokers

Q8.18. An occupant survey should account for at least _____ percent of the regular building occupants? (Choose one)

  A. 10

  B. 90

  C. 70

  D. 30

  E. 50

Q8.19. What is the minimum percentage of occupants that must have lighting controls in order to comply with EQ Credit 2.2: Controllability of Systems – Lighting? (Choose one)

  A. 10 percent

  B. 25 percent

  C. 90 percent

D. 50 percent

E. 75 percent

Q8.20. What is vision glazing? (Choose one)

A. Glazing between 30 and 60 inches from the floor

B. Glazing between 30 and 90 inches from the floor

C. Glazing between 60 and 90 inches from the floor

D. Glazing below 30 inches

E. Glazing above 60 inches

Q8.21. What is the most common failure of daylighting strategies? (Choose one)

A. Shallow floorplates

B. Interior color schemes

C. Shading devices

D. Glare control

Q8.22. Which of the following are qualifying strategies to control glare? (Choose three)

A. Blinds

B. Louvers

C. Interior light shelves

D. Reflective glazing

E. Building orientation

F. Lower ceiling heights

Q8.23. In addition to addressing light levels, what are other strategies are to be considered when design for daylighting? (Choose three)

A. Photovoltaic system energy contribution

B. Direct beam penetration

C. Integration with the electric lighting system

D. Mechanical heat and cooling

E. Interior color schemes

Q8.24. At what height is the line of sight drawn in section view in order to comply with EQ Credit 2.4: Daylight and Views? (Choose one)

A. 30 inches

B. 32 inches

C. 34 inches

D. 36 inches

E. 42 inches

Q8.25. Which one of the following most closely represents an appropriate level of overall illumination on an office work surface, including daylighting, ambient artificial lighting, and task lighting? (Choose one)

A. 1–2 footcandles

B. 5–10 footcandles

C. 15–25 footcandles

D. 40–60 footcandles

E. 75–120 footcandles

F. 150–200 footcandles

GREEN CLEANING

Think about the chemicals you smell after a space is "cleaned." What kind of health impacts do they pose on building occupants and maintenance personnel? What happens when those chemicals evaporate into the atmosphere or are disposed of and introduced into the waste stream? What kind of detriments do they have on water and air quality or aquatic ecology? It is for these reasons the EBOM rating system encourages project teams to address hazardous chemical, biological and particulate contaminants from building finishes and systems that impact air quality, human health, and the environment. This not only includes the products used but the equipment as well.

Green Cleaning in Relation to LEED Compliance

EQ Prerequisite 1: Green Cleaning Policy. Just as with most other prerequisites in the rating system, the owner will need to develop and execute a green cleaning policy that sets the standard for the following purchasing and operating procedures:

- Procurement of cleaning products and equipment in accordance with EQ Credit 3.3 and EQ Credit 3.4

- Operating strategies for effective cleaning that will be executed, coordinated, and audited

- Means to improve hand hygiene

- Guidelines for handling and storage of cleaning chemicals, including spill accidents

- Training and staffing requirements

- Continuous surveys and audits

   EQ Credit 3.1: Green Cleaning – High Performance Cleaning Program. Develop a program to set standards for the building and site (tenant spaces not required) for the following:

- Staffing plan

- Training of the operations and maintenance personnel

- Chemical use for concentrates and dilution

- Use of cleaning products and equipment in accordance with EQ Credit 3.3 and EQ Credit 3.4

   EQ Credit 3.2: Green Cleaning – Custodial Effectiveness Assessment. This credit requires the completion of an Association of Physical Plant Administrators

Create a flashcard to remember the credit synergies of EQ Prerequisite 1 and EQ Credit 3.1; both refer to EQ Credits 3.3 and 3.4.

Notice EQ Credit 3.1 only requires the program to be created and does not require it to be implemented with the performance tracked.

(APPA) "Custodial Staffing Guidelines" audit and should be carried out be an independent party to avoid biased results. The guidelines assess custodial effectiveness will need to result in a score of 3 or less to comply. Audits should be conducted annually with a plan for corrective action. Should a facility earn a score of 2 or less, the team can pursue an exemplary point under the IO category.

EQ Credit 3.3: Green Cleaning – Purchase of Sustainable Cleaning Products and Materials. Whereas the previous two credits required a program to be developed, this credit requires a purchasing program be implemented to track its success. During the performance period, should 30 percent of total annual purchases meet at least one of the following criteria, the team is eligible to pursue one point. They can pursue another point under the IO category for exemplary performance should 60 percent of the total annual purchases meet at least one of the following criteria during the performance period. Just as with the previous chapter, project teams can use the weighted value of products.

Green Cleaning Products (see Figure 8.11):[10]

- Green Seal GS-37, for general-purpose, bathroom, glass, and carpet cleaners used for industrial and institutional purposes
- Environmental Choice CCD-110, for cleaning and degreasing compounds
- Environmental Choice CCD-146, for hard surface cleaners
- Environmental Choice CCD-148, for carpet and upholstery care

Disinfectants, metal polish, floor finishes, strippers, or other products not addressed by the above standards:[11]

- Green Seal GS-40, for industrial and institutional floor care products
- Environmental Choice CCD-112, for digestion additives for cleaning and odor control
- Environmental Choice CCD-113, for drain or grease traps additives
- Environmental Choice CCD-115, for odor control additives
- Environmental Choice CCD-147, for hard floor care
- California Code of Regulations maximum allowable VOC levels for the specific product category

Figure 8.11 Requiring the use of green cleaning products will ensure that no harmful chemicals are used to contaminate the air. *Image courtesy of Absolute Green*

Figure 8.12 Using sustainable paper products can help preserve raw materials for future generations. *Image courtesy of Absolute Green*

Disposable janitorial paper products and trash bags (see Figure 8.12):[12]

■ Environmental Protection Agency (EPA) Comprehensive Procurement Guidelines for Janitorial Paper and Plastic Trash Can Liners

■ Green Seal GS-09, for paper towels and napkins

■ Green Seal GS-01, for tissue paper

■ Environmental Choice CCD-082, for toilet tissue

■ Environmental Choice CCD-086, for hand towels

■ Janitorial paper products derived from rapidly renewable resources or made from treefree fibers

Hand soaps meet 1 or more of the following standards:[13]

■ No antimicrobial agents (other than as a preservative), except where required by health codes and other regulations (e.g., food service and health care requirements)

■ Green Seal GS-41, for industrial and institutional hand cleaners

■ Environmental Choice CCD-104, for hand cleaners and hand soaps

EQ Credit 3.4: Green Cleaning – Sustainable Cleaning Equipment. Just as with the previous credit, a program needs to be implemented in order to earn this 1-point credit. This program specifically relates to janitorial equipment purchased during the performance period. All purchases must comply with the following criteria, but that does not imply the equipment in use (previously purchased) must comply in order to pursue this credit. Only 20 percent of the equipment in use must be in accordance with the following:[14]

■ Vacuum cleaners are certified by the Carpet and Rug Institute "Green Label" Testing Program for vacuum cleaners and operate with a sound level of less than 70 dBA.

■ Carpet extraction equipment used for restorative deep cleaning is certified by the Carpet and Rug Institute's "Seal of Approval" Testing Program for deep-cleaning extractors.

- Powered floor maintenance equipment, including electric and battery-powered floor buffers and burnishers, is equipped with vacuums, guards, and/or other devices for capturing fine particulates and operates with a sound level of less than 70 dBA.

- Propane-powered floor equipment has high-efficiency, low-emission engines with catalytic converters and mufflers that meet the California Air Resources Board (CARB) or Environmental Protection Agency (EPA) standards for the specific engine size and operate with a sound level of less than 90 dBA.

- Automated scrubbing machines are equipped with variable-speed feed pumps and on-board chemical metering to optimize the use of cleaning fluids. Alternatively, the scrubbing machines use only tap water with no added cleaning products.

- Battery-powered equipment is equipped with environmentally preferable gel batteries.

- Powered equipment is ergonomically designed to minimize vibration, noise and user fatigue.

- Equipment is designed with safeguards, such as rollers or rubber bumpers, to reduce potential damage to building surfaces.

The facility manager shall document all existing equipment, log all purchases and the sustainability criteria met, and track any repair and maintenance for any new and existing cleaning equipment.

EQ Credit 3.5: Green Cleaning – Indoor Chemical and Pollutant Source Control. Project teams will need to comply with two strategies in order to earn this credit. First, all regularly used entrances must employ an **entryway system** that is at least 10 feet long in the primary direction of travel to reduce the amount of dirt and contaminants from entering the building (see Figure 8.13). Second, the team must ensure containment is provided for any hazardous materials to be

Figure 8.13 Implementing grate entryway systems, such as this one at the Waterfront Tech Center in Camden, New Jersey, contributes to earning EQ Credit 5: Indoor Chemical & Pollutant Source Control. *Image courtesy of Stephen Martorana, LEED AP BD+C of the NJ Economic Development Authority*

properly disposed of and separate drains where the mixing of hazardous materials occurs for laboratory purposes.

QUIZ TIME!

Q8.26. An existing facility is pursuing EQ Credit 3.3: Green Cleaning – Purchase of Sustainable Cleaning Products and Materials. The team has documented that 34.5 percent of their cleaning products meet the requirements of Environmental Choice CCD-110, 15 percent of their paper products are Environmental Choice – CCD-082 certified, and 26.2 percent of their hand soap purchases meet the requirements of the California Code of Regulations for biodegradable products. How many points is the team eligible to pursue? (Choose one)

   A. 1
   B. 2
   C. 3
   D. 4
   E. None

Q8.27. Which of the following best describes the LEED strategy applicable to ASHRAE Standard 62.1-2007? (Choose one)

   A. Exterior lighting levels
   B. Thermal comfort by the means of controllability of systems
   C. Environmental tobacco smoke (ETS) control
   D. Ventilation and indoor air quality
   E. Building flush-out parameters and guidelines

Q8.28. Which of the following are standards teams should refer to when creating a purchasing plan? (Choose two)

   A. I-BEAM
   B. Green Seal
   C. Environmental Choice
   D. ASHRAE
   E. APPA

Q8.29. Which of the following have opportunities for exemplary performance? (Choose four)

   A. EQ Prerequisite 1: Minimum IAQ Performance
   B. EQ Credit 3.3: Green Cleaning – Purchase of Sustainable Cleaning Products and Materials
   C. EQ Credit 2.2: Controllability of Systems – Lighting
   D. EQ Credit 3.2: Green Cleaning – Custodial Effectiveness Assessment
   E. EQ Credit 1.1: IAQ Best Management Practices – IAQ Management Program
   F. EQ Credit 2.4: Daylight and Views

Q8.30. To which standards should engineers design the ventilation systems for a LEED project? (Choose two)

A. ASHRAE 55

B. California Air Resources Board

C. ASHRAE 62.1

D. ASHRAE 90.1

E. ASTM 44

Q8.31. Which of the following strategies have proven to increase productivity and occupant satisfaction in green buildings? (Choose two)

A. Providing access to daylight

B. Selecting a site adjacent to a shopping center

C. Improving indoor air quality

D. Implementing a recycling program

E. Offering incentives for carpooling

Q8.32. Which of the following reference standard should be used when conducting a custodial effectiveness assessment? (Choose one)

A. ASHRAE 62.1

B. ENERGY STAR

C. I-BEAM

D. APPA

E. ASHRAE 55

Q8.33. Where must sensors be located in order to comply with the requirements of EQ Credit 2.3: Occupant Comfort – Thermal Comfort Monitoring? (Choose one)

A. Above 72 inches

B. Between 4 and 72 inches from the floor

C. Between 30 and 60 inches from the floor

D. Above 60 inches from the floor

E. Below 30 inches

Q8.34. Which of the following credits are referenced as part of EQ Prerequisite 3: Green Cleaning Policy and EQ Credit 3.1: Green Cleaning – High Performance Cleaning Program? (Choose two)

A. EQ Credit 3.2: Green Cleaning – Custodial Effectiveness Assessment

B. EQ Credit 3.3: Green Cleaning – Purchase of Sustainable Cleaning Products and Materials

C. EQ Credit 3.4: Green Cleaning – Sustainable Cleaning Equipment

D. EQ Credit 3.5: Green Cleaning – Indoor Chemical and Pollutant Source Control

E. EQ Credit 1.3: Indoor Air Quality Management Best Management Practices – Increased Ventilation

Q8.35. Although_____ percent of cleaning equipment purchased during the performance period must comply with the criteria detailed in EQ Credit 3.4: Green Cleaning – Sustainable Cleaning Equipment, only_____ percent of equipment in use must comply? (Choose one)

A. 100, 20

B. 90, 100

C. 20, 100

D. 50, 50

E. 80, 20

Q8.36. Which of the following is not required as part of the purchasing policy for EQ Credit 3.3: Green Cleaning Policy – Purchase of Sustainable Cleaning Products and Materials? (Choose one)

A. Hand soap

B. Disinfectants

C. Trash bags

D. Floor finishes

E. Vacuum cleaners

F. Janitorial paper products

Q8.37. Which of the following comply with EQ Credit 3.3: Green Cleaning Policy – Purchase of Sustainable Cleaning Products and Materials? (Choose three)

A. APPA certified scrubbers

B. Environmental Choice CCD-115, for odor control additives

C. GS-01 tissue paper

D. CARB compliant equipment

E. GS-41 hand cleaners

Q8.38. Which of the following is required to comply with EQ Credit 3.5: Green Cleaning – Indoor Chemical and Pollutant Source Control? (Choose two)

A. Entryway systems at least 8 feet in the primary direction of travel

B. Entryway systems at least 10 feet in the primary direction of travel

C. MERV 8 filters

D. MERV 13 filters

E. Separately plumbed hazardous liquid waste

F. Separately exhaust areas with hazardous gases or chemicals

Q8.39. Which of the following credits require MERV filters? (Choose two)

A. EQ Credit 1.3: Indoor Air Quality Management Best Management Practices – Increased Ventilation

B. EQ Credit 1.4: Indoor Air Quality Management Best Management Practices – Reducing Particulates in Air Distribution

C. EQ Credit 1.2: Indoor Air Quality Management Best Management Practices – Outdoor Air Delivery Monitoring

D. EQ Credit 1.5: Indoor Air Quality Management Best Management Practices – Indoor Air Quality Management for Facility Additions and Alterations

Q8.40. What are the two most common IAQ problems with existing buildings? (Choose two)

A. Mold

B. Acoustics

C. Moisture

D. Lighting

E. Odors

Plan	**EQ Prerequisite 1:** **Minimum Indoor Air Quality Performance**

Plan	**EQ Credit 1.3:** **Indoor Air Quality Best Management Practices Increased Ventilation**

PURPOSE

To improve the _____ air quality in buildings to enhance the _____ and _____-being of the occupants by establishing a _____ and _____ indoor air quality _____.

REQUIREMENTS

Case 1: For projects able to meet ASHRAE 62.1:

Prerequisite:

Comply with the standard's _____ Rate _____ by maintaining each outside air intake, supply air fan and/or ventilation distribution system.

Test all local, dedicated building exhaust systems, including bathroom, shower, kitchen, and parking exhaust systems for the following functions:

o _____ speed

o voltage

o control _____

o _____ points

Credit:

Provide at least _____ percent more _____ air than that required by the Prerequisite.

Case 2: For projects unable to meet ASHRAE 62.1:

Prerequisite:

Supply at least _____ cubic _____ per _____ of _____ air person.

Credit: Meet recommendations of Carbon trust "Good _____ Guide _____" for occupied spaces and one of the following options:

Option 1: Design building to meet recommendations described in _____ Applications Manual 10

Option 2: Predict room-by-room _____ with an analytic model to meet the minimum ventilation rates required by ASHRAE 62.1 – 2007 for at least _____ percent of the _____ spaces.

CALCULATIONS (for mechanically ventilated spaces)

_____ Zone Outdoor Airflow (vbz) = required design outdoor airflow in the breathing zone of an occupied space

$$vbz = Rp \times Pz + Ra \times Az$$

Rp = outdoor airflow rate required/person

Pz = zone population

Ra = outdoor airflow rate

Az = zone floor area

Zone _____ Airflow (Voz) = the outdoor airflow required for the zone for the supply air distribution system

$$Voz = \frac{Vbz}{Ez}$$

Ez = zone air distribution effectiveness

REFERENCED STANDARDS

ASHRAE Standard 62.1 – 2007, _____ for Acceptable Indoor Air Quality

_____ Applications Manual 10 -2005, Natural Ventilation in Non-Domestic Buildings

1 pt. for credit	**RESPONSIBLE PARTY:** **BUILDING ENGINEER**

	EQ Prerequisite 1: Minimum Indoor Air Quality Performance

	EQ Credit 1.3: Indoor Air Quality Best Management Practices

ANSWER KEY

PURPOSE

To improve the **indoor** air quality in buildings to enhance the **comfort** and **well**-being of the occupants by establishing a **minimum** and **increased** indoor air quality **performance**

REQUIREMENTS

Case 1: For projects able to meet ASHRAE 62.1:

Prerequisite:

Comply with the standard's **Ventilation** Rate **Procedure** by maintaining each outside air intake, supply air fan and/or ventilation distribution system.

Test all local, dedicated building exhaust systems, including bathroom, shower, kitchen, and parking exhaust systems for the following functions:

- o **fan** speed
- o voltage
- o control **sequences**
- o **set** points

Credit:

Provide at least **30** percent more **outdoor** air than that required by the Prerequisite.

Case 2: For projects unable to meet ASHRAE 62.1:

Prerequisite:

Supply at least **10** cubic **feet** per **minute** of **outside** air person.

Credit: Meet recommendations of Carbon trust "Good **Practice** Guide **237**" for occupied spaces and one of the following options:

Option 1: Design building to meet recommendations described in **CIBSE** Applications Manual 10

Option 2: Predict room-by-room **airflows** with an analytic model to meet the minimum ventilation rates required by ASHRAE 62.1 - 2007 for at least **90** percent of the **occupied** spaces.

CALCULATIONS (for mechanically ventilated spaces)

Breathing Zone Outdoor Airflow (vbz) = required design outdoor airflow in the breathing zone of an occupied space

$$vbz = Rp \times Pz + Ra \times Az$$

Rp = outdoor airflow rate required/person

Pz = zone population

Ra = outdoor airflow rate

Az = zone floor area

Zone **Outdoor** Airflow (Voz) = the outdoor airflow required for the zone for the supply air distribution system

$$Voz = \frac{Vbz}{Ez}$$

Ez = zone air distribution effectiveness

REFERENCED STANDARDS

ASHRAE Standard 62.1 - 2007, **Ventilation** for Acceptable Indoor Air Quality

CIBSE Applications Manual 10 -2005, Natural Ventilation in Non-Domestic Buildings

Program Development	EQ Prerequisite 2:
	Environmental Tobacco Smoke (ETS) Control

PURPOSE

To _____ or _____ environmental _____ smoke (ETS) from contaminating the indoor environment, including _____, surfaces, and _____ systems.

REQUIREMENTS

Option 1:

Do not allow smoking in the building.

Provide a dedicated smoking area on site that is at least _____ feet away from any building _____, outdoor air _____ and _____ windows.

Option 2:

o Do not allow smoking within the building except in dedicated areas with separate and isolated ventilation and exhaust systems. Interior smoking areas also to have _____ deck-to-deck partitions.

o Provide a _____ smoking area on site that is at least 25 _____ away from any building entrances, outdoor air intakes, and operable windows.

Option 3: Residential and Mixed-Use Projects Only

o Do not allow smoking in the _____ areas of the building.

o Provide a dedicated exterior smoking area on site that is at least 25 feet away from any building entrances, outdoor air intakes, and operable windows (this includes _____ as well).

o _____ all openings and _____ all penetrations in each unit.

o Conduct a blower door test in accordance with reference standard to demonstrate acceptable sealing of units.

o Conduct _____ air testing.

REFERENCED STANDARD

ANSI/ASTM _____-03, Standard Test Method for Determining Air Leakage Rate by Fan Pressurization

_____ Residential Alternative Calculation Method Approval Manual

Required	RESPONSIBLE PARTY:
	OWNER

| EQ Prerequisite 2: |
| Environmental Tobacco Smoke (ETS) Control |

ANSWER KEY

PURPOSE

To **prevent** or **minimize** environmental **tobacco** smoke (ETS) from contaminating the indoor environment, including **occupants**, surfaces, and **ventilation** systems.

REQUIREMENTS

Option 1:

Do not allow smoking in the building.

Provide a dedicated smoking area on site that is at least **25** feet away from any building **entrances,** outdoor air **intakes,** and **operable** windows.

Option 2:

Do not allow smoking within the building except in dedicated areas with separate and isolated ventilation and exhaust systems. Interior smoking areas also to have **impermeable** deck-to-deck partitions.

Provide a **dedicated** smoking area on site that is at least 25 **feet** away from any building entrances, outdoor air intakes, and operable windows.

Option 3: Residential and Mixed-Use Projects Only

Do not allow smoking in the **common** areas of the building.

Provide a dedicated exterior smoking area on site that is at least 25 feet away from any building entrances, outdoor air intakes, and operable windows (this includes **balconies** as well).

Weatherstrip all openings and **seal** all penetrations in each unit.

Conduct a blower door test in accordance with reference standard to demonstrate acceptable sealing of units.

Conduct **periodic** air testing.

REFERENCED STANDARD

ANSI/ASTM **E779**-03, Standard Test Method for Determining Air Leakage Rate by Fan Pressurization

California Residential Alternative Calculation Method Approval Manual

| **Program Development** | **EQ Prerequisite 3:** |
| | **Green Cleaning Policy** |

| **Program Development** | **EQ Credit 3.1:** |
| | **Green Cleaning High Performance Cleaning Policy** |

PURPOSE

To reduce the impacts on _____ quality, human _____, building _____, building _____ and the environment by hazardous _____, biological, and particulate _____ by reducing exposure to building occupants and maintenance personnel.

REQUIREMENTS

Prerequisite:

Create and execute a green cleaning policy that require the following:

- The purchase of sustainable _____ products in compliance with EQ Credit _____
- The purchase of cleaning _____ in compliance with EQ Credit _____
- Standard operating _____ for effective _____ that will be consistently implemented and audited
- Strategies for promoting and improving _____ hygiene and mindful of _____ codes
- Guidelines addressing the safe handling and storage of cleaning _____
- _____ and _____ of maintenance personnel
- Guidelines for collecting occupant _____ for continuous improvement

Credit:

Implement a green cleaning _____ to include:

_____ needs and goals

- Efficient use of _____ and supplies
- Meet _____ and cleanliness goals
- _____ building occupants

Implement a green cleaning policy to include:

- _____ plan
- _____ plan for staff
- Chemical use for concentrates and _____
- Use of cleaning products and equipment in accordance with EQ Credits _____ and _____

| **1 pt. for credit** | **RESPONSIBLE PARTY:** |
| | **OWNER** |

EQ Prerequisite 3:

Green Cleaning Policy

EQ Credit 3.1:

Green Cleaning Policy
High Performance Cleaning Policy

ANSWER KEY

PURPOSE

To reduce the impacts on **air** quality, human **health**, building **finishes**, building **systems** and the environment by hazardous **chemical**, biological, and particulate **contaminants** by reducing exposure to building occupants and maintenance personnel.

REQUIREMENTS

Create and execute a green cleaning policy that require the following:

o The purchase of sustainable **cleaning** products in compliance with EQ Credit **3.3**

o The purchase of cleaning **equipment** in compliance with EQ Credit **3.4**

o Standard operating **procedures** for effective **cleaning** that will be consistently implemented and audited

o Strategies for promoting and improving **hand** hygiene and mindful of **health** codes

o Guidelines addressing the safe handling and storage of cleaning **chemicals**

o **Staffing** and **training** of maintenance personnel

o Guidelines for collecting occupant **feedback** for continuous improvement

Credit:

Implement a green cleaning **program** to include:

o **Cleanliness** needs and goals

o Efficient use of **chemicals** and supplies

o Meet **hygiene** and cleanliness goals

o **Protect** building occupants

Implement a green cleaning policy to include:

o **Staffing** plan

o **Training** plan for staff

o Chemical use for concentrates and **dilution**

o Use of cleaning products and equipment in accordance with EQ Credits **3.3** and **3.4**

Program Development

PURPOSE

Promote occupant comfort and well-being by _____ IAQ by optimizing _____ and _____ practices.

REQUIREMENTS

Create and execute, on an ongoing basis, an _____ management _____ to comply with the _____'s Indoor Air Quality Building Education and Assessment Model (_____).

REFERENCED STANDARD

Indoor Air Quality _____ Education and _____ Model (I-BEAM)

1 pt.

RESPONSIBLE PARTY:

FACILITY MANAGER

	EQ Credit 1.1:
	IAQ Best Management Practices **Indoor IAQ Management Program**

ANSWER KEY

PURPOSE

Promote occupant comfort and well-being by **enhancing** IAQ by optimizing **prevention** and **correction** practices.

REQUIREMENTS

Create and execute on an, ongoing basis, an **IAQ** management **program** to comply with the **EPA's** Indoor Air Quality Building Education and Assessment Model **(I-BEAM)**.

REFERENCED STANDARD

Indoor Air Quality **Building** Education and **Assessment** Model (I-BEAM)

Audit	**EQ Credit 1.2:** **IAQ Best Management Practices** **Outdoor Air Delivery Monitoring**

PURPOSE

Promote occupant _____ and well-_____ by providing ventilation system _____.

REQUIREMENTS

Install _____ monitoring _____ sensors to report _____ on effectiveness and one of the following:

Case 1: Mechanically Ventilated Spaces

Monitor outdoor airflow rates to ensure ventilation effectiveness within _____% of the design minimum outdoor air rate.

Case 2: Mechanical Ventilation Systems serving predominately Densely Occupied Areas

Use _____ or _____ zone _____ locations in each _____ occupied space and compare it with _____ ambient CO_2 concentrations.

Case 3: Naturally Ventilated Spaces

Install permanent monitoring CO_2 sensors within the breathing _____ (_____ to _____ feet above the floor) for all densely occupied spaces.

Sensors must provide an audible or visual alarm if CO_2 levels are greater than _____ ppm above _____ levels or _____ ppm _____.

REFERENCED STANDARD

ASHRAE Standard _____ -2007, Ventilation for Acceptable Indoor Air Quality

1 pt.	**RESPONSIBLE PARTY:** **BUILDING ENGINEER**

EQ Credit 1.2:
IAQ Best Management Practices
Outdoor Air Delivery Monitoring

ANSWER KEY

PURPOSE

Promote occupant **comfort** and well-**being** by providing ventilation system **monitoring**.

REQUIREMENTS

Install **permanent** monitoring CO_2 sensors to report **feedback** on effectiveness and one of the following:

Case 1: Mechanically Ventilated Spaces

Monitor outdoor airflow rates to ensure ventilation effectiveness within **15%** of the design minimum outdoor air rate.

Case 2: Mechanical Ventilation Systems serving predominately Densely Occupied Areas

Use **sensors** or **breathing** zone **sampling** locations in each **densely** occupied space and compare it with **outdoor** ambient CO_2 concentrations.

Case 3: Naturally Ventilated Spaces

Install permanent monitoring CO_2 sensors within the breathing **zone** (**3** to **6** feet above the floor) for all densely occupied spaces.

Sensors must provide an audible or visual alarm if CO_2 levels are greater than **530** ppm above **outdoor** levels or **1,000** ppm **absolute**.

REFERENCED STANDARD

ASHRAE Standard **62.1** - 2007, Ventilation for Acceptable Indoor Air Quality

Audit	EQ Credit 1.4:
	IAQ Best Management Practices **Reducing Particulates in Air Distribution**

PURPOSE

To reduce the impacts on _____ quality, human _____ , building _____ , building _____ and the environment by potentially particulate _____ by reducing exposure to building occupants and maintenance personnel.

REQUIREMENTS

Install MERV _____ or better filters on all outside air intakes and inside air recirculation returns.

Filters must be maintained and replaced on a _____ schedule.

REFERENCED STANDARD

ASHRAE Standard _____ - 1999, Method of Testing General Ventilation Air-Cleaning Devices for Removal Efficiency by Particle Size

1 pt.

RESPONSIBLE PARTY:

BUILDING ENGINEER

EQ Credit 1.4:

IAQ Best Management Practices
Reducing Particulates in Air Distribution

ANSWER KEY

PURPOSE

To reduce the impacts on **air** quality, human **health**, building **finishes**, building **systems** and the environment by potentially particulate **contaminants** by reducing exposure to building occupants and maintenance personnel.

REQUIREMENTS

Install MERV **13** or better filters on all outside air intakes and inside air recirculation returns.

Filters must be maintained and replaced on a **regular** schedule.

REFERENCED STANDARD

ASHRAE Standard **52.2** - 1999, Method of Testing General Ventilation Air-Cleaning Devices for Removal Efficiency by Particle Size

Plan	**EQ Credit 1.5:**
	IAQ Best Management Practices
	IAQ Management for Facility Alterations and Additions

PURPOSE

Promote occupant and construction worker comfort and well-being by _____ indoor _____ quality problems caused during _____ or _____ projects.

REQUIREMENTS

Create and implement a _____ management plan for the construction and occupancy phases to comply with _____ control measures and include a _____-out procedure after construction, prior to occupancy.

All _____ materials must be protected from moisture damage whether they are installed or stored on site.

Use a minimum of MERV _____ filters at all return air grilles for any permanently installed air handlers are during construction, per ASHRAE Standard _____. All filters to be replaced prior to occupancy.

STRATEGIES

IAQ management plan should be coordinated by an accredited professional _____ hygienist, professional _____ consultant) or by an accredited organization (_____ 9001 or ISO 17075).

_____ Guideline control measures:

    _____ Control

Pathway _____

Housekeeping

Scheduling

    _____ Protection

_____-out Procedure:

Provide _____ cubic feet of outside air per square foot of floor area maintaining an average of _____ °F with a maximum of _____ percent relative humidity.

If _____ is desired, provide at least _____ cubic feet of _____ air per square foot of floor area. After occupancy, begin ventilation at least three hours prior to occupancy each day at a minimum rate of _____ cubic feet per minute per square foot of outside air until _____ cubic feet of outside air per square foot of floor area has been delivered.

REFERENCED STANDARD

Sheet Metal and Air Conditioning Contractors National Association (_____) IAQ Guidelines for Occupied Buildings Under Construction, 2nd Edition 2007, ANSI/SMACNA 008-2008 (Chapter 3)

| **1 pt.** | **RESPONSIBLE PARTY:** |
| | **CONTRACTOR** |

ANSWER KEY

PURPOSE

Promote occupant and construction worker comfort and well-being by **reducing** indoor **air** quality problems caused during **construction** or **renovation** projects.

REQUIREMENTS

Create and implement a **IAQ** management plan for the construction and occupancy phases to comply with **SMACNA** control measures and include a **flush**-out procedure after construction, prior to occupancy.

All **absorptive** materials must be protected from moisture damage whether they are installed or stored on site.

Use a minimum of MERV **8** filters at all return air grilles for any permanently installed air handlers are during construction, per ASHRAE Standard **52.2.** All filters to be replaced prior to occupancy.

STRATEGIES

IAQ management plan should be coordinated by an accredited professional (**certified** hygienist, professional **engineer, environmental** consultant) or by an accredited organization **(ISO** 9001 or ISO 17075).

SMACNA Guideline control measures:

> **Source** Control
>
> Pathway **Interruption**
>
> Housekeeping
>
> Scheduling
>
> **HVAC** Protection

Flush-out Procedure:

> Provide **14,000** cubic feet of outside air per square foot of floor area maintaining an average of **60**°F with a maximum of **60** percent relative humidity.
>
> If **occupancy** is desired, provide at least **3,500** cubic feet of **outside** air per square foot of floor area. After occupancy, begin ventilation at least three hours prior to occupancy each day at a minimum rate of **0.30** cubic feet per minute per square foot of outside air until **14,000** cubic feet of outside air per square foot of floor area has been delivered.

REFERENCED STANDARD

Sheet Metal and Air Conditioning Contractors National Association **(SMACNA)** IAQ Guidelines for Occupied Buildings Under Construction, 2nd Edition 2007, ANSI/SMACNA 008-2008 (Chapter 3)

Performance Period/Certification

PURPOSE

Assess occupant satisfaction with thermal comfort, _____, IAQ, lighting levels, building cleanliness, and any other comfort issues.

REQUIREMENTS

At least _____ time during the _____ period, conduct a _____-point occupant survey to assess _____ comfort, acoustics, IAQ, _____ levels, building _____, and any other comfort issues.

Collect _____ responses for at least _____percent of the number of regular building _____ and have a plan for corrective action should more than _____percent of respondents be _____.

REFERENCED STANDARD

ASHRAE Standard _____ - 2004

1 pt.

RESPONSIBLE PARTY:

FACILITY MANAGER

	EQ Credit 2.1:
	Occupant Comfort
	Occupancy Survey

ANSWER KEY

PURPOSE

Assess occupant satisfaction with thermal comfort, **acoustics**, IAQ, lighting levels, building cleanliness and any other comfort issues.

REQUIREMENTS

At least **one** time during the **performance** period, conduct a **seven**-point occupant survey to assess **thermal** comfort, acoustics, IAQ, **lighting** levels, building **cleanliness**, and any other comfort issues.

Collect **anonymous** responses for at least **30** percent of the number of regular building **occupants** and have a plan for corrective action should more than **20** percent of respondents be **dissatisfied.**

REFERENCED STANDARD

ASHRAE Standard **55** - 2004

Audit

PURPOSE

Increase the _____ comfort, and well-being for occupants by providing a high level of _____ system _____ to _____ occupants and groups in _____ spaces.

REQUIREMENTS

Provide individual lighting controls for at least _____ percent of _____, _____ percent of individual _____, and _____ percent of shared _____ spaces. _____ spaces are _____ from compliance _____.

EXEMPLARY PERFORMANCE

Provide individual lighting controls for at least _____ percent of individual workstations and shared multi-occupant spaces.

1 pt.

RESPONSIBLE PARTY:

BUILDING ENGINEER

| EQ Credit 2.2: |
| Controllability of Systems, Lighting |

ANSWER KEY

PURPOSE

Increase the **productivity**, comfort, and well-being for occupants by providing a high level of **lighting** system **control** to **individual** occupants and groups in **multioccupant** spaces.

REQUIREMENTS

Provide individual lighting controls for at least **50** percent of **occupants**, **50** percent of individual **workstations**, and **50** percent of shared **multioccupant** spaces.

Non-occupied spaces are **excluded** from compliance **calculations**.

EXEMPLARY PERFORMANCE

Provide individual lighting controls for at least **95** percent of individual workstations and shared multioccupant spaces.

Audit

PURPOSE

To support the productivity and well-being of occupants by providing a comfortable _____ environment by maintaining appropriate _____ and _____ of building and their systems to meet target _____ goals.

REQUIREMENTS

Ensure thermal comfort criteria is in accordance with ASHRAE 55.

Install a _____ and _____ monitoring system to examine air _____ and relative _____ every 15 minutes. At least _____ air temperature _____ is required within each HVAC zone and at least _____ humidity sensor is required within each humidity _____. _____ must be located between _____ and _____ inches above the finish floor to comply.

Periodic _____ of air _____ and radiant _____ will also need to be conducted in occupied spaces using hand-held meters or other monitoring equipment.

_____ are required to signify when the system is out of alignment with the thermal comfort criteria and needs adjustment and/or repair.

REFERENCED STANDARD

_____ Standard _____ - 2004, Thermal Environmental Conditions for Human Occupancy

1 pt.

RESPONSIBLE PARTY:

BUILDING ENGINEER

EQ Credit 2.3:

Occupant Comfort
Thermal Comfort Monitoring

ANSWER KEY

PURPOSE

To support the productivity and well-being of occupants by providing a comfortable **thermal** environment by maintaining appropriate **operations** and **maintenance** of building and their systems to meet target **performance** goals.

REQUIREMENTS

Ensure thermal comfort criteria is in accordance with ASHRAE 55.

Install a **continuous** and **permanent** monitoring system to examine air **temperature** and relative **humidity** every 15 minutes. At least **one** air temperature **sensor** is required within each HVAC zone and at least **one** humidity sensor is required within each humidity **zone. Sensors** must be located between **4** and **72** inches above the finish floor to comply.

Periodic **testing** of air **speed** and radiant **temperature** will also need to be conducted in occupied spaces using handheld meters or other monitoring equipment.

Alarms are required to signify when the system is out of alignment with the thermal comfort criteria and needs adjustment and/or repair.

REFERENCED STANDARD

ASHRAE Standard **55** - 2004, Thermal Environmental Conditions for Human Occupancy

Audit	EQ Credit 2.4: Daylight and Views

PURPOSE

For regularly occupied areas, introduce _____ and _____ to provide the building occupants with a _____ to the _____ environment.

REQUIREMENTS

DAYLIGHT:

Provide daylight to _____% of the regularly _____ spaces in compliance with one of the options below.

VIEWS:

Provide _____ line of _____ to the exterior for at least _____ percent of regularly occupied areas.

Direct line of sight is measured between _____in. and _____in. above the finish floor.

COMPLIANCE PATH OPTIONS FOR DAYLIGHTING:

OPTION 1: Simulation

Prove 75 percent of the spaces are daylit with between _____ and _____ footcandles.

OPTION 2: Prescriptive

Calculate the daylight zone for side-lighting and/or top-lighting strategies.

OPTION 3: Measurement

Record indoor light footcandle levels on a 10-foot grid to prove a minimum of _____ footcandles.

OPTION 4: Combination

Choose from Options 1 through 3 to prove compliance.

STRATEGIES

All strategies must include _____ control.

OPTION 2: Prescriptive

_____-Lighting Daylight Zone:

Determine the _____ light _____ (VLT) for windows _____ in. above the floor. Multiply VLT by the window-to-floor area ration (WFR) to prove a value between 0.150 and 0.180.

For ceiling obstructed daylight, the related floor area must be excluded from the calculations.

_____-lighting Daylight Zone:

Determine the daylight zone area under each skylight and add the *lesser* of the following three factors:

_____ percent of the _____ height

One-half the distance to the edge of the closest skylight

The distance to a fixed solid partition farther than 70 percent of the distance between the top of the wall and the ceiling

Skylight roof coverage must be between 3 and 6 percent of the roof area.

Skylights must have a minimum VLT of 0.5 and not be spaced apart more than 1.4 times the ceiling height.

If using a skylight diffuser, it is required to have a measured haze value of at least 90 percent and a direct line of sight to the diffuser must be avoided.

EXEMPLARY PERFORMANCE

Provide the _____ occupied spaces with_____ percent daylight and _____ percent views.

REFERENCED STANDARD

_____ D1003-07E1, Standard Test for Method for Haze and Luminous Transmittance of Transparent Plastics

1 pt.	RESPONSIBLE PARTY: ARCHITECT/FACILITY MANAGER

EQ Credit 2.4:
Daylight and Views

ANSWER KEY

PURPOSE

For regularly occupied areas, introduce **daylight** and **views** to provide the building occupants with a **connection** to the **outdoor** environment.

REQUIREMENTS

DAYLIGHT:

Provide daylight to **50** percent of the regularly **occupied** spaces in compliance with one of the options below.

VIEWS:

Provide **direct** line of **sight** to the exterior for at least **45** percent of regularly occupied areas.

Direct line of sight is measured between **30** in. and **90** in. above the finish floor.

COMPLIANCE PATH OPTIONS FOR DAYLIGHTING:

OPTION 1: Simulation

Prove 75 percent of the spaces are daylit with between **25** and **500** footcandles.

OPTION 2: Prescriptive

Calculate the daylight zone for side-lighting and/or top-lighting strategies.

OPTION 3: Measurement

Record indoor light footcandle levels on a 10-foot grid to prove a minimum of **25** footcandles.

OPTION 4: Combination

Choose from Options 1 through 3 to prove compliance.

STRATEGIES

All strategies must include **glare** control.

OPTION 2: Prescriptive

Side-Lighting Daylight Zone:

Determine the **visible** light **transmittance** (VLT) for windows **30** in. above the floor. Multiply VLT by the window-to-floor area ration (WFR) to prove a value between 0.150 and 0.180.

For ceiling obstructed daylight, the related floor area must be excluded from the calculations.

Top-lighting Daylight Zone:

Determine the daylight zone area under each skylight and add the *lesser* of the following three factors:

70 percent of the **ceiling** height

One-half the distance to the edge of the closest skylight

The distance to a fixed solid partition farther than 70 percent of the distance between the top of the wall and the ceiling

Skylight roof coverage must be between 3 and 6 percent of the roof area.

Skylights must have a minimum VLT of 0.5 and not be spaced apart more than 1.4 times the ceiling height

If using a skylight diffuser, it is required to have a measured haze value of at least 90 percent and a direct line of sight to the diffuser must be avoided

EXEMPLARY PERFORMANCE

Provide the **regularly** occupied spaces with **75** percent daylight and **95** percent views.

REFERENCED STANDARD

ASTM D1003-07E1, Standard Test for Method for Haze and Luminous Transmittance of Transparent Plastics

	EQ Credit 3.2:
Performance Period/Certification	**Green Cleaning**
	Custodial Effectiveness Assessment

PURPOSE

Implement, manage, and _____ cleaning procedures and processes to reduce the impacts on _____ quality, human _____, building _____, building _____ and the environment by hazardous _____, biological and particulate _____ by reducing exposure to building occupants and maintenance personnel.

REQUIREMENTS

Conduct an audit to assess the custodial effectiveness in accordance with _____'s "Custodial _____ Guidelines."

Audits must result in a score of _____ or less and should be conducted _____.

REFERENCED STANDARD

Association of Physical Plant Administrators (APPA) Leadership in Educational Facilities "_____ Staffing _____"

EXEMPLARY PERFORMANCE

To receive EP, audits must result in a score of _____ or _____.

1 pt.

RESPONSIBLE PARTY:

FACILITY MANAGER

	EQ Credit 3.2:
	Green Cleaning
	Custodial Effectiveness Assessment

ANSWER KEY

PURPOSE

Implement, manage, and **audit** cleaning procedures and processes to reduce the impacts on **air** quality, human **health,** building **finishes,** building **systems,** and the environment by hazardous **chemical,** biological, and particulate **contaminants** by reducing exposure to building occupants and maintenance personnel.

REQUIREMENTS

Conduct an audit to assess the custodial effectiveness in accordance with **APPA's** "Custodial **Staffing** Guidelines."

Audits must result in a score of **3** or less and should be conducted **annually**.

REFERENCED STANDARD

Association of Physical Plant Administrators (APPA) Leadership in Educational Facilities **"Custodial** Staffing **Guidelines"**

EXEMPLARY PERFORMANCE

To receive EP, audits must result in a score of **2** or **less**.

| **Performance Period/Certification** | **EQ Credit 3.3:**
Green Cleaning - Purchase of
Sustainable Cleaning Products & Materials |

PURPOSE

To lessen the environmental impacts of _____ products, _____ janitorial _____ products, and _____ bags.

REQUIREMENTS

Track the purchases of the following during the _____ period to meet at least _____ of the sustainable criteria listed:

Green _____ Products:

- o _____ Seal GS-_____, for general-purpose, bathroom, glass, and carpet cleaners used for industrial and institutional purposes
- o Environmental Choice _____-_____, for cleaning and degreasing compounds
- o _____ Choice CCD-_____, for hard surface cleaners
- o Environmental _____ CCD-_____, for carpet and upholstery care

_____, metal polish, floor finishes, strippers, or other products not addressed by the above standards:

- o Green _____ GS-_____, for industrial and institutional floor care products
- o Environmental Choice CCD-_____, for digestion additives for cleaning and odor control
- o Environmental _____ CCD-_____, for drain or grease traps additives
- o _____ Choice CCD-_____, for odor control additives
- o Environmental Choice _____-_____, for hard floor care
- o _____ Code of Regulations maximum allowable _____ levels for the specific product category

_____ janitorial _____ products and trash bags:

- o _____ Protection _____ (EPA) Comprehensive Procurement Guidelines for Janitorial Paper and Plastic Trash Can Liners
- o _____ Seal GS-_____, for paper towels and napkins
- o Green _____ GS-_____, for tissue paper
- o _____ Choice CCD-_____, for toilet tissue
- o Environmental _____ CCD-_____, for hand towels
- o Janitorial paper products derived from rapidly _____ resources or made from _____ fibers

Hand _____:

- o No antimicrobial agents (other than as a preservative) except where required by health codes and other regulations (e.g., food service and health care requirements)
- o _____ Seal GS-_____, for industrial and institutional hand cleaners
- o _____ Choice CCD-_____, for hand cleaners and hand soaps

Credit is awarded if _____ percent of total annual purchases (by cost) meet at least one of the sustainable criteria.

REFERENCED STANDARDS

_____ Code of Regulations Maximum Allowable VOC Levels

Environmental _____ Certified Products

_____ Seal® Certified

The _____ Comprehensive Procurement Guidelines

EXEMPLARY PERFORMANCE

Credit is awarded if _____ percent of total annual purchases (by cost) meet at least one of the sustainable criteria.

1 pt.

RESPONSIBLE PARTY:

FACILITY MANAGER

	EQ Credit 3.3:
	Green Cleaning - Purchase of **Sustainable Cleaning Products & Materials**

ANSWER KEY

PURPOSE

To lessen the environmental impacts of **cleaning** products, **disposable** janitorial **paper** products, and **trash** bags.

REQUIREMENTS

Track the purchases of the following during the **performance** period to meet at least **one** of the sustainable criteria listed:

Green Cleaning Products:

- o **Green** Seal GS-**37**, for general-purpose, bathroom, glass, and carpet cleaners used for industrial and institutional purposes
- o Environmental Choice **CCD-110**, for cleaning and degreasing compounds
- o **Environmental** Choice CCD-**146**, for hard surface cleaners
- o Environmental **Choice** CCD-**148**, for carpet and upholstery care

Disinfectants, metal polish, floor finishes, strippers, or other products not addressed by the above standards:

- o Green **Seal** GS-**40**, for industrial and institutional floor care products
- o Environmental Choice CCD-**112**, for digestion additives for cleaning and odor control
- o Environmental **Choice** CCD-**113**, for drain or grease traps additives
- o **Environmental** Choice CCD-**115**, for odor control additives
- o Environmental Choice **CCD-147**, for hard floor care
- o **California** Code of Regulations maximum allowable **VOC** levels for the specific product category

Disposable janitorial paper products and trash bags:

- o **Environmental** Protection **Agency** (EPA) Comprehensive Procurement Guidelines for Janitorial Paper and Plastic Trash Can Liners
- o **Green** Seal GS-**09**, for paper towels and napkins
- o Green **Seal** GS-**01**, for tissue paper
- o **Environmental** Choice CCD-**082**, for toilet tissue
- o Environmental **Choice** CCD-**086**, for hand towels
- o Janitorial paper products derived from rapidly **renewable** resources or made from **treefree** fibers

Hand soaps:

- o No antimicrobial agents (other than as a preservative), except where required by health codes and other regulations (e.g., food service and health care requirements)
- o **Green** Seal GS-**41**, for industrial and institutional hand cleaners
- o **Environmental** Choice CCD-**104**, for hand cleaners and hand soaps

Credit is awarded if **30** percent of total annual purchases (by cost) meet at least one of the sustainable criteria.

REFERENCED STANDARDS

California Code of Regulations Maximum Allowable VOC Levels

Environmental **Choice** Certified Products

Green Seal® Certified

The **EPA** Comprehensive Procurement Guidelines

EXEMPLARY PERFORMANCE

Credit is awarded if **60** percent of total annual purchases (by cost) meet at least one of the sustainable criteria.

Performance Period/Certification

PURPOSE

To reduce the impacts on _____ quality, human _____, building _____, building _____, and the environment by hazardous _____, biological and particulate _____ from _____ cleaning _____ by reducing _____ to building occupants and maintenance personnel.

REQUIREMENTS

Log all equipment purchased and in use during the performance period to ensure compliance with the following criteria:

o _____ cleaners are certified by the Carpet and Rug Institute "Green Label" Testing Program for vacuum cleaners and operate with a sound level of less than _____ dBA.

o Carpet extraction equipment used for restorative deep cleaning is certified by the _____ and Rug _____'s "Seal of _____" Testing Program for deep-cleaning extractors.

o Powered floor _____ equipment, including electric and battery-powered floor buffers and burnishers, is equipped with _____, guards and/or other devices for capturing fine particulates and operates with a sound level of less than _____ dBA.

o Propane-powered _____ equipment has high-efficiency, low-emissions engines with catalytic _____ and _____ that meet the California Air Resources Board (_____) or Environmental Protection Agency (_____) standards for the specific _____ size and operate with a sound level of less than _____ dBA.

o Automated _____ machines are equipped with variable-speed feed pumps and on-board chemical metering to _____ the use of cleaning _____. Alternatively, the scrubbing machines _____ only _____ water with _____ added cleaning products,

o _____-powered equipment is equipped with environmentally preferable _____ batteries.

o Powered equipment is _____ designed to minimize vibration, noise, and user fatigue.

o _____ is designed with _____, such as rollers or rubber bumpers, to reduce potential damage to building surfaces.

Credit is awarded if _____ percent of equipment in use during the performance period complies with the criteria listed.

REFERENCED STANDARDS

_____ Air Resources Board (CARB)

Environmental _____ Agency

_____ and Rug _____ (CRI) Green _____

Carpet and _____ Institute (_____) Seal of Approval

1 pt.

RESPONSIBLE PARTY:

FACILITY MANAGER

EQ Credit 3.4:

Green Cleaning
Sustainable Cleaning Equipment

ANSWER KEY

PURPOSE

To reduce the impacts on **air** quality, human **health,** building **finishes,** building **systems,** and the environment by hazardous **chemical,** biological, and particulate **contaminants** from **powered** cleaning **equipment** by reducing **exposure** to building occupants and maintenance personnel.

REQUIREMENTS

Log all equipment purchased and in use during the performance period to ensure compliance with the following criteria:

- o **Vacuum** cleaners are certified by the Carpet and Rug Institute "Green Label" Testing Program for vacuum cleaners and operate with a sound level of less than **70** dBA.

- o Carpet extraction equipment used for restorative deep cleaning is certified by the **Carpet** and Rug **Institute's** "Seal of **Approval**" Testing Program for deep-cleaning extractors.

- o Powered floor **maintenance** equipment, including electric and battery-powered floor buffers and burnishers, is equipped with **vacuums,** guards and/or other devices for capturing fine particulates and operates with a sound level of less than **70** dBA.

- o Propane-powered **floor** equipment has high-efficiency, low-emission engines with catalytic **converters** and **mufflers** that meet the California Air Resources Board **(CARB)** or Environmental Protection Agency **(EPA)** standards for the specific **engine** size and operate with a sound level of less than **90** dBA.

- o Automated **scrubbing** machines are equipped with variable-speed feed pumps and on-board chemical metering to **optimize** the use of cleaning **fluids.** Alternatively, the scrubbing machines **use** only **tap** water with **no** added cleaning products

- o **Battery**-powered equipment is equipped with environmentally preferable **gel** batteries.

- o Powered equipment is **ergonomically** designed to minimize vibration, noise, and user fatigue.

- o **Equipment** is designed with **safeguards,** such as rollers or rubber bumpers, to reduce potential damage to building surfaces

Credit is awarded if **20** percent of equipment in use during the performance period complies with the criteria listed.

REFERENCED STANDARDS

California Air Resources Board (CARB)

Environmental **Protection** Agency

Carpet and Rug **Institute** (CRI) Green **Label**

Carpet and **Rug** Institute **(CRI)** Seal of Approval

Audit	EQ Credit 3.5:
	Green Cleaning
	Indoor Chemical and Pollutant Source Control

PURPOSE

To reduce the impacts on _____ quality, human _____, building _____, building _____, and the environment by hazardous _____, biological, and particulate _____ by reducing exposure to building occupants and maintenance personnel.

REQUIREMENTS

Install _____ entryway system, such as grilles, grates, and mats, at least _____ ft long in the direction of travel at building entrances and create strategies to _____ the system employed.

Provide for appropriate _____ of _____ liquid wastes for _____ spaces.

1 pt.	**RESPONSIBLE PARTY:**
	FACILITY MANAGER

EQ Credit 3.5:

Green Cleaning
Indoor Chemical and Pollutant Source Control

ANSWER KEY

PURPOSE

To reduce the impacts on **air** quality, human **health,** building **finishes,** building **systems,** and the environment by hazardous **chemical,** biological, and particulate **contaminants** by reducing exposure to building occupants and maintenance personnel.

REQUIREMENTS

Install **permanent** entryway system, such as grilles, grates, and mats, at least **10** ft long in the direction of travel at building entrances and create strategies to **maintain** the system employed.

Provide for appropriate **disposal** of **hazardous** liquid wastes for **laboratory** spaces.

Performance Period/Certification

PURPOSE

To reduce the impacts on _____ quality, human _____, building _____, building _____, and the environment by hazardous _____, biological, and particulate _____ by reducing exposure to building occupants and maintenance personnel.

REQUIREMENTS

During the performance _____, create, execute, and maintain an _____ integrated _____ management (IPM) plan to keep insects and animal pest _____ under control and to _____ pests from entering the building.

_____ products must meet the requirements of _____ Credit _____.

_____ and _____ strategies to evaluate their effectiveness.

STRATEGIES

To be implemented at least _____ percent of the time during the _____ period:

- o Removal of _____ plants and fungi
- o Site or pest _____ and _____
- o Sanitation, _____ repairs, mechanical and living biological controls, other _____ methods
- o Least toxic and nontoxic pesticides
- o _____ notification for pesticide application. In _____, at least _____ hour notice is required.
- o _____ maintenance to avoid _____
- o _____ sources of attraction, such as trash receptacles

1 pt.

RESPONSIBLE PARTY:

FACILITY MANAGER

ANSWER KEY

PURPOSE

To reduce the impacts on **air** quality, human **health,** building **finishes,** building **systems,** and the environment by hazardous **chemical,** biological, and particulate **contaminants** by reducing exposure to building occupants and maintenance personnel.

REQUIREMENTS

During the performance **period,** create, execute, and maintain an **indoor** integrated **pest** management (IPM) plan to keep insects and animal pest **populations** under control and to **prevent** pests from entering the building.

Cleaning products must meet the requirements of **EQ** Credit **3.3**.

Monitor and **record** strategies to evaluate their effectiveness.

STRATEGIES

To be implemented at least **20** percent of the time during the **performance** period:

- o Removal of **invasive** plants and fungi
- o Site or pest **inspection** and **monitoring**
- o Sanitation, **structural** repairs, mechanical and living biological controls, other **nonchemical** methods
- o Least toxic and nontoxic pesticides
- o **Universal** notification for pesticide application. In **emergencies**, at least **24** hour notice is required.
- o **Envelope** maintenance to avoid **intrusions**
- o **Monitoring** sources of attraction, such as trash receptacles

CHAPTER 9

INNOVATION IN OPERATIONS AND REGIONAL PRIORITY

THE PREVIOUS FIVE CHAPTERS detailed the main categories of the Leadership in Energy and Environmental Design (LEED®) for Existing Buildings: Operations & Maintenance™ (EBOM) rating system, while this chapter focuses on the two bonus categories of the rating system: Innovation in Operations (IO) and Regional Priority (RP). These categories are treated as bonus categories, as neither contains any prerequisites. The IO category encourages projects to explore new and innovative strategies and technologies, while the RP category offers additional point-earning opportunities focused on geographic environmental achievements.

 Remember to switch back to the white flashcards for IO and RP topics.

INNOVATION IN OPERATIONS

The IO category encourages the exploration and implementation of new green building technologies, as well as exceeding the thresholds defined in the existing LEED credits. As seen in Table 9.1, the EBOM rating system offers up to six points for projects within the IO category by addressing four different strategies:

1. Exemplary performance
2. Innovation in Operations
3. Including a LEED Accredited Professional on the project team
4. Documenting sustainable building cost

 Create a flashcard to remember the strategies to earn IO points.

IO Credit 1: Innovation or Exemplary Performance

Three of the available six IO points can be used toward the achievement of exemplary performance. As mentioned in the previous chapters, Exemplary Performance credits are achieved once projects surpass the minimum performance-based thresholds defined in the existing LEED credits, typically the

Table 9.1 The Innovation in Operations Category

Timeframe	Credit	Title	Points
To be determined	Credit 1	Innovation or Exemplary Performance	1–4
To be determined	Credit 2	LEED Accredited Professional	1
Education/Recertification	Credit 3	Documenting Sustainable Building Cost	1

next incremental percentage threshold. For example, projects can earn Exemplary Performance credits (within the IO category) for achieving the following:

- Diverting 95 percent of construction waste per the requirements of MR Credit 9: Solid Waste Management – Facility Alterations and Additions

- Reducing nonpotable makeup water consumption by more than 95 percent per the requirements of WE Credit 4: Cooling Tower Water Management – Chemical Management

- Earning a score of 2 or less for an APPA "Custodial Staffing Guidelines" audit for EQ Credit 3.2 Green Cleaning – Custodial Effectiveness Assessment

If the team uses all three opportunities for exemplary performance achievements, they still have at least one more point opportunity for implementing an innovative strategy. If the team pursues less than three credits within the IO category for exemplary performance, then they can pursue more innovative strategies. The teams should research credit interpretation requests (CIRs) to see if their proposed strategy has been incorporated or presented in the past, or issue a new CIR to inquire about the award potential. Successful IO solutions include strategies that demonstrate quantitative performance with environmental benefits and can be replicated by other project teams. Some examples previously submitted and awarded include:

- Incorporating cradle-to-cradle (C2C) certified products (see Figure 9.1)

- Implementing an educational program for occupants and visitors (see Figures 9.2 and 9.3)

- Performing an infrared scan of the facility to improve envelopment performance and integrity (see Figure 9.4)

- Inspiration of strategies from other LEED rating systems, such as achieving compliance with the requirements of Acoustical Performance from the LEED for Schools™ rating system

- Instituting an employee wellness program and provide access to exercise classes or facilities, clinics, stress management programs, and educational sessions

Figure 9.1 C2C products help to extend the life of materials, although repurposed, reducing the need for virgin materials. *Photo courtesy of Armstrong Ceiling and Wall Systems*

Figure 9.2 Providing opportunities to educate the end users and community about the benefits and strategies of green building helps to further transform the market and, therefore, contribute to pursuing LEED certification. In this photo, a student works in the permaculture garden at the EcoDorm at Warren County College with building integrated photovoltaic panels doubling as shading devices on the south windows. *Image Courtesy of Liina Laufer and Samsel Architects*

- Participating in a local or state peak demand/load program
- Documenting environmental benefits of implementing new sustainable purchasing policy

When submitting for an Innovation in Operations credit, each of the following four components need to be addressed for each credit being pursued:

1. Intent of strategy
2. Suggested requirements for compliance

Figure 9.3 Solar hot water storage tanks, pumps, valves, and boilers are labeled and visible from the main living space at the EcoDorm, enabling students to see the equipment that maintains their comfort in the building. *Image Courtesy of Samsel Architects*

Figure 9.4 This hotel project utilized thermal scanning technologies to study the envelope performance. *Image courtesy of John Cannamela of infraredsurvey.com*

3. Suggested documentation proving compliance with requirements
4. A narrative describing the strategy implemented

IO Credit 2: LEED Accredited Professional

The EBOM rating system also offers another point opportunity for including a LEED Accredited Professional (AP) on the project team. Including a LEED AP on the project team can add efficiencies, as they are aware of the requirements of the LEED certification process. They are familiar with integrated design processes and understand how to evaluate the trade-offs and synergies of green building strategies and technologies. For the purposes of the exam, it is critical to remember that only **one point** can be awarded to projects for this credit; it does not matter how many LEED APs are on the project team, just as long as there is one. Note, LEED Green Associates do not qualify for the bonus point under this credit. The LEED AP credential certificate is required to prove compliance and earn the point.

IO Credit 3: Documenting Sustainable Building Cost

This credit is unique to the EBOM rating systems as it requires a project team to provide documentation for the building operating costs for the previous five years, including the performance period. If the building was occupied less than five years, documentation is required for the duration of occupancy. This credit should be started as early as possible and will need to continue after the performance period ends. The intentions of this credit include documenting the operating costs and financial impacts of pursuing EBOM certification, including the changes during the performance period. The documentation must include internal staff time commitments, consultant fees, and actual certification costs.

Table 9.2 The Regional Priority Category

Timeframe	Credit	Title	Points
To be determined	Credit 1	Regional Priority	1–4

The team is encouraged to use BOMA's Experience Exchange Report as a guideline to track operating costs such as cleaning expenses, repair/maintenance expenses, grounds keeping expenses, and utility expenses, including electricity/fuel, water, and waste.

REGIONAL PRIORITY

As seen in Table 9.2, the RP category offers the opportunity to earn up to four bonus points for achieving compliance of previously mentioned existing LEED credits. U.S. Green Building Council's (USGBC®'s) eight regional councils have consulted with the local chapters to determine which existing LEED credits are more challenging to achieve within certain zip codes. Based on the results of their findings, USGBC compiled a database of all the zip codes in the United States (available on the USGBC website) and choose six existing LEED credits to coordinate with each corresponding geographic region. For example, a project located in Orlando, Florida, could earn a bonus point within the RP category for purchasing 25 percent of their food products in compliance with MR Credit 5: Sustainable Purchasing – Food and purchased within 100-mile radius of the project, as USGBC has recognized that South Florida has a few opportunities to obtain food products to comply with this credit. A project could earn up to four Regional Priority credits (RPCs) out of the six opportunities presented. For the purposes of the exam, it is critical to remember that RPCs are not *new* credits.

 TIP Do you remember the point structure for LEED? How many points does a project need to achieve to earn Platinum status?

QUIZ TIME!

Q9.1. Exemplary performance generally requires which of the following? (Choose one)

A. Develop an innovative strategy not presented in any existing LEED credit.

B. Achieve either 20 percent or the next incremental percentage threshold established by the existing LEED credit that is being exceeded, whichever is greater.

C. Meet or exceed the next percentage threshold as listed within the existing credit.

D. Surpass the defined threshold of an innovative strategy being proposed by the team.

E. Regardless of the LEED credit being pursued, achieve at least double the minimum effort described within the existing LEED credit, regardless of which credit is being exceeded.

Q9.2. Pursuing an Innovation in Operations opportunity is appropriate when *at least one* of which of the following are true? (Choose two)

  A. The project is unable to meet the requirements established by an existing LEED credit.

  B. The compliance paths offered within an existing LEED credit are not possible to pursue.

  C. The project has exceeded or is projected to exceed the minimum performance established by an existing LEED credit.

  D. The project has achieved measurable performance in a LEED credit within another rating system.

Q9.3. Is it possible for the same building to earn multiple LEED certifications?

  A. Yes

  B. No

Q9.4. Which of the following statements are true regarding RPCs? (Choose three)

  A. Earning an RPC adds a bonus point to the project's total points.

  B. RPCs are new credits included in the LEED rating systems.

  C. Projects that are not registered with the 2009 versions of LEED are not awarded points within the Regional Priority category.

  D. Each zip code is assigned eight RPC opportunities.

  E. A project may earn up to four RPC bonus points.

Q9.5. How many points can be earned in the RP category? (Choose one)

  A. Six

  B. Three

  C. Two

  D. Four

  E. Ten

Q9.6. There are five LEED APs on the Botanical Center project, including three from the architectural firm, one from the mechanical engineering firm, and one from the electrical engineering firm. How many points can be achieved within the IO category for achieving this effort? (Choose one)

  A. One

  B. Two

  C. Three

  D. Four

Q9.7. If a building has been occupied for eight years, what is the minimum duration in which operating cost documentation must be provided to comply with IO Credit 3: Documenting Sustainable Building Cost? (Choose one)

A. 1 year

B. When the performance period started

C. 2 years

D. 3 years

E. 5 years

F. When the project was registered with GBCI

Q9.8. What reference should the team utilize to track operating costs? (Choose one)

A. ASHRAE

B. ACEEE

C. BOMA Experience Exchange Report

D. EPEAT

E. ENERGY STAR Portfolio Manager

Q9.9. Implementing a building automation system (BAS) might contribute to earning which of the following credits? (Choose three)

A. EQ Credit 2.2: Controllability of Systems, Lighting

B. EA Credit 2.2: Existing Building Commissioning, Implementation

C. IO Credit 1: Innovation in Operations

D. SS Credit 8: Light Pollution Reduction

E. EA Credit 3.1: Performance Measurement, Building Automation System

Q9.10. Which of the following prerequisites are addressed during the performance period? (Choose one)

A. MR Prerequisite 1: Sustainable Purchasing Policy

B. MR Prerequisite 2: Solid Waste Management Policy

C. WE Prerequisite 1: Minimum Indoor Plumbing Fixture and Fitting Efficiency

D. EQ Prerequisite 2: Environmental Tobacco Smoke Control

E. None of the above

Q9.11. Which of the following must be included in the documentation to comply with IO Credit 3: Documenting Sustainable Building Cost? (Choose three)

A. Internal staff time commitments

B. Utility costs

C. Consultant fees

D. Actual certification costs

E. Permitting fees

Q9.12. What of the following is not part of the five phases of a project seeking EBOM certification? (Choose one)

A. Audit

B. Program Development

C. Recertification

D. Plan

E. Construction

Q9.13. Which of the following is not required to be part of a policy proving compliance with EBOM? (Choose one)

A. Scope

B. Goals

C. Cost Benefits

D. Strategies

E. Performance metric

Q9.14. Which of the following does not permit a 10 percent floor area exemption for compliance? (Choose one)

A. MR Prerequisite 2: Solid Waste Management Policy

B. EQ Credit 2.2: Controllability of Systems, Lighting

C. EA Credit 2.2: Existing Building Commissioning, Implementation

D. EQ Prerequisite 2: Environmental Tobacco Smoke Control

E. EA Credit 3.1: Performance Measurement, Building Automation System

DESIGN	**IO Credit 1:**
	Innovation in Operations

PURPOSE

Allow for the opportunity to achieve _____ performance and/or _____ performance for green _____ and _____ strategies not addressed by the LEED for Existing Buildings: Operations and Maintenance Rating System.

STRATEGIES

PATH 1: Innovation in Operations (Up to _____ points)

1. Propose a quantifiable and innovative performance achieved with an environmental benefit

2. Proposed innovation must be applied comprehensively to the entire project

3. Must be achievable by other projects and considerably better than sustainable design strategies

PATH 2: Exemplary Performance (Up to _____ points)

Double the requirement of an existing LEED credit and/or achieve the stated _____ percentage _____

DOCUMENTATION

PATH 1:

_____ of proposed strategy

_____ of proposed strategy

Submittals _____ compliance with proposed requirements _____/technologies to achieve innovative performance

1–4 pts.

RESPONSIBLE PARTY:

PROJECT TEAM

	IO Credit 1:
	Innovation in Operations

ANSWER KEY

PURPOSE

Allow for the opportunity to achieve **exemplary** performance and/or innovative performance for green **operations** and **maintenance** strategies not addressed by the LEED for Existing Buildings: Operations and Maintenance Rating System.

STRATEGIES

PATH 1: Innovation in Operations (Up to **4** points)

1. Propose an quantifiable and innovative performance achieved with an environmental benefit

2. Proposed innovation must be applied comprehensively to the entire project

3. Must be achievable by other projects and considerably better than sustainable design strategies

PATH 2: Exemplary Performance (Up to **3** points)

Double the requirement of an existing LEED credit and/or achieve the stated **incremental** percentage **threshold**

DOCUMENTATION

PATH 1:

Intent of proposed strategy

Requirements of proposed strategy

Submittals **proving** compliance with proposed requirements

Strategies/technologies to achieve innovative performance

CONSTRUCTION

PURPOSE

_____ the _____ and _____ process by encouraging the integration required by the LEED Green Building Rating Systems.

REQUIREMENTS

Engage at least _____ LEED AP as a integral project team member.

REFERENCED STANDARDS

LEED _____ Professional (AP)

Green Building _____ Institute (GBCI), www.gbci.org

1 pt.

RESPONSIBLE PARTY:

PROJECT TEAM

	IO Credit 2:
	LEED Accredited Professional (AP)

ANSWER KEY

PURPOSE

Streamline the **application** and **certification** process by encouraging the integration required by the LEED Green Building Rating Systems.

REQUIREMENTS

Engage at least **one** LEED AP as a integral project team member.

REFERENCED STANDARDS

LEED **Accredited** Professional (AP)

Green Building **Certification** Institute (GBCI), www.gbci.org

EDUCATION/RECERTIFICATION

PURPOSE

To document _____ building _____ impacts.

REQUIREMENTS

For the previous _____ years (or occupancy length if shorter), document _____ costs and _____ impact for pursuing EBOM _____, including the _____ period.

Use _____'s Experience _____ Report as a guideline.

Internal _____ hours, _____ fees, and _____ costs should be included.

1 pt.

RESPONSIBLE PARTY:

OWNER

<table>
<tr><td></td><td align="right">**IO Credit 3:**

**Documenting Sustainable
Building Cost Impacts**</td></tr>
</table>

ANSWER KEY

PURPOSE

To document **sustainable** building **cost** impacts.

REQUIREMENTS

For the previous **5** years (or occupancy length if shorter), document **operating** costs and **financial** impact for pursuing EBOM **certification**, including the **performance** period.

Use **BOMA's** Experience **Exchange** Report as a guideline.

Internal **staff** hours, **consultant** fees, and **certification** costs should be included.

PART III

STUDY TIPS AND APPENDICES

CHAPTER **10**
STUDY TIPS

AS MENTIONED EARLIER, IN THE INTRODUCTION OF THIS BOOK, this chapter is dedicated to providing an approach for the rest of your study efforts. It includes tips for taking online practice exams and resources on where to find additional information while you continue to study, as well as providing an insight to the Prometric testing center environment and the exam format structure.

PREPARING FOR THE LEED AP O+M EXAM: WEEK EIGHT

By the time you read this section, it should be Week Eight of your study efforts. You should have your white set of flashcards covering the basics of Leadership in Energy and Environmental Design (LEED®); including Innovation in Operations [IO] and Regional Priority [RP] bonus categories and your color-coded cards separated into the five main categories of the LEED for Existing Buildings: Operations & Maintenance™ (EBOM) rating system. This week will be a great opportunity to rewrite your cheat sheet at least three times. Note that your cheat sheet may evolve as you take a few online practice exams.

 TIP Download and read through two of the references from the *LEED AP O+M Candidate Handbook*:
- Guidance on Innovation in Design (ID) Credits
- LEED-Online v2—Sample Credit Templates

During Week Eight, you may need to refer to additional resources while studying. For example, if you want to learn more about the integrated design process, refer to *Sustainable Building Technical Manual: Part II* by Anthony Bernheim and William Reed. Although a sample credit is provided in Appendix I, I would recommend downloading the free version of the EBOM rating system from the U.S. Green Building Council (USGBC) website and skimming through it to see how the categories, prerequisites, and credits are organized and presented. I would also recommend reading through another reference: *Guidance on Innovation & Design (ID) Credits*. All of these references are available to download from the *LEED AP Operations + Maintenance Candidate Handbook* on the GBCI website for free. Again, it is highly recommended that you download the most current candidate handbook from the GBCI website, but as a point of reference, at the time of printing the primary references included:

- ■ *LEED for Operation & Maintenance Reference Guide* (USGBC)
- ■ *Sustainable Building Technical Manual: Part II*, by Anthony Bernheim and William Reed (1996)
- ■ Guidance on Innovation & Design (ID) Credits (USGBC, 2004)
- ■ LEED-Online v2 – Sample Credit Templates

The ancillary references at the time of printing included:

- ■ Energy Star Portfolio Manager (U.S. EPA; www.epa.gov)

- Sub-Metering Energy Use in Colleges and Universities: Incentives and Challenges (U.S. EPA; www.epa.gov)
- ADA Architectural Barriers Act (www.access-board.gov)
- Buildings and Plants (www.energystar.gov)
- IESNA Technical Memorandum on Light Emitting Diode (LED) Sources and Systems (Illuminating Engineering Society of North America, 2005)

Some other resources include:

- *www.usgbc.org.* You may want to check out some of the rating system scorecards or read about credit weightings of LEED v3. The USGBC website is also your primary source to learn about any updates to the LEED rating systems.
- *www.gbci.org.* Make sure you download the current candidate handbook, and you may want to reference the disciplinary policy and the minimum program requirements and the project registration information.
- *www.leedonline.com.* Even if you do not have any projects assigned to you, you will still be able to see what it looks like and watch a demo video.
- *www.epa.gov.* Be sure to visit the ENERGY STAR Portfolio Manager site to learn more about the performance rating tool.

Practice Exam Approach

During Week Nine, you should take some online practice exams. Although there are many sample exam questions provided in this book, it is helpful to practice for the real-life testing environment scenario. Search online, as you will find that there are a few options from which to choose for online practice exams, including www.GreenEDU.com. When you are taking a practice exam, pretend it is the real thing. For example, time yourself, have scratch paper and a pencil available, make a cheat sheet in about two to three minutes, do not use this book or your flashcards, and avoid any disruptions. Some of the online practice exams allow you to flag questions you are doubtful of to remind you to go back and answer later, so take advantage of this for practice as the real test is formatted in the same manner.

Most of the questions include multiple choices with multiple answers required. When approaching these types of questions, you are best advised to "hide" or "cover up" the provided answer options with your hand or a sheet of paper and formulate your own answers to help avoid getting sidetracked by the answer selection choices. Once you uncover or reveal the answer choices, make sure to read through all of the options before selecting your final answer(s). Be sure to read each question carefully and select the proper number of answers. After taking the practice exam, go through the answer key and evaluate your score. On the first practice exam, read through each question and answer one by one to understand how you decided on the correct answer and where you went wrong on the incorrect ones. Try to notice a pattern on your strengths and weaknesses to determine where your study efforts need to be devoted to improve your score. After taking the first practice exam, you may just want to focus on the questions you answered incorrectly.

THE TESTING CENTER ENVIRONMENT

The introduction of this book described the opportunity to make a cheat sheet after you completed the tutorial at the testing center, and Chapter 1 detailed how to schedule your exam date with a Prometric testing center. Hopefully, your exam date is still not scheduled at this point, as one more week of preparation time is suggested to review your flashcards, to refine your cheat sheet, and to give you the opportunity to take a few online practice exams. As stated earlier, it is best to assess your knowledge before scheduling your exam date.

During Week Ten, the week of your test date, there are a few things to remember before you sit for the exam:

- Remember to visit the GBCI website and download the latest version of the *LEED AP Operations + Maintenance Candidate Handbook.*

- Confirm your exam date at least one day prior.

- Find the Prometric testing center and map your path to make sure you know where you are going on your exam day.

- Keep rewriting your cheat sheet and studying your flashcards. Take your flashcards everywhere with you!

To be prepared on the day of your exam, please note the following:

- Bring your picture ID with matching name, just as it is on your GBCI profile.

- Dress comfortably and bring a sweater or a jacket, as the testing center may be cold.

- Be sure to get plenty of rest and eat something, as you will not want to take any breaks during the exam to grab a bite or a drink (the clock cannot be paused).

- Be sure to **check in** at least 30 minutes prior to your testing time. If you miss your scheduled exam time, you will be considered absent and will have to forfeit your exam fees and the opportunity to take the exam.

- Be sure to use the restroom after checking in and prior to being escorted to your workstation. Remember, no breaks!

- You will be observed during your testing session and will be audio and video recorded as well.

- You will not be allowed to bring any personal items to your workstation, such as calculators, paper, pencils, purses, wallets, food, or books.

 TIP A calculator will be provided should you be required to perform any calculations.

EXAM STRUCTURE

The exam is structured to test you on three components, as described in the candidate handbook provided by GBCI. You will be tested on recognition items, application items, and analysis items. The recognition items test your ability to remember factual data once presented in a structure similar to that of the exam references. For example, you may need to provide the definition for a term or recall a fact. The application items present a situation for you to resolve using the principles and elements described in the exam format. These questions may require you to perform a calculation or provide the process or sequence of actions (e.g., CIRs, registration, certification). The analysis items are presented to determine your ability to evaluate a problem and create a solution. These question types are more challenging, as you must be able to decipher the different components of the problem and also assess the relationships of the components.

The exam questions are separated into categories of focus areas and then coordinated with an applicable rating system category. For example, project site factors coordinate with the Sustainable Sites (SS) category, and water management issues coordinate with the Water Efficiency (WE) category. Project systems and energy impacts coordinate with the Energy & Atmosphere (EA) category, while acquisition, installation, and management of project materials coordinate with the Materials & Resources (MR) category. Improvements to the indoor environment coordinate with the Indoor Environmental Quality (EQ) category. Stakeholder involvement in innovation, project surroundings, and public outreach coordinate with the Innovation in Operations (IO) and Regional Priority (RP) categories. Therefore, you should be familiar with each of the credit categories as presented earlier in Part II, Chapters 4–9.

TIP Remember, the exam is composed of multiple-choice questions. No written answers are required!

When at the Testing Center

To give you an idea of what to expect, once you are at your workstation:

- You should dedicate 2 hours and 20 minutes to taking the exam:
  - 10-minute tutorial
  - 2-hour exam
  - 10-minute exit survey

- The tutorial is computer based, so make sure your workstation's monitor, keyboard, and mouse are all functioning properly. After completing the tutorial, remember to then create your cheat sheet in the time left over. Take advantage of the entire 10 minutes before advancing to the exam portion.

- The two-hour exam is composed of 100 multiple-choice questions. Just as with the practice exam questions, in order for the question to be counted as CORRECT, you must select **all** of the correct answers within each question, as there is no partial credit for choosing two out of the three correct answers.

- Although some of the practice exam questions in this book are formatted with a true or false statement or "All of the above" as an answer selection, you are less likely to find this on the real exam, as the questions tend to be straightforward and clear, to avoid any confusion.

- You will not see any credit numbers listed on their own, as all credit names will include the full name.

- Appendix H includes a list of commonly used acronyms. Although most of them are spelled out on the exam, it is still helpful to know what they are!

- During the exam, you will have the opportunity to mark or flag questions to come back to later. It is advised that you take advantage of this, as you may be short on time and want to revisit only the questions you were doubtful about. Note that any unanswered questions are marked INCORRECT, so it is best to at least try. This also gives you the opportunity to move on to the rest of the exam, as some of the other questions might give you the answer to a question you are unsure of.

■ The 10-minute exit survey is followed by your exam results—yes, instant and immediate results!

 Remember to rely on your instincts. Typically, the first answer that comes to mind is often the right one!

Exam Scoring

The exams are scored on a scale from 125 to 200, where 170+ is considered passing. Do not worry about how the questions are weighted, just do your best! Should you need to retake the exam, your application is valid for one year, and therefore you will have three chances within the year to earn a score of 170 or more. Consult the candidate handbook for more information.

After the Exam

Once you have passed the LEED AP O+M exam, remember to change your signature to reflect earning the credential! Although your certificate will not arrive immediately, remember, you must fulfill 30 hours of continuing education units over the next two years, including six LEED-specific continuing education units. The two-year reporting period begins the same day of your exam. Refer to the Credential Maintenance Program (CMP) handbook found on the GBCI website, for more information. There is also a code of conduct you must abide by, as stipulated in the disciplinary policy posted on the GBCI website at www.gbci.org/Files/Disc_ExamAppeals_Policy.pdf. It states that individuals with LEED credentials must:

A. Be truthful, forthcoming, and cooperative in their dealings with GBCI.

B. Be in continuous compliance with GBCI rules (as amended from time to time by GBCI).

 The disciplinary policy found on the GBCI website also includes the exam appeals policy, if needed.

C. Respect GBCI intellectual property rights.

D. Abide by laws related to the profession and to general public health and safety.

E. Carry out their professional work in a competent and objective manner.

SAMPLE LEED EBOM SCORECARD[1]

LEED 2009 for Existing Buildings: Operations & Maintenance Project Checklist

Project Name
Date

Sustainable Sites — 26 Possible Points

Y N ?

		Points
Credit 1	LEED Certified Design and Construction	4
Credit 2	Building Exterior and Hardscape Management Plan	1
Credit 3	Integrated Pest Mgmt, Erosion Control, and Landscape Mgmt Plan	1
Credit 4	Alternative Commuting Transportation	3 to 15
Credit 5	Site Development—Protect or Restore Open Habitat	1
Credit 6	Stormwater Quantity Control	1
Credit 7.1	Heat Island Reduction—Non-Roof	1
Credit 7.2	Heat Island Reduction—Roof	1
Credit 8	Light Pollution Reduction	1

Water Efficiency — 14 Possible Points

		Points
Prereq 1	Minimum Indoor Plumbing Fixture and Fitting Efficiency	
Credit 1	Water Performance Measurement	1 to 2
Credit 1	Additional Indoor Plumbing Fixture and Fitting Efficiency	1 to 5
Credit 1	Water Efficient Landscaping	1 to 5
Credit 1	Cooling Tower Water Management—Chemical Management	1
Credit 1	Cooling Tower Water Management—Non-Potable Water Source Use	1

Energy & Atmosphere — 35 Possible Points

		Points
Prereq 1	Energy Efficiency Best Management Practices	
Prereq 2	Minimum Energy Efficiency Performance	
Prereq 3	Fundamental Refrigerant Management	
Credit 1	Optimize Energy Efficiency Performance	1 to 18
Credit 2.1	Existing Building Commissioning—Investigation and Analysis	2
Credit 2.2	Existing Building Commissioning—Implementation	2
Credit 2.3	Existing Building Commissioning—Ongoing Commissioning	2
Credit 3.1	Performance Measurement—Building Automation System	1
Credit 3.2	Performance Measurement—System-Level Metering	1 to 2
Credit 4	On-site and Off-site Renewable Energy	1 to 6
Credit 5	Enhanced Refrigerant Management	1
Credit 6	Emissions Reduction Reporting	1

Materials and Resources — 10 Possible Points

		Points
Prereq 1	Sustainable Purchasing Policy	
Prereq 2	Solid Waste Management Policy	
Credit 1	Sustainable Purchasing—Ongoing Consumables	1
Credit 2.1	Sustainable Purchasing—Electric	1
Credit 2.2	Sustainable Purchasing—Furniture	1
Credit 3	Sustainable Purchasing—Facility Alterations and Additions	1
Credit 4	Sustainable Purchasing—Reduced Mercury in Lamps	1
Credit 5	Sustainable Purchasing—Food	1

Materials and Resources, Continued

Y N ?

		Points
Credit 6	Solid Waste Management—Waste Stream Audit	1
Credit 7	Solid Waste Management—Ongoing Consumables	1
Credit 8	Solid Waste Management—Durable Goods	1
Credit 9	Solid Waste Management—Facility Alterations and Additions	1

Indoor Environmental Quality — 15 Possible Points

		Points
Prereq 1	Minimum IAQ Performance	
Prereq 2	Environmental Tobacco Smoke (ETS) Control	
Prereq 3	Green Cleaning Policy	
Credit 1.1	IAQ Best Mgmt Practices—IAQ Management Program	1
Credit 1.2	IAQ Best Mgmt Practices—Outdoor Air	1
Credit 1.3	IAQ Best Mgmt Practices—Increased Ventilation	1
Credit 1.4	IAQ Best Mgmt Practices—Reduce Particulates in Air Distribution	1
Credit 1.5	IAQ Mgmt Plan—IAQ Mgmt for Facility Alterations and Additions	1
Credit 2.1	Occupant Comfort—Occupant Survey	1
Credit 2.2	Controllability of Systems—Lighting	1
Credit 2.3	Occupant Comfort—Thermal Comfort Monitoring	1
Credit 2.4	Daylight and Views	1
Credit 3.1	Green Cleaning—High Performance Cleaning Program	1
Credit 3.2	Green Cleaning—Custodial Effectiveness Assessment	1
Credit 3.3	Green Cleaning—Sustainable Cleaning Products, Materials Purchases	1
Credit 3.4	Green Cleaning—Sustainable Cleaning Equipment	1
Credit 3.5	Green Cleaning—Indoor Chemical and Pollutant Source Control	1
Credit 3.6	Green Cleaning—Indoor Integrated Pest Management	1

Innovation in Operations — 6 Possible Points

		Points
Credit 1.1	Innovation in Operations: Specific Title	1
Credit 1.2	Innovation in Operations: Specific Title	1
Credit 1.3	Innovation in Operations: Specific Title	1
Credit 1.4	Innovation in Operations: Specific Title	1
Credit 2	LEED Accredited Professional	1
Credit 3	Documenting Sustainable Building Cost Impacts	1

Regional Priority Credits — 4 Possible Points

		Points
Credit 1.1	Regional Priority: Specific Credit	1
Credit 1.2	Regional Priority: Specific Credit	1
Credit 1.3	Regional Priority: Specific Credit	1
Credit 1.4	Regional Priority: Specific Credit	1

Total — 110 Possible Points

Certified: 40 to 49 points   **Silver:** 50 to 59 points   **Gold:** 60 to 79 points   **Platinum:** 80 to 110

Appendix B

MINIMUM PROGRAM REQUIREMENTS (MPRs) FOR THE EBOM RATING SYSTEM

Minimum Program Requirements

1	**MUST COMPLY WITH ENVIRONMENTAL LAWS**
	Must comply with all applicable federal, state, and local building-related environmental laws and regulations in place where the project is located from the beginning of the performance period through the expiration date.
2	**MUST BE A COMPLETE, PERMANENT BUILDING OR SPACE**
	All LEED projects must be designed for, constructed on, and operated on a permanent location on already existing land.
	No building or space that is designed to move at any point in its lifetime may pursue LEED certification.
	LEED projects must include at least one existing commercial, institutional, or high-rise residential building in its entirety.
3	**MUST USE A REASONABLE SITE BOUNDARY**
	1. The LEED project boundary must include all contiguous land that is associated with and supports normal building operations for the LEED project building, including all land that was or will be disturbed for the purpose of undertaking the LEED project.
	2. The LEED project boundary may not include land that is owned by a party other than that which owns the LEED project unless that land is associated with and supports normal building operations for the LEED project building.
	3. LEED projects located on a campus must have project boundaries such that if all the buildings on campus become LEED certified, then 100% of the gross land area on the campus would be included within a LEED boundary. If this requirement is in conflict with MPR 7, Must Comply with Minimum Building Area to Site Area Ratio, then MPR 7 will take precedence.
	4. Any given parcel of real property may be attributed to only a single LEED project building.
	5. Gerrymandering of a LEED project boundary is prohibited: the boundary may not unreasonably exclude sections of land to create boundaries in unreasonable shapes for the sole purpose of complying with prerequisites or credits.
4	**MUST COMPLY WITH MINIMUM FLOOR AREA REQUIREMENTS**
	The LEED project must include a minimum of 1,000 square feet of gross floor area.
5	**MUST COMPLY WITH MINIMUM OCCUPANCY RATES**
	Full Time Equivalent Occupancy
	The LEED project must serve one or more full-time equivalent (FTE) occupant(s), calculated as an annual average in order to use LEED in its entirety. If the project serves less than one annualized FTE, optional credits from the Indoor Environmental Quality category may not be earned (the prerequisites must still be earned).

	Minimum Occupancy Rate
	The LEED project must be in a state of typical physical occupancy, and all building systems must be operating at a capacity necessary to serve the current occupants, for a period that includes all performance periods as well as at least the 12 continuous months immediately preceding the first submission for a review.
6	**COMMITMENT TO SHARE WHOLE-BUILDING ENERGY AND WATER USAGE DATA**
	All certified projects must commit to sharing with USGBC and/or GBCI all available actual whole-project energy and water usage data for a period of at least five years. This period starts on the date that the building is awarded certification if certifying under EBOM.
	This commitment must carry forward if the building or space changes ownership or lessee.
7	**MUST COMPLY WITH A MINIMUM BUILDING AREA TO SITE AREA RATIO**
	The gross floor area of the LEED project building must be no less than 2% of the gross land area within the LEED project boundary.

Appendix C

MAIN CATEGORY SUMMARIES

Sustainable Sites

Site Design
- SS Credit 1: LEED Certified Design and Construction
- SS Credit 5: Site Development
- SS Credit 7: Heat Island Effect
- SS Credit 8: Light Pollution Reduction

Site Management and Maintenance
- SS Credit 2: Building Exterior and Hardscape Management Plan
- SS Credit 3: Integrated Pest Management Plan, Erosion Control, and Landscape Management Plan

Transportation
- SS Credit 4: Alternative Commuting Transportation

Stormwater Management
- SS Credit 6.1: Stormwater Quantity Control

Water Efficiency

Indoor Water Use
- WE Prerequisite 1: Water Use Reduction
- WE Credit 2: Additional Indoor Plumbing Fixture and Fitting Efficiency

Water Consumption Monitoring
- WE Credit 1: Water Performance Measurement

Outdoor Water Use Reduction
- WE Credit 3: Water Efficient Landscaping

Process Water
- WE Credit 4: Cooling Tower Water Management

Energy & Atmosphere

Monitoring and Improving Building Energy Performance
- EA Prerequisite 1: Energy Efficiency Best Management Practices – Planning, Documentation, and Opportunity Assessment
- EA Prerequisite 2: Minimum Energy Efficiency Performance
- EA Credit 1: Optimize Energy Efficiency Performance
- EA Credit 2.1: Existing Building Commissioning – Investigation and Analysis
- EA Credit 2.2: Existing Building Commissioning – Implementation
- EA Credit 2.3: Existing Building Commissioning – Ongoing Commissioning
- EA Credit 3.1: Performance Measurement – Building Automation System
- EA Credit 3.2: Performance Measurement – System-Level Metering
- EA Credit 6: Emissions Reduction Reporting

Eliminating Chlorofluorocarbons
- EA Prerequisite 3: Fundamental Refrigerant Management
- EA Credit 5: Enhanced Refrigerant Management

Renewable Energy
- EA Credit 4: On-Site and Off-Site Renewable Energy
- EA Credit 6: Green Power

Materials & Resources

Sustainable Purchasing
- MR Prerequisite 1: Sustainable Purchasing Policy
- MR Credit 1: Sustainable Purchasing – Ingoing Consumables
- MR Credit 2: Sustainable Purchasing – Durable Goods
- MR Credit 3: Sustainable Purchasing – Facility Alterations and Additions
- MR Credit 4: Sustainable Purchasing – Reduced Mercury in Lamps
- MR Credit 5: Sustainable Purchasing – Food

Solid Waste Management
- MR Prerequisite 2: Solid Waste Management Policy
- MR Credit 6: Solid Waste Management – Waste Stream Audit
- MR Credit 7: Solid Waste Management – Ongoing Consumables
- MR Credit 8: Solid Waste Management – Durable Goods
- MR Credit 9: Solid Waste Management – Facility Alterations and Additions

Indoor Environmental Quality

Indoor Air Quality Management
- EQ Prerequisite 1: Minimum Indoor Air Quality Performance
- EQ Prerequisite 2: Environmental Tobacco Smoke (ETS) Control

- EQ Credit 1.1: Indoor Air Quality Best Management Practices – IAQ Management Program
- EQ Credit 1.2: Indoor Air Quality Best Management Practices – Outdoor Air Delivery Monitoring
- EQ Credit 1.3: Indoor Air Quality Best Management Practices – Increased Ventilation
- EQ Credit 1.4: Indoor Air Quality Best Management Practices – Reducing Particulates in Air Distribution
- EQ Credit 1.5: Indoor Air Quality Best Management Practices – IAQ Management for Facility Additions and Alterations

Occupant Comfort

- EQ Credit 2.1: Occupant Comfort Occupant Survey
- EQ Credit 2.2: Controllability of Systems - Lighting
- EQ Credit 2.3: Occupant Comfort - Thermal Comfort Monitoring
- EQ Credit 2.4: Daylight and Views

Green Cleaning

- EQ Prerequisite 3: Green Cleaning Policy
- EQ Credit 3.1: Green Cleaning – High Performance Cleaning Program
- EQ Credit 3.2: Green Cleaning – Custodial Effectiveness Assessment
- EQ Credit 3.3: Green Cleaning – Purchase of Sustainable Cleaning Products and Materials
- EQ Credit 3.4: Green Cleaning – Sustainable Cleaning Equipment
- EQ Credit 3.5: Green Cleaning – Indoor Chemical Pollutant Source Control
- EQ Credit 3.6: Green Cleaning – Indoor Integrated Pest Management

Appendix D

RELATED PREREQUISITES AND CREDITS FOR EBOM

Category	Credit	Description	Sustainable Sites									Water Efficiency					
			Credit 1	Credit 2	Credit 3	Credit 4	Credit 5	Credit 6	Credit 7.1	Credit 7.2	Credit 8	Prereq 1	Credit 1	Credit 2	Credit 3	Credit 4	Credit 5
Sustainable Sites	Credit 1	LEED Certified Design and Construction															
	Credit 2	Building Exterior and Hardscape Management Plan															
	Credit 3	Integrated Pest Mgmt Erosion Control, and Landscape Mgmt Plan					X	X							X		
	Credit 4	Alternative Commuting Transportation					X	X	X								
	Credit 5	Site Development, Protect or Restore Open Habitat			X			X	X	X					X		
	Credit 6	Stormwater Quantity Control					X		X	X							
	Credit 7.1	Heat Island Effect, Non-Roof					X	X							X		
	Credit 7.2	Heat Island Effect, Roof					X	X									
	Credit 8	Light Pollution Reduction															
Water Efficiency	Prerequisite 1	Minimum Indoor Plumbing Fixture and Fitting Efficiency						X						X	X	X	
	Credit 1	Water Performance Measurement										X		X	X	X	
	Credit 2	Additional Indoor Plumbing Fixture and Fitting Efficiency						X				X			X	X	
	Credit 3	Water Efficienct Landscaping			X		X	X									
	Credit 4	Cooling Tower Water Management - Chemical Management						X						X	X		
	Credit 5	Cooling Tower Water Management - Non-Potable Water Source Use															
Energy & Atmosphere	Prerequisite 1	Energy Efficiency Best Management Practices															
	Prerequisite 2	Minimum Energy Efficiency Performance															
	Prerequisite 3	Fundamental Refrigerant Management															
	Credit 1	Optimize Energy Efficiency Performance															
	Credit 2.1	Existing Building Commissioning - Investigation and Analysis															
	Credit 2.2	Existing Building Commissioning - Implementation															
	Credit 2.3	Existing Building Commissioning - Ongoing Commissioning															
	Credit 3.1	Performance Measurement - Building Automation System															
	Credit 3.2	Performance Measurement - System-Level Metering															
	Credit 4	On-Site and Off-Site Renewable Energy															
	Credit 5	Enhanced Refrigerant Management															
	Credit 6	Emissions Reduction Reporting															
Materials & Resources	Prerequisite 1	Sustainable Purchasing Policy															
	Prerequisite 2	Solid Waste Management Policy															
	Credit 1	Sustainable Purchasing - Ongoing Consumables															
	Credit 2.1	Sustainable Purchasing - Durables Goods, Electric															
	Credit 2.2	Sustainable Purchasing - Durables Goods, Furniture															
	Credit 3	Sustainable Purchasing - Facility Alterations and Additions															
	Credit 4	Sustainable Purchasing - Reduced Mercury in Lamps															
	Credit 5	Sustainable Purchasing - Food															
	Credit 6	Solid Waste Management - Waste Stream Audit															
	Credit 7	Solid Waste Management - Ongoing Consumables															
	Credit 8	Solid Waste Management - Durable Goods															
	Credit 9	Solid Waste Management - Facility Alterations and Additions															
Indoor Environmental Quality	Prerequisite 1	Minimum IAQ Performance					X										
	Prerequisite 2	Environmental Tobacco Smoke (ETS) Control															
	Prerequisite 3	Green Cleaning Policy															
	Credit 1.1	IAQ Best Mgmt Practices - IAQ Management Program															
	Credit 1.2	IAQ Best Mgmt Practices - Outdoor Air Delivery Monitoring					X										
	Credit 1.3	IAQ Best Mgmt Practices - Increased Ventilation															
	Credit 1.4	Distribution															
	Credit 1.5	Alterations															
	Credit 2.1	Occupant Comfort - Occupant Survey															
	Credit 2.2	Controllability of Systems - Lighting															
	Credit 2.3	Occupant Comfort - Thermal Comfort Monitoring															
	Credit 2.4	Daylight and Views															
	Credit 3.1	Green Cleaning - High Performance Cleaning Program		X													
	Credit 3.2	Green Cleaning - Custodial Effectiveness Assessment															
	Credit 3.3	Green Cleaning - Sustainable Cleaning Products and Materials															
	Credit 3.4	Green Cleaning - Sustainable Cleaning Equipment	X	X													
	Credit 3.5	Green Cleaning - Indoor Chemical and Pollutant Source Control	X														
	Credit 3.6	Green Cleaning - Indoor Integrated Pest Management		X													

	Prereq 1	Prereq 2	Prereq 3	Credit 1	Credit 2.1	Credit 2.2	Credit 2.3	Credit 3.1	Credit 3.2	Credit 4	Credit 5	Credit 6	Prereq 1	Prereq 2	Credit 1	Credit 2.1	Credit 2.2	Credit 3	Credit 4	Credit 5	Credit 6	Credit 7	Credit 8	Credit 9	Prereq 1	Prereq 2	Prereq 3	Credit 1.1	Credit 1.2	Credit 1.3	Credit 1.4	Credit 1.5	Credit 2.1	Credit 2.2	Credit 2.3	Credit 2.4	Credit 3.6	Credit 3.2	Credit 3.3	Credit 3.4	Credit 3.5	Credit 3.6
																																								X	X	X
																																										X
				X																																						
	X																																									
X	X			X	X	X																																			
	X		X	X	X	X																																			
X			X	X	X	X	X	X			X													X				X		X		X									
									X																																
X			X	X	X	X	X				X													X				X		X		X									
X					X	X																																			
X			X		X																																				
X			X	X																																					
			X			X		X																													X				
X			X			X	X																																		
X			X	X	X																																				
	X	X	X																																						
	X		X	X	X	X		X																																	
												X	X	X	X	X	X	X	X		X	X	X	X																	
												X									X	X	X	X																	
												X	X		X	X					X	X	X	X																	
												X	X								X	X	X	X																	
												X	X								X	X	X	X																	
												X	X								X	X	X	X																	
												X	X								X	X	X	X																	
												X	X								X	X	X	X																	
												X	X	X	X	X	X	X	X		X	X	X	X																	
													X	X	X	X	X	X	X	X		X	X																			
													X	X	X	X	X	X	X	X	X																					
				X	X	X	X	X	X																X			X							X						
X	X			X																				X			X	X	X			X								X	
				X	X			X																														X	X	X	X
				X	X	X	X	X	X															X	X			X		X	X	X	X								X
																								X	X			X			X		X	X	X				X		
X				X																				X				X													
																								X			X														
							X	X																X					X						X				X	X	X	X
X	X			X	X	X	X																											X							
X	X						X																												X						
				X												X	X													X						X					
																													X									X	X	X	X
																																				X		X	X	X	
																X											X									X					
																X											X									X					
																X											X									X					
																																				X		X	X	X	
																																				X		X	X	X	

Appendix E

EXEMPLARY PERFORMANCE FOR LEED EBOM

SUSTAINABLE SITES		
SSc4	Alternative Commuting Transportation	Demonstrate a minimum **95%** reduction in conventional commuting trips equivalent to an average vehicle ridership (as defined by SCAQMD) of 20
SSc5	Site Development – Protect or Restore Open Space	Having on-site native or adapted vegetation covering **50%** of the site area (excluding the building footprint) **- OR -**
		10% of the total site area (including the building footprint), whichever is greater. For off-site habitat protection or restoration, double the required areas **- OR -**
		Previously certified projects that earned SSc5.1: Site Development, Protect or Restore Habitat with a LEED Building Design + Construction rating system
SSc6	Stormwater Quantity Control	Demonstrating that the stormwater management plan in place during the performance period is capable of reducing stormwater runoff by **30%** or more
SSc7.1	Heat Island Effect: Nonroof	At least **95%** of nonroof impervious surfaces have been constructed with SRI-compliant materials and/or open-grid paving or will be shaded within 5 years **- OR -**
		At least **95%** of the on-site parking spaces have been located under cover (SRI compliant)
SSc7.2	Heat Island Effect: Roof	Demonstrating that **95%** of the project's roof area (excluding any mechanical equipment, photovoltaic panels, and skylights) consists of a vegetated roof system

WATER EFFICIENCY		
WEc1, Option 2	Water Performance Measurement - Submetering	Comply with WE Credit 1, Water Performance Measurement, Option 1, and provide documentation meeting the requirements of Option 2 for **two or more** water subsystems
WEc2	Additional Indoor Plumbing Fixture & Fitting Efficiency	Achieve a potable water savings of **35%** or greater
WEc4, Option 2	Cooling Tower Water Management - Nonpotable Water Source Use	Demonstrate a minimum of **95%** of cooling tower makeup water comes from nonpotable sources

ENERGY & ATMOSPHERE		
EAc1	Optimize Energy Efficiency Performance	For Case 1, buildings must receive an ENERGY STAR rating of **97** or higher
		For Case 2, Option 2, project buildings must be in the **47th** percentile above the national median

EAc4	On-Site and Off-Site Renewable Energy	Could mean **13.5%** on-site renewable energy, or the equivalent calculated combination of on-site and off-site renewable energy, provided the % sum of off-site and on-site renewable energy is 100% or less

MATERIALS & RESOURCES

MRc1	Sustainable Purchasing – Ongoing Consumables	Achieve sustainable purchases of **95%** or more of total purchases over the performance period
MRc2	Sustainable Purchasing – Durable Goods	For Option 1, project teams can earn 1 additional credit by increasing sustainable purchases of electrical equipment to **80%** of total electronics purchases **- OR -**
		For Option 2, project teams can earn 1 additional point by increasing sustainable purchases of furniture to **80%** of total furniture purchases
MRc3	Sustainable Purchasing – Facility Alterations & Additions	Sustainable purchases for materials in facility alterations and additions account for **95%** of total purchases
MRc4	Sustainable Purchasing – Reduced Mercury in Lamps	Project teams can earn an additional point if 90% of lamps purchased over the performance period have an average mercury content of **70** picograms per lumen-hour or less
MRc5	Sustainable Purchasing – Food	Sustainable food and beverage purchases account for **50%** or more of the total cost over the performance period
MRc7	Solid Waste Management – Ongoing Consumables	Document **95%** diversion of the ongoing consumables waste stream
MRc9	Solid Waste Management – Facility Alterations & Additions	Divert **95%** or more of waste generated by facility alterations and additions from disposal to landfills and incineration facilities

INDOOR ENVIRONMENTAL QUALITY

EQc2.2	Controllability of Systems – Lighting	Achieve **95%** occupant-controlled lighting in both individual workstations and multioccupant spaces
EQc2.4	Daylight & Views	Achieve both **75%** daylighting and **90%** views
EQc3.2	Green Cleaning – Custodial Effectiveness Assessment	Score a **2 or less** in appearance level
EQc3.3	Green Cleaning – Purchase of Sustainable Cleaning Products & Materials	**60%** or more of the total annual purchases of these products must meet at least 1 of the required criteria for this credit

Appendix F

REFERENCED STANDARDS OF LEED EBOM

SUSTAINABLE SITES		
SSc1	LEED Certified Design & Construction	USGBC
SSc4	Alternative Transportation – Parking Capacity	California Air Resources Board, Definition of Zero-Emission Vehicle
		American Council for an Energy-Efficient Economy, The ACEEE Green Book®: The Environmental Guide to Cars and Trucks
		South Coast Air Quality Management District, Rule 2202, *On-Road Motor Vehicle Mitigation Options Employee Commute Reduction Program Guidelines*, Chapter II, effective February 2004, and Rule 2202, *Employee Commute Reduction Program AVR Survey Support Guide*, effective July 29, 2005

WATER EFFICIENCY		
WEp1	Water Use Reduction	International Association of Plumbing and Mechanical Officials Publication IAPMO/ ANSI UPC 1-2006 section 402.0, *Water-Conservation Fixtures and Fittings*
		International Code Council, IPC 2006, section 604, *Design of Building Water Distribution System*
WEc2	Innovative Wastewater Technologies	Refer to WEp1 Standards

ENERGY & ATMOSPHERE		
EAp1	Energy Efficiency Best Management Practices - Planning, Documentation, and Opportunity Assessment	ASHRAE Level I, Walk-Through Analysis
EAp3	Fundamental Refrigerant Management	U.S. EPA Clean Air Act, Title VI, Section 608, Refrigerant Recycling Rule
EAc1	Optimize Energy Efficiency Performance	ENERGY STAR® Portfolio Manager
EAc2.1	Existing Building Commissioning - Investigation and Analysis	ASHRAE Level II, Energy Audit, Energy Survey and Analysis
EAc4	On-Site and Off-Site Renewable Energy	Center for Resource Solutions' Green-e Product Certification Requirements

MATERIALS & RESOURCES		
MRc1	Sustainable Purchasing - Ongoing Consumables	Forest Stewardship Council Certified Paper Products
MRc2	Sustainable Purchasing - Durable Goods	ENERGY STAR® Qualified Products
		Forest Stewardship Council, Certified Wood
		Electronic Product Environmental Assessment Tools (EPEAT)
MRc3	Sustainable Purchasing - Facility Alterations and Additions	Forest Stewardship Council, Certified Wood
		FloorScore
		Green Label Testing Program (1992) and Green Label Plus TestingProgram (2004)
		Green Seal GS-11 Environmental Requirements for Paints, effective May 1993
		Bay Area Air Quality Management District (BAAQMD) Regulation 8, Organic Compounds, Rule 51, Adhesive and Sealant Products, effective July 2002
		South Coast Air Quality Management District (SCAQMD) Rule 1168, Adhesive and Sealant Applications, effective October 2003
MRc4	Sustainable Purchasing - Reduced Mercury in Lamps	NEMA Voluntary Commitment on Mercury in Compact Fluorescent Lights
MRc5	Sustainable Purchasing - Food	Fairtrade Labeling Organizations Internation certification
		Food Alliance certification
		Marine Stewardship Council (MSC) Blue Eco-label
		Protected Harvest certification
		Rainforest Alliance certification
		U.S. Department of Agricultural Organic certification

INDOOR ENVIRONMENTAL QUALITY		
EQp1	Minimum IAQ Performance	ASHRAE 62.1-2007 - Ventilation for Acceptable Indoor Air Quality (Ventilation Rate Procedure)
EQp2	Environmental Tobacco Smoke (ETS) Control	ANSI/ASTM E779-03, Standard Test Method for Determining Air Leakage by Fan Pressurization
		California Residential Alternative Calculation Method Approval Manual
EQc1.1	IAQ Best Management Practices - IAQ Management Program	IAQ Building Education and Assessment Model (I-BEAM)
EQc1.2	IAQ Best Management Practices - Outdoor Air Delivery Monitoring	ASHRAE 62.1-2007 - Ventilation for Acceptable Indoor Air Quality

EQc1.3	IAQ Best Management Practices - Increased Ventilation	ASHRAE 62.1-2007 - Ventilation for Acceptable Indoor Air Quality
		CIBSE Applications Manual 10: Natural Ventilation in Non-Domestic Buildings (2005)
		The Carbon Trust Good Practice Guide 237: Natural Ventilation in Non-Domestic Buildings - A Guide for Designers; Developers & Owners (1998)
EQc1.4	IAQ Best Management Practices - Reduce Particulates in Air Distribution	ASHRAE 52.2-1999: Method of Testing General Ventilation Air-Cleaning Devices for Removal Efficiency by Particle Size
EQc1.5	IAQ Best Management Practices - IAQ Management for Facilty Additions and Alterations	ANSI/ASHRAE 52.2-1999 - Method of Testing General Ventilation Air-Cleaning Devices for Removal Efficiency by Particle Size
		SMACNA, IAQ Guidelines for Occupied Buildings Under Construction, second edition, November 2007, Chapter 3
EQc2.1	Occupant Comfort - Occupant Survey	ASHRAE 55-2004 - Thermal Comfort Conditions for Human Occupancy
EQc2.3	Occupant Comfort - Thermal Comfort Monitoring	ASHRAE 55-2004 - Thermal Comfort Conditions for Human Occupancy
EQc2.4	Daylight and Views	ASTM D1003-07E1, Standard Test Method for Haze and Luminous Transmittance of Transparent Plastics
EQc3.2	Green Cleaning - Custodial Effectiveness Assessment	Custodial Staffing Guidelines
EQc3.3	Green Cleaning - Purchase of Sustainable Cleaning Products and Materials	California Code of Regulations Maximum Allowable VOC Levels
		Environmental Choice Certified Products
		Green Seal® Certified
		The EPA Comprehensive Procurement Guidelines
EQc3.4	Green Cleaning - Sustainable Cleaning Equipment	California Air Resources Board
		Environmental Protection Agency
		Carpet and Rug Institute Green Label
		Carpet and Rug Institute Seal of Approval

| **INNOVATION IN OPERATIONS** | | |
| IOc2 | LEED Accredited Professional | LEED Accredited Professional - (GBCI) Green Building Certification Institute |

Appendix G

ANSWERS TO QUIZ QUESTIONS

CHAPTER 3: THE LEED FOR EXISTING BUILDINGS: OPERATIONS & MAINTENANCE RATING SYSTEM

Q3.1.   **D.** Remember, EBOM is the only rating system that expires and where a building can be recertified. Certification lasts for 5 years, although a team can submit every year for recertification.

Q3.2.   **E.** All of the four options listed are environmental benefits of green building design, construction, and operational efforts.

Q3.3.   **A and D.** Ultimately, it is up to the project team to decide which rating system is best suited to their project but in this case, the O+M reference guide defines the maximum limitations to guide the decision to determine the appropriate rating system.

Q3.4.   **B.** According to the EPA website, Americans typically spend about 90 percent of their time indoors.

Q3.5.   **B.** Although the strategies listed will increase the first costs for a project, it is important to remember the life-cycle costs, including purchase price, installation, operation, maintenance, and upgrade costs.

Q3.6.   **A.** Make sure to remember the point range scales of the LEED certification levels for the purposes of the exam.

Q3.7.   **A and C.** CIRs are submitted to GBCI for review, electronically through LEED-Online. CIRs are limited to 600 words and should not be formatted as a letter. Since the CIR is submitted electronically through LEED-Online, the project and credit or prerequisite information is tracked; therefore, the CIR does not need to include this type of information. It is critical to remember that CIRs are submitted specific to one credit or prerequisite.

Q3.8.   **C.** EBOM projects seeking certification must include a minimum of 1,000 square feet of gross floor area per the MPRs listed on the USGBC website.

Q3.9.   **B and E.** Be sure to remember each of the MPRs and how they pertain to each rating system, as posted on the GBCI website.

Q3.10. **E.** All projects seeking LEED certification must commit to sharing five years' worth of actual whole-project energy and water usage data with USGBC and/or GBCI.

Q3.11. **B and E.** Appeals are electronically submitted to GBCI through LEED-Online for a fee, within 25 business days after the final results from a design or construction certification review are posted to LEED-Online.

Q3.12. **C.** It is also important to remember, although the Regional Priority category is a new addition to the rating systems, no new prerequisites or credits were created to include within the new category. The Regional Priority category offers bonus points for achieving existing LEED credits detailed in the other categories.

Q3.13. **B.** Although design reviews can be beneficial, points are not awarded until final review after construction.

Q3.14. **D and E.** Registering with GBCI indicates a project is seeking LEED certification. Project registration can be completed at any time, although it is strongly encouraged to do so as early as possible. GBCI does not grant the award of any points regardless when registration occurs. Registration will, however, grant the project team access to a LEED-Online site specific for the project, but does not include any free submissions of CIRs.

Q3.15. **A and C.** Although registering a project requires some information, including contact information, project location, and indication of compliance with MPRs, a team must submit all credit submittal templates for all prerequisites and attempted credits during the certification application. Required supplemental documentation, such as plans and calculations, must be uploaded as well.

Q3.16. **D.** All prerequisites and any credits under pursuit must be submitted for review no more than 60 calendar days after the performance periods have been completed.

Q3.17. **A.** It is important to remember that the details of the certification process specific to the EBOM rating system for the purposes of the exam.

Q3.18. **B.** Project teams have 25 business days to issue an appeal to GBCI after receiving the final review comments.

Q3.19. **B, C, and F.** CIRs can be submitted through LEED-Online, any time after registration. CIRs specifically address one MPR, prerequisite, or credit. Although the project administrator submits the CIR, the response is viewable by all team members invited to the LEED-Online site for the project. CIRs are project specific, and therefore CIR responses will no longer be published to a database as they once were.

Q3.20. **A.** GBCI is responsible for the appeals process as well as managing the certification bodies. It is best to remember USGBC as an education provider for the LEED rating systems they create, and GBCI as being responsible for the professional accreditation and project certification processes.

Q3.21. **C.** Be sure to use flashcards to remember the details and characteristics of performance periods as they relate to the EBOM rating system.

CHAPTER 4: SUSTAINABLE SITES

Q4.1. **B.** Where a project is located and how it is developed can have multiple impacts on the ecosystem and water resources required during the life of a building.

Q4.2. **D.** Remember to use your flashcards to help you to remember these types of details.

Q4.3. **A, C, and D.** The exam will test your knowledge of credit and strategy synergies. Remembering all of the benefits of green building strategies, such as green roofs and stormwater reuse, is key for exam purposes.

Q4.4. **C.** Be sure to use your flashcards to remember these types of details.

Q4.5. **B and D.** The process of elimination might be helpful to deduce the most appropriate answers.

Q4.6. **C.** The key to reducing heat island effects is to avoid implementing materials that will absorb and retain heat. Deciduous trees lose their leaves and, therefore, are not the best decision. Xeriscaping to reduce evaporation and increasing impervious surfaces to recharge groundwater are great strategies for sustainable site design, but they do not help to reduce heat island effects. They, in turn, reap the benefits of reduced heat island effects. Implementing paving and roofing products with a higher albedo, or SRI, is therefore the best answer to reduce heat island effects.

Q4.7. **F.** It is best to involve all the players related to designing and installing a green roof in a collaborative setting. Understanding the requirements of a green roof will indicate the team members required, especially what type of vegetation will be utilized. Remember, a green roof impacts the thermal elements of a building, structural integrity, stormwater management, and the coordination of construction trades.

Q4.8. **D.** Emissivity is the ability of a material surface to give up heat in the form of radiation. It may be helpful to remember emittance is the opposite of reflectivity. Infrared reflectivity applies to low-emissivity materials. Therefore, these materials reflect the majority of long-wave radiation and emit very little, such as metals or special metallic coatings. High-emissivity surfaces, such as painted building materials, absorb a majority of long-wave radiation as opposed to reflecting it, and emit infrared or long-wave radiation more willingly.

Q4.9. **A, B, and C.** The LEED rating systems recommend to combine the following three strategies to reduce heat island effects: provide shade (within five years of occupancy), install paving materials with an SRI of at least 29, and implement an open-grid pavement system (less than 50 percent impervious).

Q4.10. **C.** Remember, some material in this book can be presented for the first time in the format of a question. Use these opportunities to test your knowledge, and if you are not familiar with the content, be sure to make a flashcard or make a note on your cheat sheet in order to remember the information.

Q4.11. **D.** Be sure to use the study worksheets at the end of each chapter to help remember the details of each prerequisite and credit.

Q4.12. **B.** The process of elimination might be helpful to use to deduce the most appropriate answers.

Q4.13. **A, C, and D.** Remembering the intentions behind each prerequisite and credit will help you remember the requirements.

Q4.14. **E.** This requirement is consistent across a number of credits and, therefore, should be remembered for the purposes of the exam.

Q4.15. **B and C.** Create a list of integrated and associated credits such as this example to help remember for the exam.

Q4.16. **A, B, and D.** Remember, incineration is not a compliant method unless the biofuel can be used for energy.

Q4.17. **A.** The process of elimination might be helpful to use to deduce the most appropriate answers.

Q4.18. **D.** In order to calculate the answer, first the commuting round trips need to be determined for the five-day work week occupants and the compressed four-day work week occupants. For the compressed work week: $80 \times 2 \times 4 = 640$ and $20 \times 2 \times 5 = 200$ determine the commuting round trips for the five-day work week. Adding the two results, produces 840. If everyone commuted for five days, then there would be 1,000 commuting round trips. To find the reduction subtract 840 from 1,000 and divide the result by 1,000 = 16 percent.

Q4.19. **A, B, and C.** According to the *Green Building and LEED Core Concepts Guide,* transportation is most affected by location, vehicle technology, fuel, and human behavior.

Q4.20. **A, C, D, and E.** If a LEED project's site does not offer mass transit accessibility and is, therefore, dependent on car commuting, it is best to encourage the occupants to carpool, offer alternative fuel-efficient vehicles, or incorporate conveniences within the building or on site.

Q4.21. **A, B, and C.** Selecting a site near public transportation, limiting parking, and encouraging carpooling are all strategies to consider when working on a project seeking LEED certification. It is always best to redevelop a previously developed site, avoiding greenfield sites.

Q4.22. **E.** Use your flashcards to remember these types of requirements.

Q4.23. **B.** This might be a note to keep on your cheat sheet if you cannot remember the requirement.

Q4.24. **A, C, and D.** Impervious asphalt does not allow rainwater to percolate through and, therefore, allows stormwater to leave the site, carrying pollutants and debris, heading to storm sewers and nearby bodies of water.

Q4.25. **D and E.** Selecting products with the highest SRI values is best suited for compliance with LEED.

Q4.26. **C.** This might be a note to keep on your cheat sheet if you cannot remember the requirement.

Q4.27. **E.** Trust your memory and your instincts!

Q4.28. **B.** In order to qualify for this credit, 50 percent of the roof surface must comply by the means of a high-SRI roofing material and/or a green roof. Photovoltaic panels and mechanical equipment square footage is subtracted from the compliant roof surface calculations. Therefore, 50,000 – 15,000 – 5,000 = 30,000 eligible roof surface, where 50 percent would need to comply with the minimum SRI level.

Q4.29. **A and E.** See Appendix E for a summary of all of the opportunities to pursue Exemplary Performance within the EBOM rating system.

Q4.30. **A.** Be sure to use the study worksheets at the end of each chapter to help remember the details of each prerequisite and credit.

Q4.31. **A, B, and D.** Remember to use your cheat sheet for details difficult to remember!

Q4.32. **B, C, and E.** Use your flashcards to remember these types of details.

Q4.33. **A and D.** Use your flashcards to remember these types of details.

CHAPTER 5: WATER EFFICIENCY

Q5.1. **C.** Use your flashcards to remember these types of details. It might be helpful to add this to your cheat sheet as well.

Q5.2. **B and F.** Remember flow fixture and flush fixture types for the exam.

Q5.3. **E.** Use your flashcards and the study worksheets at the end of each chapter to remember these types of details.

Q5.4. **A and F.** Remember the fixtures to include in the prerequisite calculations to differentiate the calculations for exemplary performance for the credit.

Q5.5. **E.** It is recommended to create a flashcard to remember the percentage thresholds and the year of cutoff specific to calculating water reduction.

Q5.6. **E.** The process of elimination might help derive the correct answer for this question.

Q5.7. **D.** Use those flashcards!

Q5.8. **C.** The study worksheets might help to remember the requirements of the prerequisites and credits.

Q5.9. **D.** If monitoring for water leakage problems, a weekly inspection is logical to assume.

Q5.10. **A, B, and D.** The process of elimination might help derive the correct answer for this question. Trust your instincts!

Q5.11. **A, B, and E.** Turf grass poses a maintenance, economic, and environmental concern by the amount of watering it requires. Reducing pervious surfaces does not address saving water for landscaping, and from an environmental aspect, project teams are encouraged to *increase* pervious surfaces to recharge groundwater.

Q5.12. **A, B, C, and D.** The site design strategies do not address increasing the density factor. Density can be increased by development design strategies, such as increasing floor-to-area ratio (FAR).

Q5.13. **C, D, and E.** Installing open-grid pavers in lieu of asphalt minimizes the contributions to the urban heat island effect, as pavers do not absorb the heat from the sun as opposed to asphalt. By reducing heat gain, energy use is optimized, as the building has less of a demand for cooling loads. The pavers also allow stormwater to penetrate through to reduce runoff.

Q5.14. **B.** Remember the types of high-efficiency irrigation systems, as traditional sprinkler or spray-type systems do not comply.

Q5.15. **A, B, and C.** Process water is the water needed for building systems and business operations.

Q5.16. **B, C, and E.** Blackwater is wastewater from a toilet. Remembering the different types of nonpotable water can help answer other questions about specific design strategies as related to water efficiency.

Q5.17. **B and D.** Sometimes the process of elimination helps to determine the correct answers. Although captured rainwater is used for custodial uses, cleaning dishes and clothes is best with potable water sources.

Q5.18. **A, B, C, and E.** Make a flashcard to remember this information if necessary.

Q5.19. **C.** Collecting stormwater for reuse does not meet the intentions for WE Credit 1, as this credit requires metering equipment for irrigation, indoor plumbing fixtures, cooling towers, domestic hot water, or other process water uses.

Q5.20. **E.** Evapotranspiration refers to water loss from a vegetated surface and, therefore, is not related to process water.

Q5.21. **B.** WE Credit 2 does not incorporate any requirements for process water for cooling towers.

Q5.22. **D.** Use your flashcards to remember this type of information.

Q5.23. **C.** Asphalt and lead-containing roof surface materials can contaminate collected water and are, therefore, not recommended.

Q5.24. **C and F.** Be sure to pay attention to the key words to ensure you select the correct answers.

Q5.25. **A.** Be sure to know the purpose of the requirements associated with WE Credit 4: Cooling Tower Water Management. Make a note to remember Evapotranspiration is associated with sustainable landscaping strategies.

CHAPTER 6: ENERGY AND ATMOSPHERE

Q6.1. **A and D.** Learning the concepts to comply with each of the credits and prerequisites is key for the exam. Try to remember the intent behind each to help decipher the appropriate strategy or technology. Refer to Appendix C for a summary of concepts and related credits/prerequisites.

Q6.2. **C.** Remember to use your cheat sheet for details difficult to remember!

Q6.3. **B.** Use your flashcards to quiz yourself on these types of details.

Q6.4. **C.** Be sure to remember what tasks are required to be completed during the performance period. Notice that most of the prerequisites are not addressed during the performance period, but instead the audit or program development stages except for this one.

Q6.5. **B.** Refer to Appendix H for a summary of acronyms to recognize. This acronym not only includes CO_2 but also five other greenhouse gases.

Q6.6. **B and C.** Be sure to make a flashcard to quiz yourself on the inclusive items for this credit.

Q6.7. **A.** Use your flashcards to quiz yourself on these types of details or make a note on your cheat sheet.

Q6.8. **A and D.** Be sure to make a flashcard to quiz yourself on the inclusive items for this credit.

Q6.9. **B.** The process of elimination works best to help narrow down the possible correct answers.

Q6.10. **A, C, and D.** Be sure to use the study worksheets at the end of each chapter to help remember the details of each prerequisite and credit.

Q6.11. **C.** Use the study worksheets and your cheat sheet to remember these types of details. Be sure to remember what kinds of appliances can be eliminated from the compliance calculations as well, such as water coolers and refrigerators.

Q6.12. **A.** Be sure to know this refrigerant is mainly disqualified for LEED certification purposes.

Q6.13. **A, D, and E.** This question relates to question 6.11 to give an example how the exam might question the same topic differently.

Q6.14. **B, D, and E.** Refrigerants do not apply to boilers, fan motors, or variable-frequency drives, which eliminates answer options A and C.

Q6.15. **A and C.** It is critical to remember the details about refrigerants for the purposes of the exam.

Q6.16. **B, D, and E.** Use your flashcards to remember these types of details specific to energy efficiency calculation.

Q6.17. **D.** This detail might be appropriate for your cheat sheet. If you write it enough times, you will remember it for the exam!

Q6.18. **B, E, and F.** Passive solar design features and off-site strategies do not contribute to earning the on-site compliance path for the Renewable Energy credit. Ground-source heat pumps do not qualify either, as they require power to function the pump.

Q6.19. **C.** Be sure to use the study worksheets to connect the purpose (or intent) for each prerequisite and credit.

Q6.20. **C and E.** Although a CxA will be responsible for verifying the installation, calibration, and performance of the cogeneration system, the strategy described in the question does not indicate any information involving a CxA, thus eliminating answer A. The question does not indicate any renewable energy to be generated on site, nor does it refer to any offsetting green power procurement, thus eliminating answers B, D, and F.

Q6.21. **A, C, and D.** There are a few credits that have a direct correlation between them such as the ones pointed out in this question. Be sure to remember these for the exam.

Q6.22. **A, D, and F.** The process of elimination might help derive the correct answers to this question as options B and C pull smaller amounts of energy as compared to energy-related building systems, such as lighting. Employee turn-over is not a BAS related component as it is not related to the functionality or operations of a building.

Q6.23. **A, D, and E.** There are a few credits that have a direct correlation between them such as the ones pointed out in this question. Be sure to remember these for the exam.

Q6.24. **A, B, and D.** On the real exam, there will be questions you might be unfamiliar with. Although not presented in the chapter material use the practice questions to learn new information relevant to the exam. It should be known that the WRI/WSBC Greenhouse Gas Reporting protocol is the most widely used international accounting tool to help governmental and business leaders comprehend, measure, and coordinate emissions.

Q6.25. **B.** Use the study worksheets and your flashcards to remember these types of details.

Q6.26. **A.** Refer to the study worksheets to remember this detail.

Q6.27. **D.** The process of elimination might have worked here as EA Credit 1 determines efficiency of consumed power from the grid.

Q6.28. **A, B, and D.** Remember—no CFCs allowed as per the prerequisite! Projects that can prove compliance is economically unfeasible will still be able to pursue certification. If CFCs are used and feasibility is determined then the refrigerant must be phased out within five years.

Q6.29. **A, C, D, and E.** Make a note on your cheat or use your flashcards to remember eligible sources of off-site renewables.

CHAPTER 7: MATERIALS AND RESOURCES

Q7.1.   **A, B, and E.** Use the study worksheets and your flashcards to remember these types of details.

Q7.2.   **B.** Remember this credit has three compliance options and, therefore, more opportunities to earn points.

Q7.3.   **D.** Use your flashcards to remember chain-of-custody documentation is required to prove compliance for FSC certification.

Q7.4.   **A, C, D, and E.** The process of elimination could be used to derive the four correct answers. Remember the cost of labor is never included in compliance documentation.

Q7.5.   **A, C, and F.** Use your flashcards to quiz yourself on these types of details or make a note on your cheat sheet.

Q7.6.   **C, D, and E.** Remember, preconsumer recycled content refers to scrap and trim material generated from the manufacturing process, but does not enter into the consumer cycle of goods. Preconsumer recycled materials are used to manufacture a different product than what it was originally intended for.

Q7.7.   **A, D, and E.** Use your flashcards to quiz yourself on these types of details or make a note on your cheat sheet.

Q7.8.   **B.** Rapidly renewable products must be able to be grown or raised in 10 years or less, thus eliminating B from qualifying.

Q7.9.   **A, B, D, and G.** As you can see, there are a lot of details to memorize for the exam. Therefore, it is suggested that you utilize any tool to assist you, such as writing and rewriting your cheat sheet or taking your flashcards everywhere you go. Without actually applying the concepts on a project, this is the best way for the material to eventually become second nature.

Q7.10.   **B and D.** If you have not worked on a project seeking LEED certification during construction, using the study worksheets will help you remember this type of information.

Q7.11.   **A.** Remembering details that affect multiple credits is the best game plan when preparing for the O+M exam. 100 miles for Credit 5 and 500 miles for Credits 1, 2, and 3.

Q7.12.   **B.** This is a flashcard opportunity if you did not answer correctly.

Q7.13.   **A.** As mentioned previously there is a lot of information to remember; therefore, it is suggested to focus your efforts on the synergies between credits or how they correlate.

Q7.14.   **C.** This is a flashcard opportunity if you did not answer correctly.

Q7.15.   **B and C.** For the purposes of the exam, it is important to remember the difference between ongoing consumables and durable goods and examples of each.

Q7.16.   **B.** Landfills produce methane, a powerful greenhouse gas. Although methane can be captured and burned to generate energy, if it is emitted, it is harmful to the environment.

Q7.17.   **B and C.** Cradle-to-cradle products can be recycled while cradle-to-grave materials are landfilled. Products with either or both preconsumer and postconsumer recycled content can contribute to earning the LEED credit.

Q7.18.   **D.** Waste is calculated in tonnage for the purposes of LEED documentation.

Q7.19.   **C and D.** Use your flashcards to quiz yourself to remember which materials are required to be collected for recycling.

Q7.20.   **A, B, and D.** Use the study worksheets and your flashcards to remember these requirements. If you are still challenged to remember the information, add it to your cheat sheet and then write and rewrite your cheat sheet until you know it by heart!

Q7.21. **A, E, and F.** Be sure to refer to Appendix E to review all of the opportunities for Exemplary Performance.

Q7.22. **A and E.** Remember all of the MR credits are either addressed during the program development or performance period/certification phases.

Q7.23. **E.** This is a flashcard opportunity if you did not answer correctly.

Q7.24. **E.** This is a flashcard opportunity if you did not answer correctly. The study worksheet for the credit might also help you to remember this requirement.

Q7.25. **C.** This question is typical of the exam. You must be able to recognize or determine how many points a team can pursue for certain strategies.

Q7.26. **B, E, and F.** Knowing the requirements to participate in pursuing certification under the EBOM rating system is pertinent for exam success.

Q7.27. **B.** Be sure to remember the referenced standards specific to the EBOM rating system for the exam.

Q7.28. **B.** Be sure to remember the suggested tools, such as EPEAT and the EPA's EPP program, and when to use each specific to the EBOM rating system for the exam.

Q7.29. **E.** Look for applicable details in the question as this is typical of the real exam. There are three qualifying sustainable criteria justifying a triple-weighted average for the carpet.

Q7.30. **C and D.** Remember all of the MR credits are either addressed during the program development or performance period/certification phases.

CHAPTER 8: INDOOR ENVIRONMENTAL QUALITY

Q8.1. **B.** Use your flashcards to quiz yourself on these types of details or make a note on your cheat sheet.

Q8.2. **B and C.** Remember all prerequisites are required to ensure that all LEED projects meet a minimum level of performance.

Q8.3. **D.** These types of details are critical to passing the exam; use your flashcards and study worksheets to quiz yourself. If necessary, add this to your cheat sheet to write and rewrite.

Q8.4. **B.** Use your flashcards to quiz yourself on these types of details or make a note on your cheat sheet.

Q8.5. **E.** Use your flashcards and study worksheets to quiz yourself on these types of details.

Q8.6. **D.** LEED requires a minimum of MERV 8 filters to be installed for compliance for EQ Credit 1.5 and 13 for EQ Credit 1.4.

Q8.7. **C.** Be sure to know all of the flush-out requirements such as maximum humidity levels and minimum temperature.

Q8.8. **A.** Remembering 60-60 is easier than the other answer selections. Now test your memory about the two options for delivering outdoor air (based on occupancy). The next question will help add a layer of more detail!

Q8.9. **A.** Use your flashcards to quiz yourself to ensure that you remember the flush-out requirements for facility alterations and additions.

Q8.10. **D.** Be sure to make a flashcard and make a note on your cheat sheet to remember the SMACNA standards.

Q8.11. **C.** Remember maximum and minimum levels within the different categories. Try dividing your cheat sheet into the categories to list each relative requirement within each.

Q8.12. **A.** Try to make a connection to between credits or rating systems to find unique ways to remember important facts.

Q8.13. **C.** Know those referenced standards and which prerequisite and credit they apply to. Be sure to refer to Appendix F.

Q8.14. **A, B, and E.** The process of elimination could help with a question such as this one. Although a LEED AP could help earn a point in the IO category, it is not applicable to any other category. A LEED Green Associate and LEED Fellow are not applicable throughout the rating system and if a general contractor were eligible to oversee the plan, who would double-check their work?

Q8.15. **D.** Use your flashcards and study worksheets to quiz yourself on these types of details.

Q8.16. **B and D.** ASHRAE 55 defines the three environmental components that impact thermal comfort, including humidity, air speed, and temperature.

Q8.17. **D.** Remember to read questions and answer options carefully to eliminate the incorrect answers and to depict the correct answer.

Q8.18. **D.** Each credit required a different percentage of participation for compliance. Be sure to list these thresholds on your cheat sheet to help remember them.

Q8.19. **D.** Use your flashcards to quiz yourself on these types of details or make a note on your cheat sheet.

Q8.20. **B.** Think about the logic behind this, as vision glazing is the glass we see out of whether we are sitting or standing.

Q8.21. **D.** Glare control is required for each of the compliance paths as it is the most commonly forgotten element of most daylight strategies.

Q8.22. **A, B, and C.** Learning the strategies to comply with each of the credits and prerequisites is key for the exam. Try to remember the intent behind each to help decipher the appropriate strategy or technology.

Q8.23. **B, C, and E.** Remember, some material in this book can be presented for the first time in the format of a question. Use these opportunities to test your knowledge, and if you are not familiar with the content, be sure to make a flashcard or make a note on your cheat sheet in order to remember the information.

Q8.24. **E.** Use your flashcards to quiz yourself on these types of details or make a note on your cheat sheet.

Q8.25. **D.** Create a flashcard to remember this technical detail.

Q8.26. **A.** Although the 34.5 percent cleaning product purchases and 15 percent paper product purchases qualify, the minimum threshold is 30 percent, whereas two points are only achieved after surpassing 60 percent. The hand soap purchases do not meet the requirements of the credit; therefore they do not qualify for inclusion for the calculations.

Q8.27. **D.** 62 IAQ, IAQ 62!

Q8.28. **B and C.** Knowing your referenced standards helps you to pick the correct answer for this type of question. Refer to Appendix F for a listing of all of them you should know and recognize.

Q8.29. **B, C, D, and F.** Refer to Appendix E for all of the Exemplary Performance opportunities.

Q8.30. **A and C.** Remember ASHRAE 55 = thermal comfort and 62 = IAQ, as both relate to ventilation system design.

Q8.31. **A and C.** Proximity to a shopping mall may increase satisfaction because of convenience, but not necessarily increase production as related to work. Carpooling and recycling are benefits to the environment and operations, not necessarily related to productivity or satisfaction.

Q8.32. **D.** Know those referenced standards and which prerequisite and credit they apply to. Be sure to refer to Appendix F.

Q8.33. **B.** Use your flashcards to quiz yourself on these types of details or make a note on your cheat sheet.

Q8.34. **B and C.** Use your flashcards to remember these types of synergies.

Q8.35. **A.** Each credit required a different percentage of participation for compliance. Be sure to list these thresholds on your cheat sheet to help remember them.

Q8.36. **E.** Try the process of elimination to determine the correct answer based on your knowledge of the other credits and find similarities.

Q8.37. **B, C, and E.** Try to group similar products to determine which ones would apply to the question. Knowing your reference standards helps as well in this case.

Q8.38. **B and E.** Use your flashcards and study worksheets to quiz yourself on these types of details.

Q8.39. **B and D.** Remember which MERV filters are required for each as well.

Q8.40. **A and C.** Be sure to know these types of details for the exam as common and typical challenges facility managers are faced with are typically quizzed.

CHAPTER 9: INNOVATION IN OPERATIONS AND REGIONAL PRIORITY

Q9.1. **C.** Earning exemplary performance is credit specific, so be aware of statements such as "regardless of which credit is being exceeded."

Q9.2. **C and D.** If unclear about IO credits, be sure to read through the Guidance on Innovation and Design (ID) credits on the GBCI website at www.gbci.org/ShowFile.aspx?DocumentID=3594.

Q9.3. **A.** A new green building project can earn the LEED for New Construction and Major Renovations certification and then earn the LEED EBOM certification during operations or a LEED for Core & Shell building can be built and then earn multiple LEED for Commercial Interiors certifications.

Q9.4. **A, C, and E.** Remember, the Regional Priority category is new but does not include any new credits. RPCs are earned by achieving existing LEED credits from other categories. Although earning a maximum of four RPCs is allowed, there are six opportunities available from which to choose.

Q9.5. **D.** Although earning a maximum of four RPCs is allowed, there are six opportunities available from which to choose for each zip code.

Q9.6. **A.** Regardless of how many LEED APs are on a project, only one point can be earned.

Q9.7. **E.** Use your flashcards to quiz yourself on these types of details or make a note on your cheat sheet.

Q9.8. **C.** Create a flashcard to help remember the referenced standards. Be sure to review Appendix F as well.

Q9.9. **A, D, and E.** Be sure to remember credit synergies for the exam.

Q9.10. **E.** Remember prerequisites are typically addressed during the auditing or program development phases of an EBOM project.

Q9.11. **A, C, and D.** The process of elimination might help derive the correct answers as permitting costs might not apply and utility data is tracked as part of EA credits.

Q9.12. **E.** Remember all the phases of the EBOM certification process. A flashcard might help to quiz your memory.

Q9.13. **C.** Cost benefits are approached in the IO category under Credit 3.

Q9.14. **D.** Be sure to remember this detail for the purposes of the exam.

Appendix H

ABBREVIATIONS AND ACRONYMS

4-PCH	4-phenylcyclohexene
ACEEE	American Council for an Energy-Efficient Economy
AFV	alternative-fuel vehicle
AIA	American Institute of Architects
ANSI	American National Standards Institute
AP	LEED Accredited Professional
APPA	Association of Physical Plant Administrators
ASHRAE	American Society of Heating, Refrigerating, and Air-Conditioning Engineers
ASTM	American Society for Testing and Materials
BAAQMD	Bay Area Air Quality Management District
BAS	building automation system
BD+C	Building Design and Construction (LEED AP credential and also a reference guide)
BEES	Building for Environmental and Economic Sustainability software by NIST
BIFMA	Business and Institutional Furniture Manufacturer's Association
BIPV	building integrated photovoltaics
BIM	building information modeling
BMP	best management practice
BOD	basis of design
BOMA	Building Owners and Managers Association
Btu	British thermal unit
CAE	combined annual efficiency
CARB	California Air Resources Board
CBECS	Commercial Building Energy Consumption Survey (by DOE)
CDs	construction documents
CDL	construction, demolition, and land clearing
CE	controller efficiency
CFA	conditioned floor area
CFC	chlorofluorocarbon
CFL	compact fluorescent lamp
CFM	cubic feet per minute
CFR	U.S. Code of Federal Regulations
CI	Commercial Interiors (LEED CI rating system)
CIBSE	Chartered Institution of Building Services Engineers
CIR	credit interpretation request
CMP	Credentialing Maintenance Program
CO	carbon monoxide
CO_2	carbon dioxide
CO2e	CO_2 equivalent
COC	chain of custody
COP	coefficient of performance
CRI	Carpet and Rug Institute
CS	Core & Shell (LEED CS rating system)
CSI	Construction Specifications Institute

CWMP	construction waste management plan
Cx	commissioning
CxA	commissioning agent or authority
dBA	A-weighted decibel
DHW	domestic hot water
DOE	U.S. Department of Energy
EA	Energy & Atmosphere category
EBOM	Existing Buildings: Operations & Maintenance (LEED EBOM rating system)
ECB	energy cost budget
ECM	energy conservation measure
EEM	energy efficiency measures
EER	energy efficiency rating
EERE	U.S. Office of Energy Efficiency and Renewable Energy
EF	energy factor
EPA	U.S. Environmental Protection Agency
EPAct	U.S. Energy Policy Act of 1992 or 2005
EPEAT	electronic product environmental assessment tools
EPP	environmentally preferable purchasing
ESA	environmental site assessment
ESC	erosion and sedimentation control
ET	evapotranspiration
ETS	environmental tobacco smoke
EUI	Energy Use Intensity
EQ	Indoor Environmental Quality category
fc	footcandle
FEMA	U.S. Federal Emergency Management Agency
FEV	fuel-efficient vehicle
FF&E	fixtures, furnishings, and equipment
FLO	Fairtrade Labeling Organizations
FSC	Forest Stewardship Council
FTE	full-time equivalent
GBCI	Green Buildings Certification Institute
GBOM	*Green Buildings Operations + Maintenance Reference Guide*
GF	glazing factor
GHG	greenhouse gas
GPF	gallons per flush
g/L	grams per Liter
GPM	gallons per minute
GWP	global warming potential
HCFC	hydrochlorofluorocarbon
HEPA	high-efficiency particle absorbing
HERS	Home Energy Rating Standards
HET	high-efficiency toilet
HFC	hydrofluorocarbon
HVAC	heating, ventilation, and air conditioning
HVAC&R	heating, ventilation, air conditioning, and refrigeration
IAQ	indoor air quality
I-BEAM	Indoor Air Quality Building Education and Assessment Model
ICF	insulated concrete form
ID	Innovation & Design category

ID+C	Interior Design + Construction (LEED AP credential and also a reference guide)
IE	irrigation efficiency
IEQ	Indoor Environmental Quality category
IESNA	Illuminating Engineering Society of North America
IPC	International Plumbing Code
IPD	integrated project delivery
IPM	integrated pest management
IPMVP	International Performance Measurement and Verification Protocol
ISO	International Organization for Standardization
KW	kilowatt
KWH	kilowatts per hour
LCA	life-cycle assessment/analysis
LCC	life-cycle cost
LCGWP	life-cycle global warming potential
LCODP	life-cycle ozone depletion potential
LED	light-emitting diode
LEED	Leadership in Energy and Environmental Design
LPD	lighting power density
MBtus	million Btus
MDF	medium density fiberboard
MERV	minimum efficiency reporting value
MPR	Minimum Program Requirement
MR	Materials & Resources category
MSDS	material safety data sheet
M&V	measurement and verification
NBI	New Building Institute
NC	New Construction (LEED NC rating system)
ND	Neighborhood Development (LEED ND rating system)
NEMA	National Electrical Manufacturers Association
NH_3	ammonia
NIST	National Institute of Standards and Technology
NRC	noise reduction coefficient
ODP	ozone-depleting potential
O&M	operations and maintenance
O+M	Operations + Maintenance (LEED AP credential)
OPR	owner's program requirements
OSB	oriented strand board
PV	photovoltaic
PVC	polyvinyl chloride
REC	renewable energy certificate/credit
RESNET	Residential Energy Services Network
RFC	request for clarification
RFI	request for information
RFP	request for proposal
RP	Regional Priority category
RT	reverberation time
SCAQMD	South Coast Air Quality Management District
SCS	Scientific Certification Systems
SEER	seasonal energy efficiency rating
SHGC	solar heat gain coefficient

SIP	structural insulated panels
SMACNA	Sheet Metal and Air-Conditioning Contractor's Association
SS	Sustainable Sites category
SRI	solar reflective index
STC	standard transmission class
TAG	Technical Advisory Group
TASC	Technical Advisory Subcommittee
TP	total phosphorus
TRACI	Tool for the Reduction and Assessment of Chemical and Other Environmental Impacts
TSS	total suspended solids
Tvis	visible transmittance
UL	Underwriter's Laboratory
UPC	Uniform Plumbing Code
USGBC	U.S. Green Building Council
VAV	variable air volume
VFD	variable frequency drives
VLT	visible light transmittance
VOC	volatile organic compound
WBCSD	World Business Council for Sustainable Development
WE	Water Efficiency category
WF	water factor
WFR	window-to-floor ratio
WRI	World Resources Institute
WWR	window-to-wall ratio
ZEV	zero-emission vehicle

Appendix I

SAMPLE CREDIT[1]

SS CREDIT 2: BUILDING EXTERIOR AND HARDSCAPE MANAGEMENT PLAN

1 Point

Intent

To encourage environmentally sensitive building exterior and hardscape management practices that provide a clean, well-maintained and safe building exterior while supporting high-performance building operations.

Requirements

Employ an environmentally sensitive, low-impact building exterior and hardscape management plan that helps preserve surrounding ecological integrity. The plan must employ best management practices that significantly reduce harmful chemical use, energy waste, water waste, air pollution, solid waste, and/or chemical runoff (e.g., gasoline, oil, antifreeze, salts) compared with standard practices. The plan must address all of the following operational elements that occur on the building and grounds:

- Maintenance equipment
- Snow and ice removal
- Cleaning of building exterior
- Paints and sealants used on building exterior
- Cleaning of sidewalks, pavement and other hardscape

Potential Technologies and Strategies

During the performance period, have in place a low-impact site and green building exterior management plan that addresses overall site management, chemicals, snow and ice removal, and building exterior cleaning and maintenance. Include green cleaning and maintenance practices and materials that minimize environmental impacts. An outline of acceptable material for a low-impact plan is available in the *LEED Reference Guide for Green Building Operations & Maintenance*, 2009 Edition. Replace conventional gas-powered machinery with electric-powered equivalents (either battery or corded). Examples include, but are not limited to, maintenance equipment and vehicles, landscaping equipment, and cleaning equipment.

Credits

CHAPTER 1

1. GBCI. *LEED AP Operations + Maintenance Candidate Handbook*, November 2010 (2008), p. 7.

CHAPTER 2

1. USGBC website,www.usgbc.org/ShowFile.aspx?DocumentID=5961.
2. USGBC website, www.usgbc.org/DisplayPage.aspx?CMSPageID=124.
3. GBCI website, www.gbci.org/org-nav/about-gbci/about-gbci.aspx.

CHAPTER 3

1. USGBC, *LEED Reference Guide for Green Buildings: Operations & Maintenance* (2009), p. xxiii.
2. Ibid.
3. USGBC website, www.usgbc.org/ShowFile.aspx?DocumentID=6715.

CHAPTER 4

1. USGBC, *LEED Reference Guide for Green Buildings: Operations & Maintenance* (2009), p. 37.
2. Ibid., p. 51.
3. Ibid.
4. Ibid.
5. Ibid., p. 55.
6. Ibid., p. 75.
7. Ibid., p. 9.
8. Ibid.
9. Ibid., p. 15.
10. USGBC. *Green Building and LEED Core Concepts Guide*, 1st edition (2009), p. 27.
11. Ibid.
12. Wikipedia website. http://en.wikipedia.org/wiki/Vehicle_Emissions.
13. USGBC. *Green Building and LEED Core Concepts Guide*, 1st edition (2009), p. 28.
14. "IPCC AR4 SYR Appendix Glossary" (PDF). Retrieved on April 20, 2010.
15. USGBC, *LEED Reference Guide for Green Buildings: Operations & Maintenance* (2009), p. 23.
16. Ibid., p. 27–8.
17. Ibid., p. 34.
18. Ibid., p. 29.
19. Ibid., p. 34.
20. Ibid., p. 42–43.

CHAPTER 5

1. USGBC, *LEED Reference Guide for Green Buildings: Operations & Maintenance* (2009), p. 102.
2. Ibid., p. 105.
3. Ibid., p. 120.
4. Ibid., p. 115.
5. Ibid.

CHAPTER 6

1. USGBC website, www.usgbc.org/DisplayPage.aspx?CMSPageID=1718.
2. USGBC, *LEED Reference Guide for Green Buildings: Operations & Maintenance* (2009), p. 124.
3. Ibid., p. 170.
4. Ibid., p. 175.
5. Ibid., p. 131.
6. Ibid., p. 507.
7. Ibid., p. 169.
8. USGBC, *Green Building and LEED Core Concepts Guide*, p. 51.
9. USGBC, *LEED Reference Guide for Green Buildings: Operations & Maintenance* (2009), p. 185.
10. Ibid., p. 197.
11. Ibid., p. 497.

CHAPTER 7

1. U.S. Environmental Protection Agency, Office of Solid Waste. Municipal Solid Waste Generation, Recycling, and Disposal in the United States: Facts and Figures for 2005. 2006. www.epa.gov/osw/rcc/resources/msw-2005.pdf (accessed December 2010).
2. Ibid.
3. USGBC, *LEED Reference Guide for Green Buildings: Operations & Maintenance* (2009), p. 239.
4. Ibid., p. 267.
5. Ibid., p. 254.
6. Ibid., p. 259.
7. Ibid., p. 283.
8. Ibid., p. 289.
9. Ibid., p. 291.
10. Ibid. p. xi.
11. Ibid., p. 304.
12. Ibid., p. 301–302.
13. Ibid., p. 305

CHAPTER 8

1. Environmental Protection Agency. *The Total Exposure Assessment Methodology (TEAM) Study* (1987).
2. USGBC, *Green Building and LEED Core Concepts Guide*, p. 59.

3. USGBC, *LEED Reference Guide for Green Building Operations and Maintenance* (2009), pgs. 325–327.

4. Ibid., p. 337.

5. USGBC, *Green Building and LEED Core Concepts Guide*, p. 60.

6. USGBC, *LEED Reference Guide for Green Building Operations and Maintenance* (2009), pgs. 332–333.

7. Ibid., p. 332.

8. USGBC, *Green Building and LEED Core Concepts Guide*, p. 60.

9. USGBC, *LEED Reference Guide for Green Building Operations and Maintenance* (2009), p. 408.

10. Ibid., p. 439.

11. Ibid.

12. Ibid., pgs. 439–440.

13. Ibid., p. 440.

14. Ibid., p.447.

APPENDIX A

1. USGBC website. www.usgbc.org/DisplayPage.aspx?CMSPageID=221.

APPENDIX I

1. USGBC website. www.usgbc.org/DisplayPage.aspx?CMSPageID=221.

Index

The letter t following a page number indicates a table.

Sample Flashcards

1

Q. What are the typical major energy-consuming systems to be analyzed during a walk-through?

2

Q. What are the three referenced standards applicable to SS Credit 4: Alternative Commuting Transportation?

3

Q. What are the reference standards applicable to MR Credit 3: Sustainable Purchasing – Facility Alterations and Additions?

4

Q. What savings have green buildings achieved?

5

Q. What are the five strategies to address solid waste management?

6

Q. What are the seven strategies to improve IAQ?

7

Q. What are the four ways to earn Innovation in Operations Credits?

8

Q. What are the five SMACNA guidelines?

2

A South Coast Air Quality Management District (SCAQMD)

California Air Resources Board (CARB)

American Council for an Energy-Efficient Economy, The ACEEE Green Book®: The Environmental Guide to Cars and Trucks

1

A. Site equipment, air distribution systems, chilled and/or heating water systems, domestic hot water systems, HVAC controls, and lighting

4

A. Up to 50 percent energy use reduction

40 percent water use reduction

70 percent solid waste reduction

13 percent reduction in maintenance costs

3

A CRI Green Label Plus Carpet Testing Program for carpet

CRI Green Label Testing Program for carpet cushion

Green Seal's Standard GS-11 for paints and coatings

FloorScore for noncarpet flooring

SCAQMD Rule #1168 for adhesives and sealants

FSC for wood products

6

A. EQ Prerequisite 1: Minimum IAQ Performance

EQ Prerequisite 2: Environmental Tobacco Smoke (ETS) Control

EQ Credit 1.1: IAQ Best Management Practices – IAQ Management Program

EQ Credit 1.2: IAQ Best Management Practices – Outdoor Delivery Monitoring

EQ Credit 1.3: IAQ Best Management Practices – Increased Ventilation

EQ Credit 1.4: IAQ Best Management Practices – Reduce Particulates in Air Distribution

EQ Credit 1.5: IAQ Best Management Practices – IAQ Management for Facility Additions and Alterations

5

A MR Prerequisite 2: Solid Waste Management Policy

MR Credit 6: Solid Waste Management – Waste Stream Audit

MR Credit 7: Solid Waste Management – Ongoing Consumables

MR Credit 8: Solid Waste Management – Durable Goods

MR Credit 9: Solid Waste Management – Facility Alterations and Additions

8

A. HVAC protection, source control, pathway interruption, housekeeping, and scheduling

7

A. Exemplary Performance

Innovation in Design

LEED Accredited Professional

Documenting Sustainable Building Cost

9

Q. What are four lighting zones and their associated footcandle range of the IESNA RP-33 referenced standard for SS Credit 8: Light Pollution Reduction?

10

Q. What four components are required for a team to submit for an Innovation in Design credit?

11

Q. What are the procedures to use for refrigerant management, reporting, and maintaining acceptable leakage rates for CFC refrigerants?

12

Q. Name the four types of corrective action should more than 20 percent of building occupants be dissatisfied with existing building conditions.

13

Q. What are the three compliance path options for MR Credit 2: Sustainable Purchasing – Durable Goods?

14

Q. What are the five comfort criteria an occupant survey should address?

15

Q. What is relative humidity?

16

Q. What are the five differences of EBOM prerequisites and credit opportunities versus the other rating systems?

10

A. Intent of strategy

Suggested requirements for compliance

Suggested documentation proving compliance with requirements

A narrative describing the strategy implemented

9

A. LZ1 Rural/Dark 0.01 fc

LZ2 Low 0.10 fc

LZ3 Medium 0.20 fc

LZ4 High/Urban 0.60 fc.

12

A. HVAC control adjustments, diffuser airflow adjustments, solar control, and acoustical and lighting modifications.

11

A. The EPA Clean Air Act, Title VI, Rule 608 procedures.

14

A. Thermal comfort

Acoustics

Indoor Air Quality

Lighting levels

Building cleanliness

13

A. Option 1: electric powered equipment, prove 40 percent of the equipment is either ENERGY STAR® qualified or replaces conventional gas-powered equipment.

Option 2: furniture, prove 40 percent of the performance period purchases comply with at least one of the defined sustainable criteria.

Option 3: purchase durable goods in compliance with both the electric-powered equipment and the furniture compliance path options

16

A. Evaluate their exterior site maintenance programs

Purchasing policies for environmentally preferred services and products

Cleaning programs and policies

Waste stream

Ongoing indoor environmental quality

15

A. The ratio of partial density of airborne water vapor to the saturation density of water vapor at the same temperature and total pressure

17

Q. What are the two requirements to comply with EQ Credit 3.5: Green Cleaning – Indoor Chemical and Pollutant Source Control?

18

Q. What are the five operational tasks to be included in an exterior and hardscape management plan for SS Credit 2?

19

Q. What are the two differences between prerequisites and credits?

20

Q. What two components are credit weightings based on?

21

Q. What are the certification levels and coordinating point ranges for LEED?

22

Q. According to the minimum program requirements (MPRs), how many occupants must occupy an EBOM project?

23

Q. Describe the MPR for whole-building energy and water use data.

24

Q. How would a project team earn EA Credit 4: On-Site and Off-Site Renewable Energy? What are the minimum percentage thresholds?

18

A. Maintenance equipment

Snow and ice removal

Cleaning of building exterior

Paints and sealants used on building exterior

Cleaning of sidewalks, pavement, and other hardscape

17

A. Entryway systems at least 10 feet in the primary direction of travel

Separately plumbed hazardous liquid waste

20

A. Environmental impacts and human benefits

19

A. Prerequisites are mandatory, as they address minimum performance achievements, and credits are optional.

Prerequisites are not worth any points, whereas credits are.

22

A. The LEED project must serve one or more full-time equivalent (FTE) occupant(s), calculated as an annual average in order to use LEED in its entirety.

EBOM projects also have a Minimum Occupancy Rate. The LEED project must be occupied and operating during the performance period, and a minimum of one year before submitting the first certification review to GBCI.

21

A. Certified: 40–49 points

Silver: 50–59 points

Gold: 60–79 points

Platinum: 80 and higher

24

A. Project teams can implement an on-site renewable energy system, purchase green power from off site, or pursue a combination of both strategies during the performance period. For on-site, minimum of 3 percent of annual energy for the facility

For off-site, owners would need to purchase at least 25 percent of the project's estimated energy demand for at least two years based on quantity, not cost.

23

A. All certified projects must commit to sharing with USGBC and/or GBCI all available actual whole-project energy and water usage data for a period of at least five years starting from the date that the LEED certification was awarded for an EBOM project.

25

Q. What are the MPRs for reasonable site boundaries for EBOM projects?

26

Q. Name the MPR for permanent buildings or spaces, applicable to all LEED rating systems.

27

Q. What is are the five credits that address sustainable site design strategies?

28

Q. CO_2 concentrations above _____ ppm typically indicate inadequate ventilation.

29

Q. At what rate must the space be ventilated at in order for the newly renovated space to be occupied prior to the delivery of the required total outdoor air volume, to be in accordance with EQ Credit 1.5: Indoor Air Quality Management Best Management Practices – Indoor Air Quality Management for Facility Additions and Alterations?

30

Q. What must be achieved in order for a project to be eligible for certification?

31

Q. What is the maximum humidity level and minimum temperature to comply with the flush-out requirements of EQ Credit 1.5: Indoor Air Quality Management Best Management Practices – Indoor Air Quality Management for Facility Additions and Alterations?

32

Q. How many cubic feet of outdoor air per square foot of floor area must be delivered prior to occupancy to comply with the flush-out requirements of EQ Credit 1.5: Indoor Air Quality Management Best Management Practices – Indoor Air Quality Management for Facility Additions and Alterations?

26

A. All LEED projects must be designed for, constructed on, and operated on a permanent location on already existing land. No building or space that is designed to move at any point in its lifetime may pursue LEED certification.

25

A.
1. Boundary must include all contiguous land that is associated with and supports normal building operations.
2. Land in boundary must be owned by the same party that owns the LEED project.
3. For campus projects, 100 percent of the gross land area on the campus would be included within a LEED boundary if all buildings eventually get certified.
4. A property may be attributed to only a single LEED building.
5. Boundary may not unreasonably exclude land to achieve prerequisites or credits (e.g., gerrymandering).

28

A. 530 ppm

27

A. SS Credit 1: LEED Certified Design and Construction

SS Credit 5: Site Development – Protect or Restore Open Habitat

SS Credit 7.1: Heat Island Reduction – Nonroof

SS Credit 7.2: Heat Island Reduction – Roof

SS Credit 8: Light Pollution Reduction

30

A. Complying with all minimum program requirements, achieving all prerequisites, and earning a minimum of 40 points

29

A. 0.30 cfm per square foot of outdoor air

32

A. 3,500 cubic feet of outdoor air per square foot of floor area

31

A. 60 percent humidity; 60°

33

Q. If a project team has learned the facility will not be able to meet the requirements of ASHRAE 62.1 to be in compliance with EQ Prerequisite 1: Minimum Indoor Air Quality Performance because of the limitations of the current HVAC system, how much air must the ventilation system supply to still be in compliance?

34

Q. How far must exterior dedicated smoking areas be located away from building entrances, outdoor air intakes, and any operable windows to comply with EQ Prerequisite 2: ETS Control?

35

Q. What are the two synergistic credits of EQ Prerequisite 1: Green Cleaning Policy and EQ Credit 3.1: Green Cleaning – High Performance Cleaning Program?

36

Q. What are the nonpotable water sources as according to the O&M reference guide?

37

Q. What are the three factors certification fees are based on?

38

Q. What are the five water uses that can be submetered in order to achieve WE Credit 1: Water Performance Measurement?

39

Q. Should a project type be eligible to participate with the ENERGY STAR Portfolio Manager software, what is the minimum score required to meet the requirements of EA Prerequisite 1: Energy Efficiency Best Management Practices, Planning, Documentation, and Opportunity Assessment and pursue Option 1, under EA Credit 1: Optimize Energy Performance?

40

Q. What are the strategies of the Sustainable Sites category?

34

A. 25 feet

33

A. 10 cfm per person

36

A. Harvested rainwater, harvested stormwater, air-conditioner condensate, swimming pool filter backwash water, cooling tower blowdown, pass-through (once-through) cooling water, recycled treated wastewater from toilet and urinal flushing, foundation drain water, municipally reclaimed water or any other appropriate on-site water source that is not naturally occurring groundwater or surface water

35

A. EQ Credit 3.3: Green Cleaning – Purchase of Sustainable Cleaning Product and Materials

EQ Credit 3.4: Green Cleaning – Sustainable Cleaning Equipment

38

A. Irrigation

Indoor plumbing fixtures and fittings

Cooling towers

Domestic hot water

Other process water uses

37

A. Rating system, membership, and square footage

40

A. Site design

Site management and maintenance

Transportation

Stormwater management

39

A. 69 for the prerequisite and 71 for the credit

41

Q. What are the two strategies that address indoor water consumption?

42

Q. What is source energy?

43

Q. What is site energy?

44

Q. What is the tool in which to compare building performance? What is the average building performance score? What is the range of scores possible?

45

Q. What are the three types of calculations required for EA Prerequisite 1: Energy Efficiency Best Management Practices, Planning, Documentation, and Opportunity Assessment?

46

Q. What are the four components required to complete the energy use analysis documentation as part of EA Prerequisite 1: Energy Efficiency Best Management Practices, Planning, Documentation, and Opportunity Assessment?

47

Q. What is stratified random sampling?

48

Q. What are some examples of stabilization control measures for erosion and sedimentation control?

42

A. The total amount of raw fuel required to operate a building; it incorporates all transmission, delivery, and production losses for a complete assessment of a building's energy use

41

A. WE Prerequisite 1: Minimum Indoor Plumbing Fixture and Fitting Efficiency

WE Credit 2: Additional Indoor Plumbing Fixture and Fitting Efficiency

44

A. ENERGY STAR Portfolio Manager is the tool

50 average building performance score

Scores range from 1 to 100

43

A. The amount of energy reflected in a project's utility bills

46

A. Building operating plan

Systems narrative

Sequence of operations

Preventative maintenance plan

45

A. Energy Use Intensity

Energy Cost Index

Utility Cost Index

48

A. Temporary or permanent seeding and mulching

47

A. A process of surveying that categorizes members of a population into discrete subgroups, based on characteristics that may affect their responses to a survey. For example, a survey of building occupants' commuting behavior might separate people by income level and commuting distance. To yield representative results, the survey should sample subgroups according to their proportions in the total population

49

Q. What are the four impacts of transportation?

50

Q. What is an alternative-fuel vehicle?

51

Q. What are the two SS credits that address sustainable site and maintenance strategies?

52

Q. What is systematic sampling?

53

Q. What are some examples of structural control measures for erosion and sedimentation control?

54

Q. What are native and adaptive plantings?

55

Q. What is potable water?

56

Q. What is imperviousness?

50

A. A vehicle that operates without the use of petroleum fuels, including gas-electric vehicle types.

49

A. Location

Vehicle technology

Fuel

Human behavior

52

A. Systematic sampling surveys every xth person in a population, using a constant skip interval. It relies on random sampling order or an order with no direct relationship to the variable under analysis (e.g., alphabetical order when sampling for commuting behavior).

51

A. SS Credit 2: Building Exterior and Hardscape Management Plan

SS Credit 3: Integrated Pest Management, Erosion Control, and Landscape Management Plan

54

A. Native vegetation occurs naturally, whereas adaptive plantings are not naturally found in a given environment, but they can adapt to their new surroundings. Both can survive with little to no human interaction or resources.

53

A. Earth dikes, silt fencing, sediment basins, and sediment traps

56

A. Surfaces that do not allow 50 percent or less of water to pass through them

55

A. Drinking water supplied by municipalities or wells

57

Q. What is perviousness?

58

Q. What is stormwater runoff?

59

Q. What is a footcandle?

60

Q. What is the heat island effect?

61

Q. What is emissivity?

62

Q. What is solar reflective index (SRI) and the associated scale?

63

Q. What is albedo and the associated scale?

64

Q. What is a building footprint?

58

A. Rainwater that leaves a project site flowing along parking lots and roadways, traveling to sewer systems and water bodies

57

A. Surfaces that allow at least 50 percent of water to percolate or penetrate through them

60

A. Heat absorption by low-SRI, hardscape materials that contribute to an overall increase in temperature by radiating heat

59

A. A measurement of light measured in lumens per square foot

62

A. A material's ability to reflect or reject solar heat gain measured on a scale from 0 (dark, most absorptive) to 100 (light, most reflective)

61

A. The ratio of the radiation emitted by a surface to the radiation emitted by a black body at the same temperature

64

A. The amount of land the building structure occupies, not including landscape and hardscape surfaces such as parking lots, driveways, and walkways

63

A. The ability to reflect sunlight based on visible, infrared, and ultraviolet wavelengths on a scale from 0 to 1

65

Q. What are the different compliant shading strategies to comply with SS Credit 7.1: Heat Island Effect, Nonroof?

66

Q. What are three strategies to manage stormwater?

67

Q. What are the four strategies of the WE category?

68

Q. What are the referenced standards used to create a baseline case for water consumption?

69

Q. What is baseline versus design case?

70

Q. What are examples of flow fixtures?

71

Q. How are flow fixtures measured?

72

Q. What are examples of flush fixtures?

66

A. Minimize impervious areas

Control stormwater

Harvest rainwater

65

A. Trees or shrubs (within five years), trellises or other types of exterior structures that support vegetation, architectural shading devices and structures, and photovoltaic systems

68

A. UPC and IPC

67

A. Indoor water use

Water consumption monitoring

Outdoor water use (for irrigation)

Process water for cooling towers

70

A. Sink faucets, showerheads, and aerators

69

A. The amount of water a conventional project would use as compared to the design case

72

A. Toilets and urinals

71

A. Gallons per minute (gpm)

73

Q. How are flow fixtures measured?

74

Q. What is graywater?

75

Q. What is the referenced standard of EQ Credit 1.1: IAQ Best Management Practices – IAQ Management Program?

76

Q. What are the strategies to reduce outdoor water consumption?

77

Q. How can nonpotable water use reduce water consumption?

78

Q. What are the uses for process water?

79

Q. What are the three referenced standards of EQ Credit 1.3: Indoor Air Quality Management Practices – Increased Ventilation?

80

Q. What are the four required tasks to comply with EA Credit 2.2: Existing Building Commissioning – Implementation?

74

A. Wastewater from showers, bathtubs, lavatories, and washing machines. This water has not come into contact with toilet waste according to the International Plumbing Code (IPC).

76

A. Implement native and adapted plants

Use xeriscaping

Specify high-efficiency irrigation systems

Use nonpotable water for irrigation

78

A. Industrial uses, such as chillers, cooling towers, and boilers

Business operations, such as washing machines, ice machines, and dishwashers

80

A. TASK 1. Implement a no-cost operational changes or low-cost repairs or upgrades and develop a capital plan for any major improvements and/ or **retrofits** (with 50 percent of improvements to be completed by the end of the performance period).

TASK 2. Conduct training for management staff (recommended time is 24 hours per staff member per year).

TASK 3. Document the financial impacts of improvements by the means of the **simple payback** period, return on investment (ROI), and cost-benefit ratio calculations.

TASK 4. Update the building operating plan as appropriate.

73

A. Gallons per flush (gpf)

75

A. EPA's Indoor air quality Building Education and Assessment Model (I-BEAM)

77

A. Indoor: toilet and urinal flushing

Outdoor: irrigation

Process: building systems

79

A. ASHRAE 62.1

Carbon Trust's Good Practice Guide 237

Chartered Institution of Building Services Engineers (CIBSE) Applications Manual 10:2005, Natural Ventilation in Nondomestic Buildings

81

Q. What are the five components of an HVAC maintenance program?

82

Q. Name some examples of ongoing consumables.

83

Q. Name some examples of a durable good.

84

Q. What two components should be evaluated when determining which refrigerants to use?

85

Q. What is ODP?

86

Q. What is GWP?

87

Q. Which two credits require MERV filters and what is the minimum MERV required for each?

88

Q. What are the three components of the Energy & Atmosphere category?

82

A. Printer paper, batteries, and printing cartridges

81

A. Visual inspections of outdoor air vents and dampers to remove obstructions and contaminants

Regularly scheduled replacement or cleaning of air filters

Regular cleaning

Cooling tower management

Testing and balancing

84

A. Refrigerants should be evaluated based on ODP and GWP impacts.

83

A. Furniture, appliances, and equipment

86

A. Global warming potential

85

A. Ozone-depleting potential

88

A. Monitoring and improving building energy performance

Eliminating chlorofluorocarbons (CFCs)

Renewable energy

87

A. EQ Credit 1.4: IAQ Management Best Management Practices – Reducing Particulates in Air Distribution; MERV 13 required

EQ Credit 1.5: IAQ Management Best Management Practices – IAQ Management for Facility Additions and Alterations; MERV 8 required

89

Q. What are the two strategies to eliminate chlorofluorocarbons within the EA category?

90

Q. Name the two types of energy audits addressing in the EBOM rating system.

91

Q. What are the nine strategies that address the monitoring and tracking of energy consumption?

92

Q. What are the six types of eligible renewable energy sources for LEED projects?

93

Q. What are the three credits that address existing building commissioning?

94

Q. What is an REC?

95

Q. What is a waste stream?

96

Q. What are two EA credits that address performance measurement?

90

A. ASHRAE Level I, Walk-Through Analysis

ASHRAE Level II, Energy Audit, Energy Survey and Analysis

89

A. EA Prerequisite 3: Fundamental Refrigerant Management

EA Credit 5: Enhanced Refrigerant Management

92

A. Solar, wind, wave, biomass, geothermal power, and low-impact hydropower

---

91

A. EA Prerequisite 1: Energy Efficiency Best Management Practices

EA Prerequisite 2: Minimum Energy Efficiency Performance

EA Credit 1: Optimize Energy Efficiency Performance

EA Credit 2.1: Existing Building Commissioning – Investigation and Analysis

EA Credit 2.2: Existing Building Commissioning – Implementation

EA Credit 2.3: Existing Building Commissioning – Ongoing Commissioning

EA Credit 3.1: Performance Measurement – Building Automation System

EA Credit 3.2: Performance Measurement – System-Level Metering

EA Credit 6: Emissions Reduction Reporting

94

A. Renewable energy credit

93

A. EA Credit 2.1: Existing Building Commissioning – Investigation and Analysis

EA Credit 2.2: Existing Building Commissioning – Implementation

EA Credit 2.3: Existing Building Commissioning – Ongoing Commissioning

---

96

A. EA Credit 3.1: Performance Measurement – Building Automation System

EA Credit 3.2: Performance Measurement – System-Level Metering

---

95

A. The overall flow of waste from the building to a landfill, incinerator, or other disposal site

97

Q. What is a rapidly renewable material?

98

Q. Define recycled content.

99

Q. What are the eight tasks of a ASHRAE Level II, Energy Audit, Energy Survey, and Analysis?

100

Q. Recycled material that was generated from a manufacturing process is referred to as _____.

101

Q. Recycled material that was generated by household, commercial, industrial, or institutional end users, which can no longer be used for its intended purpose is referred to as _____.

102

Q. What are considered regional materials according to LEED?

103

Q. What type of documentation is required to prove compliance for FSC wood?

104

Q. Which elements are excluded from the calculations for recycled content, regional materials, and rapidly renewable materials?

98

A. The percentage of materials in a product that are recycled from the manufacturing waste stream (preconsumer waste) or the consumer waste stream (postconsumer waste) and used to make new materials. Recycled content is typically expressed as a percentage of the total material volume or weight.

97

A. Fiber or animal materials that must be grown or raised in 10 years or less

100

A. Preconsumer. Examples include planer shavings, sawdust, bagasse, walnut shells, culls, trimmed materials, over issue publications, and obsolete inventories. Not included are rework, regrind, or scrap materials capable of being reclaimed within the same process that generated them.

99

A. Summary Energy Use (by major end use.

Building Systems Description

Rejected Energy Efficiency Measures

Recommended Energy Efficiency Measures

Table of Estimated Costs

Overall Project Economic Evaluation

Recommended Measurement & Verification Methods

Potential Capital Improvements for Level III Analysis

102

A. The amount of a building's materials that are extracted, processed, and manufactured close to a project site, expressed as a percentage of the total material cost. LEED considers regional materials as those that originate within 500 miles of the project site.

101

A. Postconsumer. Examples include construction and demolition debris, materials collected through recycling programs, and landscaping waste.

104

A. Mechanical, electrical, and plumbing equipment and hazardous waste materials

103

A. FSC wood requires chain-of-custody documentation.

105

Q. What are the six strategies that address sustainable purchasing?

106

Q. What are the minimum types of items to be recycled during operations to meet the requirements of the MR prerequisite?

107

Q. What are the 3R's of waste management?

108

Q. What are the six different types of labels in compliance with MR Credit 5: Sustainable Purchasing – Food?

109

Q. What are the three components discussed in the EQ category?

110

Q. What are the types of VOCs?

111

Q. What is the reference standard that depicts CFL compliance for calculations purposes for MR Credit: Sustainable Purchasing – Reduced Mercury in Lamps?

112

Q. How are VOCs measured?

106

A. Paper, corrugated cardboard, glass, plastics, and metals

105

A. MR Prerequisite 1: Sustainable Purchasing Policy

MR Credit 1: Sustainable Purchasing – Ongoing Consumables

MR Credit 2: Sustainable Purchasing – Durable Goods

MR Credit 3: Sustainable Purchasing – Facility Alterations and Additions

MR Credit 4: Sustainable Purchasing – Reduced Mercury in Lamps

MR Credit 5: Sustainable Purchasing – Food

108

A. 1. USDA Organic

2. Food Alliance certified

3. Rainforest Alliance certified

4. Protected Harvest certified

5. Fair Trade certified

6. Marine Stewardship Council's Blue Eco-Label

107

A. Reduce, reuse, and recycle

110

A. Volatile organic compounds include carbon dioxide, tobacco smoke, and particulates emitted from carpet, paints, adhesives, glues, sealants, coatings, furniture, and composite wood products

109

A. Indoor air quality (IAQ) management

Occupant comfort

Green Cleaning

112

A. Grams per liter (g/L)

111

A. National Electrical Manufacturers Association (NEMA) guidelines

113

Q. What are the two components addressed in the MR category?

114

Q. What is MERV? What is the range?

115

Q. What is a pictogram?

116

Q. What are the four environmental factors of thermal comfort defined by ASHRAE 55?

117

Q. What are the four credits that address occupant comfort?

118

Q. What are the three factors in which to measure performance for a lamp purchasing plan?

119

Q. What is a lumen?

120

Q. Of the six available Regional Priority credits, how many can count toward a project's LEED certification?

114

A. Minimum Efficiency Reporting Value (MERV) filters range from 1 (low) to 16 (highest).

113

A. Sustainable purchasing

Solid waste management

116

A. Humidity, air speed, air temperature, and radiant temperature

115

A. A trillionth of a gram

118

A. Mercury content (mg/lamp)

Lamp life (hours)

Light output (lumens)

117

A. EQ Credit 2.1: Occupant Comfort – Occupant Survey

EQ Credit 2.2: Controllability of Systems – Lighting

EQ Credit 2.3: Occupant Comfort – Thermal Comfort Monitoring

EQ Credit 2.4: Daylight and Views

120

A. Four

119

A. A unit of luminous flux equal to the light emitted in a unit solid angle by a uniform point source of 1 candle intensity.